Demystifying Exotic Products

Interest Rates, Equities and Foreign Exchange

Chia Chiang Tan

A John Wiley and Sons, Ltd., Publication

This edition first published 2010
© 2010 Chia Chiang Tan

Registered office
John Wiley & Sons Ltd, The Atrium, Southern Gate, Chichester, West Sussex, PO19 8SQ, United Kingdom

For details of our global editorial offices, for customer services and for information about how to apply for permission to reuse the copyright material in this book please see our website at www.wiley.com.

A catalogue record for this book is available from the British Library.

ISBN 978-0-470-74815-2 (H/B)

Typeset in 10/12pt Times by Aptara Inc., New Delhi, India
Printed in Great Britain by CPI Antony Rowe, Chippenham, Wiltshire

To my father and
in memory of my mother.

Contents

Foreword

It must be difficult being an investment professional in these times: miniscule bond yields and a moribund economy too weak to sustain stock market outperformance. Do you resign yourself to paltry bond coupons and put aside more cash in anticipation of future needs, or do you just unleash all you have got into the stock markets and pray for the best?

There must be another way. What if you can have better control over risks and yet participate in a rising market? This brings us into the realm of derivatives. But are they not inherently risky and dangerous instruments to deal with? In a sense the answer is yes! In the same way, a sharp kitchen knife or the driving of a car may cause fatalities if one fails to understand and control the dangers involved. However once the risks are mastered, they become indispensable "tools" of our society.

In a sense the situation is similar when derivatives and structured products are used to shape the individual portfolio allocation of an entity's assets and liabilities. Contrary to popular misconception, structured products are inherently risky only if applied without care. For example, assume a French aerospace company wins a contract to export aeroplanes to the US with payments taking place in 18 months from now upon the delivery of the products. The company faces a dilemma: the production costs occur in Euros whereas the revenues will be paid in US dollars. The company could potentially go out of business if the US dollar should collapse relative to the Euro in 18 months from now. Whether one likes it or not: The business transaction makes the company intrinsically long a currency future leaving it exposed to large risks. If derivatives are used wisely in this case, the company's risks can be minimized or even eliminated.

If this view is correct, how can one best understand the risks as well as the opportunities that derivatives can potentially offer? Why should one trust investment banks that have foremost their own sales targets in mind but not necessarily the best solution for the client's investment goals?

Bookshelves are flowing with countless technical books on derivatives describing Brownian motions and (re-) derivation of the Black–Scholes formula. However what one needs is a book that describes the potential and risks of the major derivatives products that have been around.

Chia takes a refreshingly unique approach by concentrating on how exotic products have arisen in the last decade to address investors' risk-reward preferences. He explains the economic rationales behind various esoteric products, their key features, as well as situations in which clients have inadvertently found themselves more exposed than they thought.

From my time in industry, I have seen too many occasions when users of derivatives failed to grasp the big picture risks and paid heavily for it. It is much more important for investors to understand if derivatives are suitable as per their investment circumstances, than if they got good prices for the derivatives. Like an insurance contract, you need to ascertain if specific eventualities are provided for, or whether you should consider taking out additional cover.

This book makes compelling reading for anyone interested in structured products. And if you happen to be studying the mathematics behind financial derivatives, why not have a look at why there is demand for them in the first place? It might give you a better perspective as to the products at the end of the assembly line.

Alex Langnau
Global Head of Quantitative Analytics,
Allianz Investment Management, and
Visiting Scientist at the Ludwig-Maximillians University,
Munich

Preface

As a consequence of the credit crisis of 2008, there is probably no other period in recent financial history where derivatives have received the same amount of negative publicity as today. However, the media coverage rarely provides more than a superficial explanation of derivatives. So, despite all the hype, does the public really know what derivatives are?

I make no excuses for the excesses of the credit markets and some of the esoteric instruments they trade (e.g. CDOs squared), which have wreaked extensive havoc on the financial and real economy. But derivatives are as different from each other as the animals that roam the land, and whereas the lion is to be feared, the hare is mostly harmless, while the horse can help its rider to cover great distances. In the same way, there are derivatives out there that can be quite useful in engineering an investment strategy suited to an investor's risk–reward preferences.

Whether derivatives are dangerous or not depends on the terms of the contract. A lot of negative sentiment towards derivatives comes from people who do not understand them. After all, would you feel comfortable in harnessing the power of electricity if you do not know how to avoid fire hazards from its unsafe use? It would be very helpful if we could demystify derivatives. The tendency of the existing literature to focus on an exclusive audience with stochastic calculus training has left a very wide gap. However, term sheets for most exotic products tend to involve only simple mathematics (addition, subtraction, multiplication, division, the summation notation and symbolic representation of quantities). So, why is it not possible to explain derivatives in simple terms?

The pricing of exotic products indeed involves complex mathematics. However, investment professionals should not typically need to understand pricing. (They are unlikely to possess the necessary infrastructure to price exotic products anyway.) Pricing is important to a financial institution selling these products, since it then tries to offset the risks by trading in simpler instruments. The investment professional, however, often buys these products with the aim of executing an investment strategy consistent with a market view. It is thus more important to understand whether the characteristics of this product make it suitable for her. For example, if a product pays you $100 if, on 15 December 2008, Microsoft stock trades above $30 and $0 otherwise, you would have been paid nothing since the market tanked late last year. Isn't it more important to understand that you are betting everything on the price of Microsoft stock on one particular day in the future, than whether you should have paid $40 or $45 for this product? Does neglecting pricing sound like taking too much on trust? If so, ask yourself whether you can confidently determine if the price of a stock you have just bought should really be $27.

Of course, a minority of operators have put derivatives to bad use, e.g. to take on more leverage than otherwise possible, or to window dress the profit if accounting regulations allow for different treatment of derivatives to the underlying. But should that be a reason to condemn derivatives, or rather a reason to close loopholes that allow less than scrupulous market participants to game the system? After all, a knife could be used to kill. But top chefs need it to prepare gourmet dishes too.

There are plenty of good books in finance, but they often provide a general description of assets, or give a long list of (usually first-generation exotic) products and how to price them (mainly using some simple model like Black–Scholes), or introduce the mathematics behind some sophisticated model. But very little exists that explains exotic products – what they are, why they are of interest and how to think about them intuitively – at least in terms that someone in the wider financial industry can understand.

This book is intended to provide an intuitive explanation of exotic products. We shall explore the major themes in the construction of structured products, with the discussion in the remainder of the book centred around these themes. After all, the products can fall out of favour as economic circumstances change, but the themes have far greater longevity. For instance, one such theme is to provide for full repayment of the investor's principal at maturity regardless of market conditions. Whether we are in an environment of high or low interest rates, a recession or a boom, this sort of controlled risk investment strategy will always be in demand.

Rather than provide an exhaustive product coverage, this book shall give a flavour of the types of products that exist. Nor is it going to delve into the mathematics behind the latest models. The reader will instead be shown why such strange products as constant maturity swaps exist, what they really are, who is bearing the risk, and will be given a little framework to think about pricing them.

This book covers mainly interest rates, equities and foreign exchange. I shall make almost no reference to structured products in credit and hence hopefully be spared the accusations of being an apologist for an area that is associated with the worst financial crisis in decades. After all, I am more interested in providing the readers with a framework in which to understand products that are likely to make a strong comeback in the years ahead, than in providing them with a historical insight into a catastrophic episode of financial mis-engineering.

Starting with the economic background that favoured the explosion of exotic products, the book proceeds to outline some major themes in the construction of structured products, then moves on to the basics of derivatives pricing. Next, the "building blocks" of exotic products are examined: barriers, quantoes, constant maturity swaps and range accruals. The book subsequently explains how more yield can be bought by incorporating early termination features in the products, and the remaining chapters focus on some esoteric products that involve pathwise accumulation, baskets where averages or extreme points are of interest, direct bets on volatility or correlation, and fund derivatives.

These products will illustrate some of the innovations of structured derivatives in the last decade. In fact, the reader shall see that, contrary to the misconception that derivatives are inherently dangerous, they can be either quite safe or *extremely* dangerous, dependent on the risks the investor chooses to take. And perhaps some derivatives were initially designed to satisfy certain investment requirements, but have subsequently been modified in the quest for higher yield so that their inherent protections have now disappeared. Some analysis aided by hindsight should hopefully help investment professionals to avoid these pitfalls in the days ahead.

I do not claim that derivatives are for everyone, but the reader is invited to learn for himself what they really are and decide if they can work for him. It is by understanding what one may be involved in that best serves the financial professional. The book concludes by speculating on which of these products might survive the credit crisis of 2008 and post-crisis deleveraging and risk aversion.

It is hoped that this book could assist investment professionals in seeing how derivatives can be used to construct strategies with certain desired risk–reward profiles. Quants, structurers and traders could benefit from seeing how derivatives are utilised to provide solutions to various client demands; students could benefit from seeing how derivatives theory is applied in practice; and perhaps this book could demystify derivatives for the general public. Further, as this happens to be one of the most tumultuous times in living memory for the financial industry as a whole, many products that thrived in the golden days of derivatives may not survive going forward. This book could serve as interesting reading for future generations about what existed in our times.

Acknowledgements

I am indebted to various friends and former colleagues for their encouragement and assistance in my endeavour to write this book. Firstly, I should thank Dr Alex Langnau for extremely helpful suggestions from his review of the manuscript, and his unwavering focus on getting me to reach out to the reader. His efforts were crucial to improving the readability of the material. I should also thank Dr Andrey Gal for insightful discussions on the subject matter and for a critical appraisal of the contents of the manuscript.

I am grateful to Andy Tran for providing a review from the perspective of someone in a different asset class (credit) to those I cover in the book. I further owe it to John Spalek for providing a partial review of the material. His attention to detail was instrumental in weeding out some errors in the manuscript. This book is not just written with quants or even investment bankers in mind, and their feedback is essential to ensuring that other finance professionals can understand the material.

I am indebted to Shiv Madan, Lars Schouw and Andy Tran (again) for helping me to source out data for use in the material. Such data is mainly obtained from Bloomberg. Without their assistance, it would have been more difficult for me to complete this book.

Finally, I must thank the staff at Wiley (in particular Pete Baker, Aimee Dibbens and Ilaria Meliconi) for being a real pleasure to work with prior to, and during, the book's production.

Any errors in the material are solely my responsibility.

NOTE ON FX QUOTE STYLE

In the interbank market, the quote style is ccy1/ccy2, which rather confusingly means the number of units of currency 2 per unit of currency 1. For example, the exchange rate between the dollar and the yen is quoted as USD/JPY (i.e. number of yen per dollar). On the other hand, EUR/USD is the number of dollars per euro.

Typically, the order of the currencies is chosen so that the quote is bigger than 1, e.g. USD/JPY is about 90, whereas JPY/USD (not the convention except in some US futures exchanges) would be around 0.011. Also, where possible currency 2 should be a decimal-denominated currency (not really relevant today). In the past, the Australian dollar was not divided into decimal units, so the quote was AUD/USD rather than USD/AUD.

In the CME Group, some FX pairs are quoted as number of dollars per unit of currency (e.g. JPY/USD). It makes these currency futures similar to futures in any other dollar asset.

NOTE ON THE SUMMATION NOTATION

The summation notation is defined as follows:

$$\sum_{i=1}^{N} A_i = A_1 + A_2 + \cdots + A_N.$$

NOTE ON EXPECTATION

The expectation operator with respect to measure Q is denoted $E^Q[\bullet]$.

Expectation is best understood as taking an average, based on probabilities of possible outcomes.

There is no need to understand the concept of a measure to follow the material in the book. The basic idea is that the choice of a numeraire asset (i.e. a unit to measure value) defines the associated measure, which then determines a set of probabilities (for purposes of computing the expectation). These are not real-world probabilities, but rather implied from an analysis of the process of hedging.

NOTE ON SUPERSCRIPT

In much of my material, a superscript number represents raising the quantity to a power. So,

$$A^4 = A \times A \times A \times A.$$

However, at times, I have used the superscript as another index, especially when I need the subscript to indicate time, e.g. S_t^i represents the price of stock i as seen at time t. In these cases, I always define the variable (S_t^i here) concerned.

Hopefully, the meaning of the superscript should be clear from the context.

1
Derivatives in their Golden Days
(1994 to 2007)

The years between 1994 and 2007 have seen a period of low inflation and low interest rates in most developed economies. With the exception of Japan, these years have also seen staggering rises in the prices of stocks and real estate. The periodic crises (e.g. the Asian crisis which began around July 1997, the bursting of the dotcom bubble in March 2000, or the terrorist attacks on 11 September 2001) have not significantly altered the financial landscape for the worst, at least when compared with the stagnation of the late 1960s, the periodic recessions throughout the 1970s and early 1980s, coupled with sky-high inflation in the late 1970s. The current economic climate since the burst of the sub-prime bubble in August 2007 might herald a less benign era, but that is still something unfolding at the time of writing. Nevertheless, we must approach the explosive growth of derivatives in the light of what could be considered the last two golden decades.

Derivatives are simply products whose payoffs depend on the values of other underlying market variables. For example, an agreement to buy a stock 1 year from now at a pre-agreed price is a derivative since its value depends on the value of the underlying stock.

Since the publication of the Black–Scholes model in 1973, a new framework for understanding derivatives and managing risk has taken shape. Derivatives have existed for a long time (e.g. rice futures in Japan in the 1700s) and have been used to transfer risk. The concept of the traditional insurance, which has also been around for some time, is really also based on risk transfer. However, with an improved framework for pricing and managing risk post-1973, substantial innovations in derivatives occurred as more players entered the field. The advances in technology which allowed for high-powered computing of the prices of derivatives also contributed significantly to their growth on an industrial scale.

Ultimately, however, the economic environment contributed heavily to the demand for derivatives from the investing public. In particular, in a low interest rates environment, can one be blamed for seeking higher yields through other means? And if, as policy-makers would have you believe, the boom–bust cycle has been tamed and we are now in a period of steady growth, is it not appropriate to leverage up with derivatives in our pursuit of yield? Further, corporates with hedging needs have certainly welcomed customised solutions that deal with projected cashflows.

In the following sections, we shall be visiting various products and concepts. Please do not be too bothered if you cannot follow all the products and features mentioned. They are meant more to show the myriad of innovations in derivatives stemming from the environment of the last decade or so. And the concepts will be fully discussed in the remainder of the book. Please note that there is a glossary at the end of the text in case you need to remind yourself of the definition of a new term.

1.1   USES OF DERIVATIVES

Put simply, there are two main purposes of derivatives

(1) hedging
(2) speculation

Hedging

Hedging is where an individual or firm takes a position, with the aim of protecting against an adverse movement in the market environment. As a simple example, suppose you are a US dollar investor and need to pay €100 for some item 1 year from now. It is unclear what spot EUR/USD would be worth 1 year from today. Figure 1.1 shows that as spot EUR/USD (1 year from today) varies between 0.5 and 2, the dollar cost of the €100 payment varies between $50 and $200.

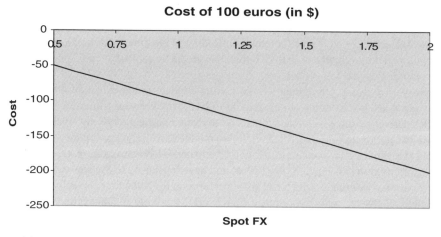

Figure 1.1   As the EUR/USD spot FX rate (1 year from today) varies from 0.5 to 2, the dollar cost of a €100 position varies from $50 to $200.

(Note that the usual style of FX quotation in ccy1/ccy2 is number of units of currency 2 per unit of currency 1. So, EUR/USD refers to number of dollars per euro. The "/" symbol can be misleading for one with mathematical training, as it wrongly suggests itself as the number of euros per dollar.)

You might want to **lock in the rate of exchange by entering a 1-year forward,** agreeing to buy EUR/USD at 1.3 (i.e. to pay $130 for €100), rather than wait until 1 year from now and be at the mercy of the exchange rate at that time. Figure 1.2 shows that as EUR/USD varies from 0.5 to 2, the forward contract has payoff varying from $80 to $70. Notice that you incur a loss on the forward contract itself if EUR/USD 1 year from now is less than $130. However, the forward contract offsets the dollar cost of buying euros, so that the net cost is always $130 (see Figure 1.3).

Suppose, instead, you are not sure you would need to enter the transaction and just want the right (but not obligation) to buy €100 for $130 at the end of 1 year. This is a **call option.** Figure 1.2 shows that the call option and the forward have the same payoff if EUR/USD is above 1.3, but otherwise the payoff of the call option is 0. Since you could walk away if EUR/USD is less

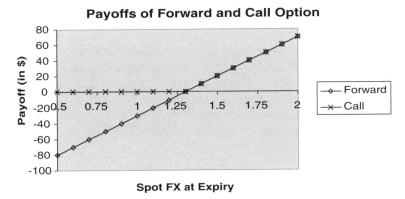

Figure 1.2 Dollar payoffs of a forward and a call option on EUR/USD based on different realised values of EUR/USD. Both the forward and the call option have increasing payoffs as EUR/USD increases but the payoff of the option does not go below zero when EUR/USD falls below 1.3.

than 1.3, the call option must cost something up front. This cost is referred to as the premium. Figure 1.3 shows that the call option allows you a lower cost of euro purchase if EUR/USD drops below 1.3, while still ensuring that you never pay more than $130.

Perhaps you think the option costs too much. Could you give away some protection for a cheaper option? Perhaps you could have the same **option with a knockout barrier so that the option expires worthless if EUR/USD drops below 1.15 any time before the end of the year**. In this case, you will be unprotected if EUR/USD drops to 1.14 after 6 months and then rises back above the strike of 1.3 by the end of the year. (See Figure 1.4 for an illustration of this.) But then, nothing in life is free.

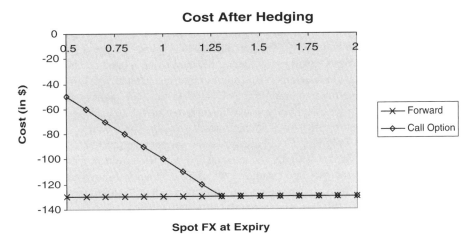

Figure 1.3 Resultant dollar payoffs when we superimpose the hedges (either forward or call option) on the short EUR/USD position (from the requirement to purchase €100). For the forward contract, the net effect is that you buy €100 at $130. For the call option, the net effect can lead to a cheaper cost of euro purchase if EUR/USD drops below 1.3.

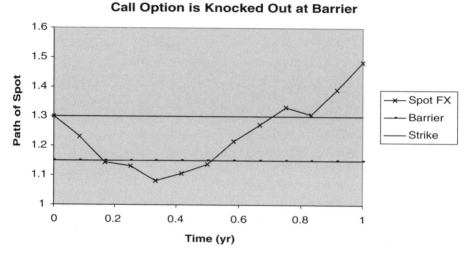

Figure 1.4 Path of spot FX. Knockout call option has barrier level 1.15. Option is knocked out at 2 months. Thus, even though at expiry of 1 year EUR/USD is above the strike of 1.3, the payoff is 0.

I hope, nevertheless, that you get the point that derivatives can be used for hedging – and optionality costs money. You can also sell some optionality, thus making the existing product cheaper.

But hedging can also be imperfect. As another example, suppose you are a huge grapefruit producer. You want to hedge your profits by entering a forward contract to sell grapefruit (i.e. a contract to sell grapefruit at a pre-agreed price in the future), so that a bumper harvest world wide in August next year will not cause depressed prices to affect you. However, you feel that orange juice contracts are much more liquidly traded, whereas the forward market cannot accommodate the volume of grapefruit you wish to sell. You also believe (or have observed historically) that grapefruit prices and orange juice prices tend to move together (at least most of the time). So instead you sell futures on orange juice (i.e. you enter into an agreement on an exchange to sell a certain quantity of orange juice next August for a pre-agreed price).

There is a significant basis risk (i.e. risk due to hedging using related assets) in that there might be a blight in oranges but a bumper harvest for grapefruit. After all, the historical relation between harvests of grapefruit and oranges may change. In this case, your grapefruit harvest will be sold at reduced prices, and yet you will lose money on the orange juice futures you have sold, since orange juice prices will spike upwards sharply. That could very well lead to ruin, so you can see that hedging may not always be the perfect solution.

It is worth pointing out that hedging tends to involve simpler products than speculation, since here you are trying to generate cashflows which protect against movements of market variables that adversely affect you, based on your existing exposure. And such exposures tend to be the result of prior simpler arrangements.

Speculation

Speculation involves taking a position in the hope of making money. If I am a dollar hedger and think that the euro will rise, I can buy euros. However, if I were a euro investor, how should I buy more euros? Perhaps, I could sell the dollar, or buy the euro by taking a long position (i.e. an agreement to buy the asset) in a 1-year EUR/USD forward contract. What differentiates me from the dollar hedger is that I have no need to buy euros, nor to sell any dollars.

No doubt huge risks can result from speculation. For instance, you could sell short a share (i.e. borrow a share you do not own to sell it) and be exposed to unlimited loss from any rises in its price. (This has nothing to do with derivatives. Going short a forward, however, involves derivatives.) But if you have bought an option, your losses are limited to the initial premium (since you are not obliged to enter the transaction at expiry).

This rather curiously takes us to the point that derivatives need not be risky in themselves. Indeed, many (but not all) retail notes are structured such that the investor's principal (or at least part of it) is safe. Of course, an investor may at times want to surrender such protection in the hope of reaping even more significant gains. The next section will discuss structured notes, and the theme will be developed further in the book.

Key Points

- Derivatives are used for hedging and speculation.
- Hedging is aimed at protecting oneself from adverse market moves, but may not be perfect as the underlying and hedge may behave differently.
- Hedges can involve, for example, a forward (i.e. agreement to fix the price of a future transaction today), an option (i.e. the right but not obligation to enter into a future transaction), or even a knockout option (i.e. an option that can become worthless under certain conditions and is thus cheaper).
- Speculation is aimed at profiting by taking outright positions.
- Not all speculation involves derivatives (e.g. buying and selling shares); derivatives need not be more risky than cash positions (e.g. limited loss in option).

1.2   STRUCTURED NOTES

Structured products are bespoke instruments that enable investors to pursue strategies tailored to their market views. They allow an investor more control over the yield–risk tradeoff in his investment. In this section, I shall start by outlining the economic environment that encourages the growth of structured notes, and then explain them in more detail. The last decade of low interest rates (especially since 2001) has perhaps been a blessing to many (at least prior to the onset of the sub-prime crisis), but it has been a boon to others. In the days when interest rates were 7–8%, it was possible for one to earn a decent nominal yield by investing in a bond. But at 4–5%, this proposition looks much less attractive. (Figures 1.5 and 1.6 show the swap rates in the USA and Eurozone countries over the past decade.) Many pension funds pay on the basis of final salary schemes. At 7–8% nominal rates of return, their liabilities look much more manageable than at 4–5%. Indeed, many will have significant increases in their deficits unless they look to other sources of investments.

One can perhaps consider investment in equities. And indeed, there is some evidence that equities tend to outperform fixed income instruments in the long term. Figures 1.7 and 1.8 show the performances of the US and UK stock indices respectively, over the last two decades.

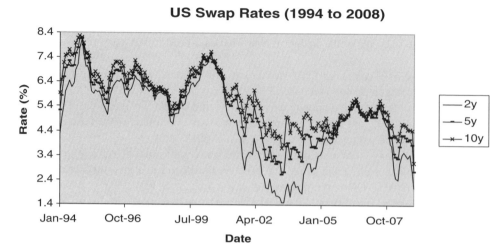

Figure 1.5 US swap rates for maturities 2y, 5y and 10y from 1994 to 2008. Notice how swap rates since 2001 have tended to be not much more than 5%, in contrast to the 7.5% around 2000 or even over 8% as in the mid-1990s.
Source: Bloomberg

Alas, it need not always hold true. A case in point is Japan. As can be seen in Figure 1.9, at its peak on 29 December 1989, the Nikkei 225 index was at 38,916. And as of 30 December 2008 (19 years later), it is merely at 8,860. In Europe, pension funds are also precluded from investing too large a proportion of their assets in equities.

Besides, after the dotcom bubble burst in March 2000, and the further deterioration of the equity markets after the 11 September attacks, an alternative to equities might seem a reasonable avenue to diversify one's portfolio. Although hedge funds have mostly filled this

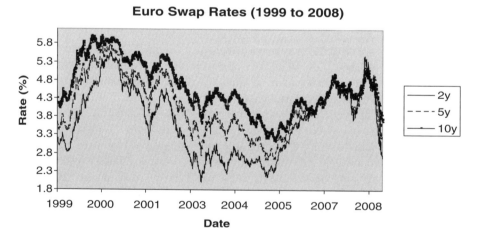

Figure 1.6 Euro swap rates for maturities 2y, 5y and 10y from 1999 to 2008. Notice how swap rates have tended to be under 5% for most of the period.
Source: Bloomberg

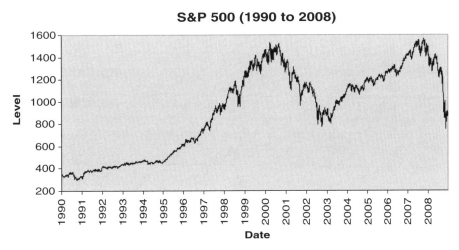

Figure 1.7　Level of S&P 500 index from 1990 to 2008. The S&P 500 index has had a meteoric rise from about 360 in January 1990 to over 1,500 by 2000, although there has been a period of decline from August 2000 to September 2003 to just over 800. Having climbed meaningful thereafter, there have been sharp declines in 2008.
Source: Bloomberg

gap, the opaque nature of their operations and their restrictive practices (e.g. lock-in periods and potential restrictions on withdrawal, especially in times of crisis) leave much to be desired.

It should also come as no surprise that structured products have catered to other investment needs. Being bespoke instruments, structured products can be used to pursue strategies involving equities, interest rates, foreign exchange, commodities, credit or real estate. Perhaps

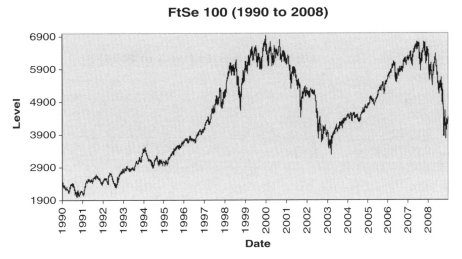

Figure 1.8　Level of FtSe 100 index from 1990 to 2008. The FtSe 100 has had a good run from 2,400 in January 1990 to a high of almost 6,900 in 2000. But like the S&P 500, the period until 2003 has been dismal, and the recovery since then has ended abruptly with the huge falls in 2008.
Source: Bloomberg

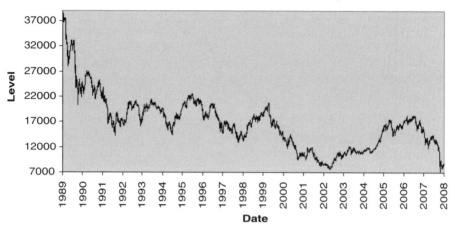

Figure 1.9 Level of Nikkei 225 index from 1990 to 2008. The Nikkei 225 index has never recovered from its peak of 38,916 on 29 December 1989. It stands only at 8,860 as of 30 December 2008.
Source: Bloomberg

an investor has a view that US inflation will stay low as per historical levels between 1.5% and 4% (see Figure 1.10). Or perhaps another investor has a view that USD/JPY will stay within historical ranges (established over the last two decades) (see Figure 1.11).

The amount of risk in structured products is very much dependent on the terms of the instrument. On one extreme, it is possible to have a contingent liability instrument where losses are not limited to one's initial investment. On the other hand, it is also possible to have notes where all (or part) of one's principal is protected and would be repaid at expiry, notwithstanding market fluctuations. In this sense, structured products often have risk profiles that are between those of a bond and a stock.

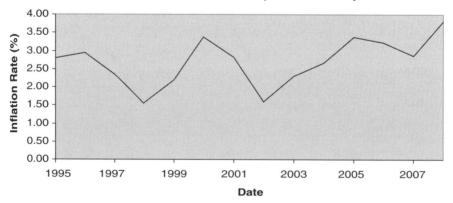

Figure 1.10 Rate of inflation in the USA (based on Consumer Price Index) from 1995 to 2008. It has been quite stable, hovering between 1.5% and 4% over the period.
Source: Bloomberg

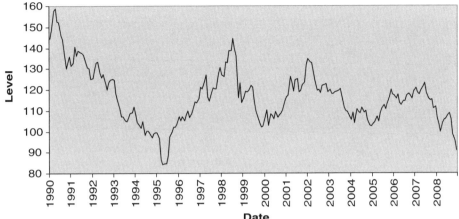

Figure 1.11   Value of spot USD/JPY from 1990 to 2008. This has ranged from a low close to 80 in 1995 to a high of 160 in 1990. However, the values have tended to be between 100 and 130 over much of the period.
Source: Bloomberg

The main idea is this: structured retail products exist because investors seek higher yield, with hopefully better control over risk.

The Concept of a Structured Note

Let me explain the basic concept. Suppose you have $1 and wish to invest it over a 5-year period. You could buy a bond and, say, get 4% interest every year. Alternatively, if you forgo the interest, your guaranteed principal is currently worth about $0.82. Figure 1.12 shows that the value of $1 paid at a future date decreases the further the payment date is. To see it another way, if you invest $0.82 now at 4% annual interest compounded yearly, it would be worth $0.82 \times 1.04^5 = \$1$ in 5 years' time.

You still have $0.18, which could be invested in something else. But what would you invest in? The choices are pretty limitless. You could buy a fraction of an option on the S&P 500 index. Or you could bet on the value of EUR/USD staying within some range for the next 5 years. You could go for a basket of equities in the hope that on average you will see a gain (even if one or two companies experience declines in fortunes). You could go for the difference between 10-year and 2-year euro swap rates, since historically the yield curve has usually been upward sloping, so that 10-year rates are typically higher than 2-year rates. (A swap rate is a rate pre-agreed for paying fixed coupons for a maturity, in exchange for floating coupons based on prevailing interest rates.) You could even go for the third best performer in a basket involving 5 stocks and 3 energy products.

Rather curiously, National Savings Premium Bonds (government backed) in the UK are based on the same concept of forgoing coupon interest. In this case, rather than being paid interest, the value of your interest is being entered into lottery prize draws. And the beauty is

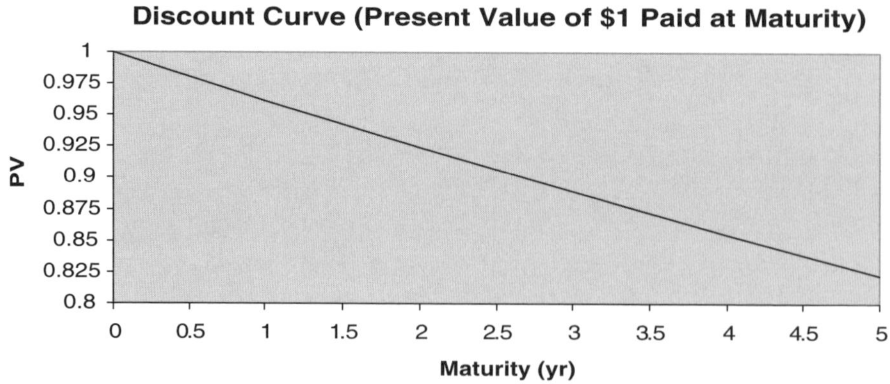

Discount Curve (Present Value of $1 Paid at Maturity)

Figure 1.12 A hypothetical discount curve, showing how $1 is worth less and less as the maturity (payment date) increases. This is because you can earn interest on $1 deposited today.

that this rather disciplined gambling means that your principal is still protected at the end of all this!

Of course, if your investment only returns your principal at expiry, you are worse off than a bond holder. But for a stock holder, it is not even assured that the stock price will not fall below current level a few years from now. **So, in this sense derivatives can be used to engineer a risk profile between that of a bond and a stock.**

It should be observed that **you might not opt for full principal protection**. Perhaps you only want to ensure that you get at least 90% of the principal back at expiry. In this case, the cost is $0.82 \times 0.9 = $0.74 today, leaving you $0.26 to invest in the structured coupons. And if you are brave or greedy, perhaps you do not need any principal protection and are happy to have your principal linked to the value of some market variable (e.g. the price of oil at expiry).

There are a few other themes I wish to mention which I hope to develop further in this book:

1. Betting against forwards
2. Upside participation
3. Protected selling of optionality
4. Benefiting from correlations.

These will be more formally introduced in the next chapter.

Caveats

Some caveats must be made regarding exotic products however.

Sacrificing Principal Protection

Investors, in their pursuit of yield, have at times given up the protection of a guaranteed principal. Take for example, the case of the Power Reverse Dual Currency (which I shall discuss in detail in Chapter 10). In their quest for a higher initial coupon, Japanese investors have often agreed to be repaid their notional (typically 30 years later) not in yen (i.e. their home currency) but in US dollars at a strike somewhat higher than the forward (say at 70 whereas the forward is 50), in the event that the product does not experience early termination.

(Note that the higher strike means they get fewer yen than if converting at the forward rate, since conversion of a yen amount into a dollar amount involves dividing by USD/JPY.) They do this partly in the belief that the realised rate for USD/JPY will be higher than suggested by the forward, and that the terms are such that early termination is very likely to occur anyway. **That is all well and good provided the investors realise the potential for huge losses.** Such features render the deal no longer as safe, and indeed such modifications when they backfire, tend to give derivatives a risky reputation.

Creditworthiness of Issuing Institution

The payments on structured notes are not only subject to market conditions, but also to the credit worthiness of the issuer. Such notes are just another claim on the issuer's assets. Even **"principal protection" merely means that the principal is not subject to market conditions, i.e. as safe as the principal payment of a bond by the same issuer.**
 When a company defaults, it will not repay the principal of fixed rate bonds either.

Illiquidity

It should be stressed that **structured products are usually illiquid**. They are tailor-made by banks to clients' investment preferences, and cannot be easily disposed of in a secondary market. You can get the issuing institution to cancel or restructure the contract (usually at a higher margin than the initial deal since the institution no longer has to price competitively). Alternatively, you can get another institution to prepare a structure whose cashflows offset the payments given by the earlier contract. The latter further exposes you to credit risk of both institutions. As such, it is **extremely important that the investor is comfortable with the structured product as is, and does not see disposal of it as an exit strategy**. For example, if you have a note that matures in 5 years, where you are happy with the worst case scenario, and do not need to dispose of it prior to maturity due to liquidity considerations, then it can be seen as a suitable investment. **If, however, you might need to realise cash from such a disposal in the event of coupons being less than you anticipated, you are best not to invest in the product, since disposal is likely to be more expensive than you think.**

Key Points

- The last decade saw low rates (e.g. 4–5%) in most developed economies, versus higher rates (e.g. 7–8%) from earlier periods. The immediate aftermath of 11 September 2001 also was a period of low yields and falling stock prices.
- Equities have been said to outperform in the long run but Japan is a counterpoint.
- Structured notes are bespoke instruments that can be tailored to an investor's preferences over assets, and also have been used to seek higher yields, with better control over risks.
- Principal protection is possible because $1 in the future is worth less than $1 today. If you forgo the coupons on a bond, these can be used to invest in structured coupons, while still ensuring that your principal is returned.
- Caveats include certain modifications that remove principal protection, creditworthiness of issuing institution, and the absence of a liquid market to dispose of structured notes.

2

Themes in Constructing Exotic Products

Notwithstanding the complexities of structured products, they often arise for simple reasons. For a yield investor, it is about obtaining a target payoff profile, with some desirable features: e.g. minimising potential losses and providing for participation in upside. For a corporate that is designing a hedging strategy, perhaps cost considerations and potential cashflow mismatches are of interest. To this end, certain common themes for structured products can be distilled. The subsequent chapters of this book will expand on many of these themes as they pertain to the various products covered. Nevertheless, the reader might benefit from a clearer statement of some of these broader ideas prior to reading specific examples of their application later in the book. We shall explore the themes *vis-à-vis* the yield investor first. One of the most powerful themes is that of principal protection (i.e. the original amount invested is repaid at maturity regardless of market conditions), which could be easily achieved by the zero-coupon bond. We next consider how an investor can achieve upside-only participation (i.e. exposure to gains but not to losses) through the use of options. This has a rather curious counterpart, in that the investor can instead sell optionality to achieve higher coupons, and if coupled with principal protection, will in any case ensure that losses are limited.

Going down the list of themes, we encounter the popular strategy of betting against the forward curve. Whereas market efficiency has been the orthodox view, historical data would bear out the success of various strategies that aim to take advantage of realised market variables being different from forwards. Next is diversification, which is a more traditional means of reducing risk in the context of a large portfolio.

Finally, we present some considerations that the hedger might wish to take into account.

There are lots of new ideas in this chapter. It can appear daunting, but please bear in mind that they will be elaborated upon throughout the book.

2.1 PRINCIPAL PROTECTION

Traditional investors typically limit themselves to bonds (government or corporate) and stocks. For government bonds (at least for developed economies), typically we can assume the probability of default to be negligible (which has become a questionable assertion since the credit crunch of 2008), so that one is assured of getting back one's principal (i.e. the original amount invested) together with a regular stream of coupons. (Even if governments can default, it is not clear what a safer alternative would be. So, we might have to live with it, short of physically hoarding cash.) For stocks, there is no such security. Stock prices fluctuate significantly even for companies in good health, and companies do go bankrupt from time to time.

Exotic products need not be any more risky than stocks. Indeed, **many structured notes are designed so that the investor gets back the principal at maturity regardless of fluctuations in market conditions. This is done simply by buying a zero-coupon bond which pays the principal at maturity.** (A note of $100 face value has a principal of $100. For a normal bond, this is the amount that is repaid at maturity.)

Principal protection refers to an arrangement that ensures that the investor's principal is repaid at maturity of the note, independent of market conditions.

The Zero-Coupon Bond

A zero-coupon bond pays no coupon during its life, but just the principal amount at maturity. Assuming interest rates are greater than zero, such a bond must be worth less than the principal amount today. This is sometimes known as the time value of money. Specifically, suppose interest rates are 3% annually compounded, then a 5-year zero-coupon bond with a principal of $100 is worth $100 \times \left(\frac{1}{1.03}\right)^5 = \$86.26$ today.

(Whereas most bonds issued are coupon-bearing, you can treat each coupon payment as a separate zero-coupon bond with face value being the coupon amount, and maturity being the coupon payment date. The principal payable at maturity is also a zero-coupon bond.)

The Sacrificed Coupon

A 5-year par bond (i.e. a bond whose present value or value today is the same as its principal) should yield annual coupons of 3% if prevailing rates were 3%. The principal repayment at maturity is worth 86.26% of the total value today, while the coupons are worth the remaining 13.74%. If the investor desires principal protection, he effectively purchases a zero-coupon bond from the issuer. The issuer, however, can then use the remaining 13.74% of the value today to purchase structured coupons as per the terms of the investment (see Figure 2.1).

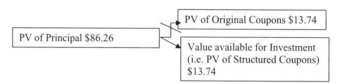

Figure 2.1   Of the $100 you have today, $86.26 is required to buy a zero-coupon bond which pays you the principal ($100) at maturity. The original coupons of a bond would be worth the remaining $13.74 but these can instead be made available to invest in structured coupons.

Note that since the remaining $13.74 is supposed to provide the yield for the entire note, it tends to be placed in a rather leveraged investment. This is not unreasonable. After all, suppose you expect a 7% per annum return on a stock. Noting that your zero-coupon bond is yielding 3%, to get a 7% overall return your $13.74 investment must now yield

$$\frac{1.07 - 1.03 \times 0.8626}{0.1374} - 1 = 32.1\%!$$

Think of it this way: This arrangement ensures that your principal is safe and, to a lesser or greater extent, you are gambling with the sacrificed coupons. On the other hand, when buying a stock, your principal is not safe.

Principal Protection is Subject to the Issuer's Credit

This may be a case of misleading terminology but principal protection only means that the principal payment is not subject to market conditions. **This means that the principal repayment is as safe as any other bond by the issuer. In the event that the issuer defaults, the**

principal repayment does not get any priority. Some investors unfortunately misunderstood this point, and were horrified to find that their Lehman-issued principal-protected structured notes were not worth very much when Lehman Brothers defaulted in September 2008.

Some banks have now added a disclaimer on their "principal protected" structured notes to say principal payment is subject to their credit risk. **Perhaps a more foolproof approach might be to buy government zero-coupon bonds and hold these on trust for the investor.** (Of course, since government bond yields are much lower than bank yields – especially in the risk-averse environment post-2008 – there will be less leftover value to invest in the structured coupons.)

We summarise the key differences between a bond, a stock and a principal protected note in Table 2.1.

Table 2.1   Key differences between a bond, a stock and a principal protected note. Note that the principal of both a bond and a principal protected note are only safe if the issuer does not default. Similarly, the coupon of a bond depends on the issuer remaining solvent.

Feature	Bond	Stock	Principal Protected Note
Principal Repayment Assured at Maturity	Yes.	No concept of maturity. Value of stock may be higher or lower than invested amount at any point in time.	Yes.
Regular Coupons	Yes.	No coupons payable. If stocks appreciate, investor can realise value in the period by selling a proportion of them.	Some notes have regular coupons while others accrue payment until maturity. Coupons are dependent on market conditions.
Potential Upside	None.	Can be very large.	Can be large but typically smaller than for a stock.
Amount at Risk	None except during default.	Entire investment.	Typically coupons are at risk if markets behave unexpectedly.

Extensions of the Principal Protection Concept

Perhaps the investor wants protection of her real principal (i.e. where the principal is adjusted to reflect inflation over the period). In that case, she can instead have an investment in a zero-coupon inflation-linked note, where the principal repayable is linked to some inflation index (e.g. Retail Price Index in the UK). Specifically, the repayment at expiry is the principal amount multiplied by $\frac{RPI_T}{RPI_0}$ (i.e. the ratio of the retail price index at maturity versus that today). Inflation-protecting the principal costs more than normal principal protection, so there is less value left over for investing in structured coupons.

Partial Principal Protection

On the other hand, perhaps the investor is willing to take some loss, e.g. 10% of notional. In that case, a zero-coupon bond with notional at 90% of the invested amount can be bought, and more value is freed to invest in the structured coupons. In this case, the cost would be $86.26 \times 0.9 = \$77.63$, leaving \$22.37 to invest in structured coupons.

Key Points

- Many structured notes are designed so that principal repayment at expiry does not depend on market conditions.
- Principal protection is achieved by buying a zero-coupon bond. This costs less than its face value (provided rates are positive), so part of the original amount remains to invest in structured coupons, usually with a fair amount of leverage.
- Principal protection is subject to the issuer's credit risk, unless the zero-coupon bond is issued by a government (however, even that is now uncertain).
- Protection of an inflation-adjusted principal is also possible, but is more expensive

---

2.2   UPSIDE-ONLY PARTICIPATION

Traditional portfolio managers will advise an investor seeking a high return to invest more of his portfolio in stocks (especially growth stocks). Historically, the stock market has yielded more than the bond market, and this has tended to be attributed to the risk premium. However, as we all are aware, stock prices can be volatile and losses over an extended period cannot be ignored. Is there a possibility of participating in the upside of a stock while eschewing any downside risk?

The Option

Consider a European **call option that gives you the right (but not the obligation) to buy** 1 stock of Walmart at the end of 1 year at a strike of $60. (A European option is exercisable only on the expiry date itself, i.e. you can only do the purchase 1 year from today, not before.)

If in 1 year's time, Walmart stock is trading over $60 (say it is $72), you will exercise the option to buy the stock at $60 and hence pocket the difference of $72 − $60 = $12. If, however, Walmart stock is trading at $55, you will allow the option to expire worthless. Figure 2.2 shows how the payoff of the call option at expiry varies based on the price of Walmart stock.

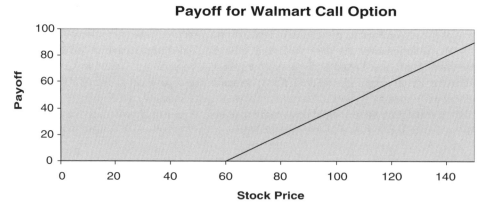

Figure 2.2   Payoff at expiry of call option with strike $60 on Walmart for different realised values of the stock. The call option has a payoff that benefits from a rising stock price but in any case is never below 0.

You can see that an option is valuable since (at worst) you can allow it to expire worthless, whereas (at best) you can exercise it to acquire a valuable asset for less than its purchase price. So, if you think the stock market is going up, a call option will allow you to participate in the upside, while not having to suffer should the stock market collapse.

Similarly, we can have a European **put option on BMW stock with expiry 6 months that allows you to sell** at strike €15. In this case, if BMW falls to X (below €15), you can sell at €15 to realise a profit of €15 − X. If the stock stays above €15 in 6 months, you simply allow the option to expire worthless. Figure 2.3 shows how the price of the put option varies based on the value of BMW stock.

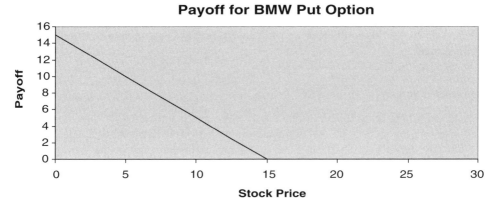

Figure 2.3 Payoff at expiry of put option on BMW with strike €15 for different realised values of the stock. The payoff of the put option is higher as the stock price falls. However, if the stock price is above €15, the payoff is zero.

In this way, options give you plenty of flexibility in tailoring your investment strategy. Much more complex optionality exists, and this will be covered in later chapters.

Cost of an Option

Since an option gives you the right but not the obligation to act, it is a valuable asset. In general, its cost depends on the volatility of the asset. Notice that if the underlying does not move, the cost of the option is wasted. For example, if Walmart is $48 today and you buy the above 1-year European call with strike $60, you clearly will waste the value of the option if Walmart stock stays at $48. In that sense, buying options is not a no-brainer.

Even so, in structured notes, options are typically used to generate coupons that reflect an investment view. Basically, having acquired a zero-coupon bond to ensure some level of principal protection, the remaining present value can then be used to acquire options to allow for upside participation if market conditions turn out as the investor expects.

Key Points

- A call option allows an investor to participate in upside moves of an asset while loss is limited to the price paid.

- A put option allows an investor to sell an asset for a given price.
- The cost of an option depends on volatility; if the price of an asset does not move sufficiently, the value of an option would be wasted.

2.3   PROTECTED SELLING OF OPTIONALITY FOR YIELD

The typical investor is hungry for yield. As the previous section discussed, options are valuable. So, **an investor can enhance the yield on the investment by protected selling of optionality**. Whereas this may sound risky, it need not be. An investor can sell optionality by limiting the coupon receivable. Or perhaps the note could terminate early in the event of it being too favourable to the investor. Or perhaps the coupons can be made conditional on some other unrelated event. **All this could be done while insisting that the principal is protected in all circumstances.**

Unprotected Selling of Optionality

Unprotected selling of optionality is extremely risky, and is unlikely to be suitable for most retail investors. In Section 2.2, we discussed the payoff of the call option. Suppose it costs $4.60 to buy the call option. That is the maximum profit the seller of the call option can make (and this only occurs if the option expires worthless). In contrast, Figure 2.4 shows that if the stock price rises significantly, the seller of the call option is subject to potentially unlimited losses. In this way, **selling options can lead to losses that are far beyond one's initial investment** (which is zero if we do not include exchange-imposed margins).

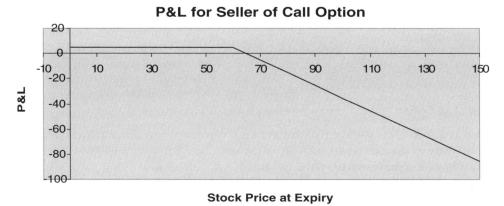

Figure 2.4   P&L for the seller of a call option based on different realised values of the stock at expiry. The maximum profit is $4.60 provided the stock price at expiry is below $60, whereas losses can be much worse if the stock price rises substantially.

In the remainder of the book, when we discuss selling optionality, we only refer to **protected selling of optionality. This is where the investor already holds either the underlying or some other options, so that the investor can deliver on the obligations of any options sold against these.** For example, suppose you have Walmart stock and sell a call option at $72. If Walmart stock rises above $72, you can deliver the stock and hence discharge your liabilities.

Capping the Coupon

Consider our call option discussed earlier. If you think it is unlikely that Walmart stock will rise above $80, then perhaps you are happy to have a cap in your payoff of $80 − $60 = $20 (i.e. in the unlikely event that Walmart stock trades at $92 in 1 year's time, you still get only a maximum of $20). Effectively, what you have done is to sell a call option with a strike of $80. Together with the call option that you have bought with strike $60, your payoff is effectively in the range $0 to $20. Figure 2.5 illustrates the payoffs of being long (i.e. to buy) a call with a strike of $60, short (i.e. to sell) a call with a strike of $80 and the capped call. Of course, you are compensated for having sold this option, and so the total cost of the structure is lower to you.

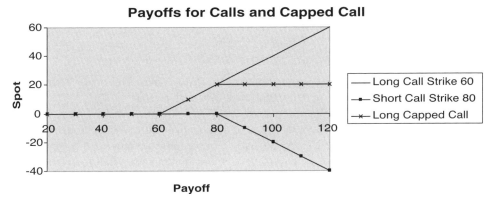

Figure 2.5   The long call option with strike $60 allows you to benefit from stock prices over $60. The short call option with strike $80 means you will incur losses as the stock price goes over $80. Combined, they create a payoff which allows you to benefit as the stock price goes above $60 but which is capped at $20 as the stock price goes beyond $80.

Barriers and Triggers

Suppose instead we have our call option with another clause: if Walmart stock drops below $35 at any time prior to the expiry date, then the option immediately becomes worthless. (Do not worry about the details. We shall cover this in the chapter on barriers.) It is clear that this structure must cost less than the original call option, since there are certain conditions under which it could become worthless.

If we take this idea further: suppose you have a structured note that pays a series of coupons tied to positive performance of EUR/USD (e.g. a coupon like $0.2 \times \max \left(EURUSD_{t_i} - 1.4, 0 \right)$). Suppose, however, that the note automatically terminates if EUR/USD rises above 1.55. This is a trigger condition, which makes the deal cheaper. (In the event of early termination, typically the principal is repaid immediately and the investor loses the chance to benefit from favourable future coupons.)

Callables

Alternatively, the note could contain a condition that allows the issuer the discretion to call it and repay the principal immediately. Let us illustrate this with a simple case. Consider an ordinary fixed rate bond of $100 notional which pays a coupon of 4% annually. If interest rates rise above 4%, this is worth less than $100 (since the investor is stuck with a below market yield). And if interest rates fall below 4%, this is worth more than $100.

If this bond were callable, the issuer would call it if rates fell sufficiently (e.g. to 2.8%), limiting the upside to the investor . However, the downside is that the investor is still stuck with the bond if rates rise. The investor would be compensated for this adverse feature by being given a higher coupon (e.g. 4.7%).

Tarns

Another idea is that perhaps the deal could terminate if the total coupons received reach some level, say 15% of notional. For example, suppose you have a note that pays

$$0.3 \times \max \left(\frac{S_{t_i}}{S_{t_{i-1}}} - 1, 0 \right),$$

where S_t is the value of the stock at time t, and t_i are coupon dates. This note basically pays some multiplier times the positive return of a stock over each period.

Maybe your returns over the first few periods are 7%, 2.4%, 0%, 4.3%, 0%, 4.1%. Then the cumulative returns reach 17.8% after the 6th period (more than the 15% condition) and so the deal terminates then (see Table 2.2). Again, early termination is accompanied by repayment of principal immediately. (Chapter 8 covers early termination in more detail.)

Table 2.2 Hypothetical cumulative coupons on a tarn. The tarn level is 15%, so that at the end of the 6th period when cumulative coupons reach 17.8%, the deal terminates.

Coupon	Cumulative coupons	Remarks
7%	7%	
2.4%	9.4%	
0%	9.4%	
4.3%	13.7%	
0%	13.7%	
4.1%	17.8%	Deal terminates after coupon is paid

Conditional Payoffs

Perhaps you could have a payoff that requires a completely different condition to be fulfilled. The payoff could be $0.3 \times \max (EURUSD_T - 1.4, 0)$ but subject to Euribor being less than 2.5% at expiry date (otherwise coupon is 0). Clearly, this additional condition means that the probability of receiving the original payoff is less, and so the structure is cheaper. This is usually compensated for by a higher coupon; e.g. without the Euribor condition, the payoff might instead have been $0.2 \times \max (EURUSD_T - 1.4, 0)$.

Range Accruals

Why bet everything on expiry? Perhaps the condition could instead be applied over a period. For example, we could have daily fixings and n can be the number of business days for which Euribor is under 2.5% while N is the total number of business days in the period. Then the payoff could be

$$0.25 \times \max\left(EURUSD_T - 1.4, 0\right) \times \frac{n}{N}.$$

This is basically a range accrual. Figure 2.6 illustrates one possible path of EUR/USD *vis-à-vis* the barrier of the range accrual. (We shall discuss range accruals further in Chapter 7.)

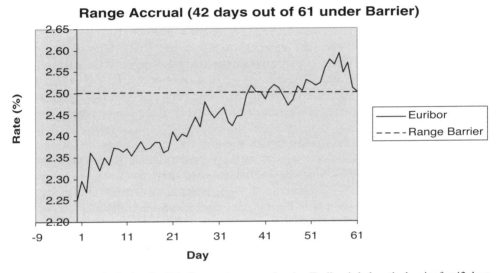

Figure 2.6 Hypothetical path of Euribor against range barrier. Euribor is below the barrier for 42 days out of 61 in the period, which gives a multiplier of $42/61 = 0.69$.

As I hope you can by now appreciate, there are lots of ways to sell optionality. I shall endeavour to make them clearer to you in the course of the book.

Key Points

- Protected selling of optionality (i.e. limiting the coupon receivable) can enhance yield while keeping principal protection. Unprotected selling (i.e. selling options without owning the underlying) exposes one to potentially unlimited downside.
- Capping the coupon (by selling an option with a higher strike than the one you have bought) can enhance yield.
- Barriers and triggers are provisions that cause a deal to terminate due to certain events. These make a deal cheaper since there is a risk of losing the payoff.
- Callability allows the issuer to terminate the note when it is in her favour.
- Tarn features provide for termination of a note when a certain amount of cumulative coupons have been paid, hence limiting the upside.
- Conditional payoffs are such that certain market conditions must occur (e.g. Euribor less than 2.5%) for the coupon to be paid.
- Range accruals are such that coupons accrue on the basis of the number of days in a period in which certain conditions are met.

2.4   BETTING AGAINST THE FORWARD CURVE

The orthodox thinking in finance is that markets are efficient. One consequence is that you cannot systematically beat the market, whereas to earn a risk premium you need to take systemic market risk.

Forward Interest Rates

Do not worry too much about forward interest rates as they will be covered in detail in Chapter 6. I must, however, outline what they are briefly to give context to the discussion below. To understand forward interest rates, consider this simple example. Suppose you can buy a 1-year bond with a coupon of 4% and a 2-year bond with a coupon of 5%. Instead of buying the 2-year bond, it must be possible for you to buy the 1-year bond and agree in advance the rate at which you deposit your money from the end of year 1 until the end of year 2. That rate would be a forward rate.

Another consequence of the efficient market hypothesis is the assumption that forward rates are the best predictors of future interest rates. But that is patently untrue. **If you look at interest rates for the USA since 1950, you will see that the yield curve has tended to be upward sloping most of the time.** If forward rates are to be realised, then an upward sloping yield curve suggests that future short-term interest rates must rise. Specifically, at some point the yield curve would be inverted. Inverted curves do exist and tend to create havoc for market participants, but they are not the norm. Upward-sloping curves tend to be the norm.

Let's assume that you do a swap. (The mechanics of a swap requires some explanation, and Section 6.1 covers this in detail. For now, it is enough to understand the main ideas.) The swap involves an exchange of cashflows: one party pays on the basis of a floating rate and the other on a fixed rate. The floating rate will be fixed, say, every 3 months, based on Libor (a benchmark rate for interbank lending), whereas the fixed rate (also termed swap rate) is determined at inception based on some averaging of forward Libor rates. Take a swap of 2 years, with annual payments. If the 1-year Libor rate is 4% today and the swap fixed rate is 5%, then the projected forward Libor rate 1 year from now has to be 6.06%. But usually, the curve 1 year hence remains upward sloping and the realised Libor rate is then 5% or even just 4% again. So it seems to be advantageous to pay the floating leg and receive the fixed leg. Similarly, it was often advantageous to borrow via floating rate notes and invest in fixed rate bonds (the essence of a swap).

But the yield curve inverts from time to time, and such strategies have tended to cause grief. Specifically, when interest rates rise dramatically, the short end rises more than the long end. So, if you have liabilities that rise with floating rates, but assets that pay on the basis of a long-term fixed rate, you are likely to find the interest on your liabilities exceeding the receipts on your assets if rates rise substantially. This was partly the cause of the savings and loans crisis of the 1980s in the USA. We shall discuss this further in Chapter 6 on Constant Maturity Swaps.

We now require the definition of a Constant Maturity Swap. This basically pays a floating long-term reference rate (e.g. 10-year rate) refixed at every coupon date (e.g. every 3 months). The idea is that long-term interest rates tend to be higher than short-term interest rates. So, **if you are not confident that rates will stay low, but still prefer to receive the long end of the curve, why not have a floating rate note, based on a long-term reference rate**?

Forward FX Rates

In the realm of foreign exchange, the bet is that the forward does not represent future realised FX rates. After all, the forward is based on the cost of carry. The logic is as follows: Suppose I have \$1. I can convert it to yen at the spot USD/JPY rate of 120. I can then deposit it to obtain whatever the yen rate of interest is (say 1%). At the end of 5 years, I have ¥120 × $1.01^5 =$ ¥126.12. I could instead have kept it in dollars at a 4% rate, earning \$1 × $1.04^5 = \$1.2167$. Suppose I had a forward to buy yen for \$1 in 5 years' time. For no arbitrage, the 5-year forward FX rate must be $\frac{126.12}{1.2167} = 103.66$. If we look at longer expiries (e.g. 30 years), the forward FX rate can be much lower than the spot (e.g. a 30-year forward of 50 versus a spot of 115 in 2007 when dollar rates were much higher than yen rates). Basically, the forward will be lower than the spot if interest rates for currency 2 are lower than rates for currency 1 in the pair ccy1/ccy2.

But **most yen investors actually do not believe that USD/JPY will drop to anywhere close to these levels predicted by the forward FX rates** (at least prior to 2008). In fact, Japanese government policy has tended to favour a weak yen to boost exports. Instead, investors think the forward FX rate would stay closer to spot. This leads to the carry trade: specifically, borrow yen at a low interest rate and invest in dollars at a higher interest rate. As long as yen does not appreciate against the dollar, you earn the interest rate differential. When yen appreciated sharply in late 2007 to 2008 following the flight to safety induced by the credit crisis, the unwinding of the carry trade contributed to an even bigger rise in the yen (to just under 90 at the beginning of 2009). **(Note that due to the quotation of USD/JPY as the number of yen per dollar, USD/JPY actually drops when the yen strengthens.)** So, there are certainly risks attached.

Key Points

- Notwithstanding efficient market hypothesis, forwards are not always good predictors of future values.
- The yield curve has tended to be upward sloping, which implies rising forward interest rates. However, future short-term interest rates often stay the same, making it advantageous to pay the floating leg of a swap.
- The yield curve inverts from time to time and can create havoc for floating rate borrowers (e.g. the savings and loans crisis of the 1980s in the USA).
- CMS refers to payments tied to a floating long-term rate (e.g. 10-year), reset every coupon period – a suitable investment when rates are rising but the curve remains upward sloping.
- Forward FX rates are determined by the interest rate differential of the two currencies. However, they do not accurately predict future spot FX rates.
- Many yen investors believe that USD/JPY will stay roughly at current levels, whereas the forward FX rate is much lower than spot. Hence, the carry trade (i.e. borrowing yen and investing in dollars) seems advantageous.
- Occasional rises in the yen (e.g. to USD/JPY of 90 in 2009) had an adverse effect on the carry trade.

2.5 DIVERSIFICATION

Diversification is perhaps a more orthodox member among the themes discussed in this chapter. Basically, portfolio theory says that you can diversify away uncorrelated risk of individual stocks, and be left mainly with market risk for which you would earn a premium. Whether you fully accept that (and certainly there are concerns of correlations increasing in times of crisis as investors dump everything and seek the safety of government securities), there is still logic not to put all your "eggs in one basket". So, rather than have a structured note based on one asset, perhaps you could have such a note based on more assets.

Baskets of Stocks

As a simple example, you could have your returns tied to a basket of stocks. Or you could use a stock index. Correlation has the effect of lowering the volatility of an average *vis-à-vis* the underlying. So, an option on the Dow Jones Industrial Average has a lower volatility than the average volatility of its underlying constituents. The higher the volatility of an option, the greater the cost to hedge it, hence the more expensive it is to buy.

Cross Asset Baskets

You could even construct bespoke baskets across asset classes. One popular choice was to have a basket involving equities and commodities (at least during the commodities boom of 2007). You could also include fixed income instruments or FX.

Asian Options

Another example is the average-rate Asian option. This is an option where the payoff is based on the average of observations of the underlying (say daily end-of-day average) rather than its value at expiry. (There is another type of Asian option where the average is used in place of a fixed strike, i.e. the average-strike Asian option. But we shall ignore that in this book, and any subsequent reference to Asian options will be to average-rate Asian options.) In some sense, it follows the same theme as the range accrual, i.e. the payoff is not overly influenced by the value of the underlying on one date (expiry).

As an added bonus, an Asian option is cheaper than a European option, since it costs much less to hedge. When 2 months of a 3-month Asian option have passed, part of the average rate has already been determined with only one third of it left. Basically, the return of an Asian option over each observation period is less than perfectly correlated and there is, therefore, less volatility.

Key Points

- Portfolio theory advises diversification to eliminate uncorrelated risk.
- A basket of stocks (e.g. stock index) has lower volatility than the average of its constituents. This makes an option cheaper since the hedging cost is lower.
- Cross asset baskets are possible.
- An Asian option has payoff based on the average of observations over a period. This reduces volatility since returns over each period are not perfectly correlated.

2.6   SOME CONSIDERATIONS IN HEDGING

Hedging is very different from yield seeking. Specifically, **the aim should be to limit exposure to adverse market conditions, rather than to make a profit**. (Indeed, it is possible to do worse with a hedge, since the market might move in your favour when you are not hedged.) So, if you are a euro producer and know you are going to receive $100 million in 3 months' time, the cleanest hedge is a 3-month forward to sell dollars and buy euros for the said amount. However, often cashflows are uncertain and perhaps there is some interest in minimising the cost of hedges, so let me offer a few thoughts on exotic products and hedging.

Inappropriate Hedges

Some exotic products, e.g. barrier options, exist because they are cheaper. Suppose you think you might receive dollars (dependent on trading conditions) and decide to buy an option to allow you to convert $50 million into euros at a EUR/USD strike of 1.3 (i.e. $1.3 per euro). Suppose, however, you feel that such an option costs too much. One possibility is to have a barrier feature that knocks out the option should EUR/USD reach 1.15 prior to expiry. Basically, you are getting a cheaper deal by betting that if the dollar strengthens so that EUR/USD reaches 1.15 during the life of the deal, you would no longer need to hedge.

Such a deal might be logical but it might not be a safe hedge. What if euro depreciates to 1.14 early in the life of the option and then appreciates (i.e. rises) to 1.44 at expiry? (See Figure 2.7.) You are no longer protected from a weakening of the dollar as per the original aims of the hedge.

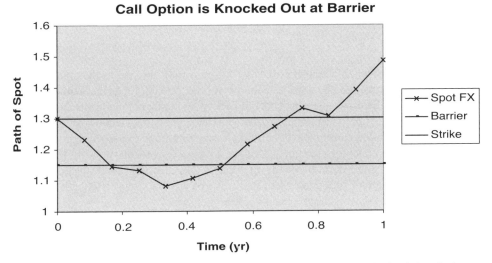

Figure 2.7 Path of spot FX. Knockout call option has a barrier level 1.15. Option is knocked out at time 2 months. Thus, even though at expiry of 1 year, EUR/USD is above the strike of 1.3, the payoff is 0. (Same as Figure 1.4.)

In 2008, as volatility skyrocketed, lots of barrier options proved worthless since the barriers were breached. This is something to bear in mind.

Uncertain Outcomes

It is worth referring once more to the issue of uncertain outcomes. Let us suppose that you have decided to hedge via a forward. However, your trading revenues in dollars are not the anticipated $100 million, but the much smaller $8 million, and if the dollar appreciates against the euro, you could lose substantially.

As another example, consider a pension fund. It might try to hedge its projected liabilities by entering into offsetting transactions. In the rare event that these liabilities are reduced, say due to demographics or changes in the company, it might have overhedged and could face losses if the markets then moved in a manner different from the intents of the hedge.

Liquidity

Another consideration about hedging is liquidity. If a hedge gives you a net present value equal to anticipated liabilities but the cashflow timings are different, then you could potentially be faced with problems of paying off liabilities even if you are solvent. A story that comes to mind is that of Metallgesellschaft, which sold long-term (e.g. 10-year) forwards on energy and hedged them with short-term futures in 1993. Futures are exchange-traded contracts where there is daily cash settlement of P&L based on traded futures prices. Forwards, on the other hand, provide for no exchange of cash until their maturity dates. As energy prices fell, Metallgesellschaft's forward positions provided a huge mark-to-market gain which, however, could only be realised in 10 years' time. The futures comprising the hedge led to correspondingly huge mark-to-market losses, which had to be settled daily. Having thus paid $900 million to satisfy margin calls on its futures, it ran out of cash, and only a bailout by a consortium of German and international banks saved it from bankruptcy.

Counterparty Risk

A final point to consider as a hedger is that the hedge is only as good as the counterparty's solvency. When Lehman Brothers went bankrupt, various pension funds that purchased protection via Liability Directed Investing strategies set up by Lehman, found these hedges to be no longer applicable. Admittedly counterparty risk is something that yield investors also face, but **for hedgers, a failed counterparty can mean a sudden huge exposure**. For instance, if you buy a forward contract for a certain quantity of oil at a strike of $50, you would usually not take any further precautionary measures as oil prices increase (to $90 say). If the counterparty who sold you the contract goes under, then suddenly you are fully impacted by the $40 surge in oil prices, from which you assumed you were immunised.

Key Points

- Hedging is meant to limit one's exposure to adverse market moves. If you have an unhedged position, the market may move in your favour or against you.
- It is tempting to minimise hedging cost, but some features may cause a hedge to provide inadequate protection in certain circumstances (e.g. barriers).
- If the outcome you are hedging is uncertain, it is possible to overhedge (and be subject to adverse market moves correspondingly).
- Liquidity considerations are important in hedging since there might be potentially serious cashflow mismatches (e.g. Metallgesellschaft).

3

Basics of Derivatives

This chapter covers the basics of derivatives pricing. If you are an experienced derivatives professional and are reading this book to broaden your product coverage, you may wish to skip this chapter. However, for those new to derivatives pricing, this chapter will present the main ideas on which all derivatives pricing relies.

First, we introduce the forward contract and plain vanilla options. Next, we shall look at how no arbitrage principles form the basis of derivatives pricing. We then go on to the Black–Scholes model. While derivatives modelling has made significant advances from its origins in the Black–Scholes model, quite a bit of insight is to be gained by examining it. Further, concepts such as volatility are best thought of in Black–Scholes terms. We then examine correlation and, finally, present some considerations involved in product modelling.

The non-technical reader may find this chapter difficult. Hopefully, if you cannot follow the minutiae of the mathematics, you can at least pick up the key ideas. The equations presented may also be referred to time and again in the remainder of the book.

3.1 THE FORWARD CONTRACT

A forward contract is an agreement to either buy or sell a fixed quantity of assets at a pre-agreed price (strike) on a future date.

Suppose I enter into a forward contract with you to buy 1 share of Yahoo 6 months from now at a strike of $K = \$11.11$. If Yahoo's share price increases, I can sell it at the prevailing market price of S_T for a profit of $S_T - K$. However, since I am obliged to buy Yahoo under the contract, I shall incur a loss if Yahoo's share price collapses. The payoff diagram is shown in Figure 3.1.

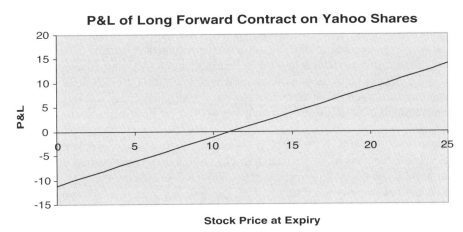

Figure 3.1 P&L of a long forward contract for different values of the underlying at maturity. If Yahoo stock price drops below the strike of $11.11 at expiry, I shall incur a loss on the position.

The Fair Value of the Strike

Suppose Yahoo today is worth $11. I can borrow or lend dollars at 2% annually. Yahoo pays no dividends on its shares. I could deposit my $11 and it would be worth $11 × (1 + 0.02 × 0.5) = $11.11 in 6 months' time. So, unless the strike for the forward contract is $11.11, there would be arbitrage.

Specifically, if the strike is less than $11.11, I should enter a forward contract to buy Yahoo shares. I then sell short (i.e. sell an asset I do not own by borrowing it) Yahoo shares at $11 and deposit my money in the bank. After 6 months, I take my $11.11, pay for the Yahoo shares as specified in the forward contract to close out my short position, and pocket the difference. (The above assumes that I can borrow Yahoo shares for free. In practice, there is a small nominal charge and that, of course, has to be taken into account in pricing the forward.)

If the strike is greater than $11.11, I instead enter a forward contract to sell Yahoo shares. I borrow $11 to buy them today and hold the shares to deliver them against the forward contract. After 6 months, I pay back $11.11 and pocket the difference.

Thus, no-arbitrage requires the fair-value forward price of a non-dividend paying stock to be

$$F_t = S(1 + rt),$$

where S is spot, r is the rate of interest, and t is the time to delivery.

Notice that in pricing the forward, we are not interested in whether the stock itself will appreciate (i.e. rise in value) or depreciate (i.e. fall in value) over time. Our static hedge (comprising a position in the stock and appropriate funding) ensures that we are protected either way. That is the essence of no-arbitrage pricing.

Contingent Liability

As it costs zero to enter into the above forward contract, this is a contingent liability instrument. Contingent liability means that the potential losses are not limited to the initial investment. Contrast this to a normal structured note. You pay a principal up front to invest in the note, and you are not liable for any future payments. In the worst case scenario, the note defaults and you are left with zero (quite bad but you need not fish for more cash to settle any liabilities). Contingent liability instruments carry the added danger that a market participant may be over-leveraged and unable to meet potential liabilities if markets move against her. Typically, financial institutions will want to protect themselves against counterparty risk by ensuring the credit-worthiness of parties with whom they enter into such deals. In any case, regulators tend to require much more disclosure and verification of investor expertise (mainly to protect unsophisticated investors) should she wish to get involved in contingent liability instruments.

In the case of forwards, it should be remarked that they are traded over-the-counter (i.e. they are private contracts with individual financial institutions). However, futures, which have similar payoffs, are traded on organised exchanges. (As the clearing house of the exchange is the central counterparty to all trades, participants do not have to worry about the credit-worthiness of their counterpart.) These exchanges require that participants who have open positions post a margin (i.e. money or liquid collateral) to cover potential adverse market moves. At the close of each business day, there is a mark-to-market based on the prices of traded contracts, and the contracts are settled daily. For example, if you have a 6-month contract to buy the S&P 500 index at 890, and the contract trades at 877 at the end of the day, you will have to pay $890 - 877 = 13$ times the notional multiplier (i.e. \$250). Futures give much better protection against counterparty risk, but the daily settlement can lead to liquidity problems if the market moves against you.

Key Points

- A forward contract is an agreement to buy or sell an asset at a given price at maturity.
- The fair-value forward price does not depend on expectations regarding the future value of the asset price, since we can construct a hedge for a forward contract.
- A contingent liability instrument is one where potential losses are not limited to the value of one's initial investment

---

3.2 THE PLAIN VANILLA OPTION

A European call option on a stock (say Walmart) allows the holder the right to buy the stock at a strike $K = 70$ on the expiry date $T = 1y$. If the stock price S_T on expiry date is greater than 70, then the holder will exercise the option to buy the stock at 70 and can sell it at S_T, at a profit of $S_T - 70$. Otherwise, the option expires worthless.

Alternatively, consider a European put option that allows the holder to sell the stock at a strike of $K = 70$ on the expiry date $T = 1y$. Now, if the stock price S_T is less than 70, the holder will make $70 - S_T$, since he could buy the stock at S_T and exercise the option to sell it at 70. If S_T is higher than 70 on the expiry date, the investor simply walks away.

It is worth mentioning that the put–call parity relationship holds independently of the pricing of a call or put. Specifically, this states that

$$C_t - P_t = S_t - \frac{K}{1 + r(T - t)},$$

where C_t is the price of a call option with expiry T and strike K as seen at prior time t (i.e. $t < T$), P_t is the price of the corresponding put option, S_t is the value of the underlying and r is the rate of interest. (Incidentally, $S_t - \frac{K}{1+r(T-t)}$ is the present value of a forward with strike K.)

This is easy to see if we consider the payoff diagrams for a call and a put (Figures 3.2 and 3.3 respectively) and that for the stock at expiry. As Figure 3.4 shows, buying 1 call and selling 1 put gives the stock minus the strike at expiry. Hence, at time t, the equation above holds (where we had to discount the strike appropriately).

For completeness, it is worth mentioning that an American option is one where the holder can exercise at any date prior to expiry.

The natural question is: How much are options worth? Derivatives pricing is about valuation of such and other instruments. In this chapter, we shall see the main ideas involved in the valuation of such instruments. Whereas I intend to devote much of the book to explaining products, it is nonetheless worth getting some insight into how these products are valued. It is after all the ability to value and risk-manage such products that encourages banks to devise new, innovative structures.

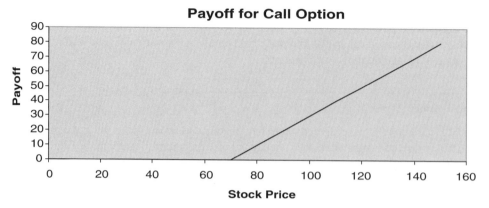

Figure 3.2 Payoff of a call option for different values of stock price at expiry. The payoff increases as the stock price increases beyond the strike 70. If the stock price is less than the strike, the payoff is 0.

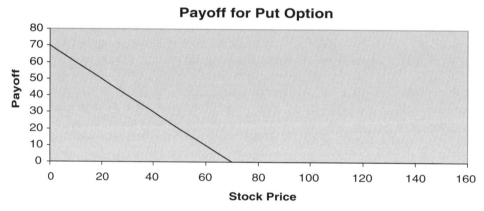

Figure 3.3 Payoff of a put option for different values of stock price at expiry. The payoff increases as the stock price decreases beyond the strike 70. If the stock price is higher than the strike, the payoff is 0.

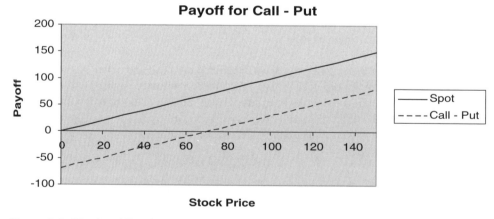

Figure 3.4 The dotted line shows the payoff at expiry based on one long call and one short put. See how it mirrors the payoff of the stock but shifted downwards by the strike.

> **Key Points**
>
> - European options give one the right to buy or sell an asset at a certain strike on the expiry date.
> - American options can be exercised at any time prior to expiry.

3.3   NO-ARBITRAGE PRICING

The basic idea in pricing derivatives is that arbitrage should not be possible. Arbitrage is defined as making a riskless profit. In more concrete terms, this implies that if you can produce a portfolio that achieves the **same payoff as a particular contract in all circumstances**, then the portfolio must be **worth the same** as the contract.

If this portfolio can be set up today and left intact, this is a **static hedge** for your contract. A static hedge is preferable where possible since it does not involve modelling assumptions, and the quality of the payoff replication tends to be higher. Section 3.1 discussed the forward contract. We saw how no-arbitrage considerations dictate the fair value of the strike of the forward. And this is via a static hedge.

However, more usually, you are required to rebalance the composition of your portfolio over time, and the rebalancing may depend on your model. If, however, such a portfolio will achieve the same payoff as the contract of interest, then you have a **dynamic hedge**.

In much of our analysis, we shall assume continuous trading, unlimited ability to buy or sell without affecting market price, no bid–offer spreads and infinite liquidity. Such assumptions are not strictly correct but good enough for liquid assets under normal market conditions, unless you are a huge player trading in an asset in which you own a substantial market share.

A Simple Illustration of Hedging

To ease our understanding of the considerations in pricing, let us consider a simple (but somewhat contrived) example. For simplicity, suppose that interest rates are 0. There is a stock with spot at 100. Over a 1-month period, it can either go up to 110 (with probability 0.65) or down to 90 (with probability 0.35). Consider an option to buy the stock at strike 100 with expiry 1 month.

We would like to construct a hedge comprising Δ amount of stock and B amount of cash. (Notice that 0 rates means that it costs nothing to borrow and a deposit earns nothing.) This is illustrated in Figure 3.5.

For our hedge to work, it must be worth the same as the option under both scenarios. In this case, we require that Δ, B satisfy the simultaneous equations

$$110\Delta + B = 10$$
$$90\Delta + B = 0.$$

Solving the above gives $\Delta = 0.5$, $B = -45$. Furthermore, the price of the option today is

$$100\Delta + B = 100 \times 0.5 - 45 = 5.$$

(There is no need to discount as we have taken interest rates as 0.)

Notice that the price of the option does not depend on the probabilities of the stock reaching either 110 or 90. Indeed, we did not use those probabilities in constructing our hedge.

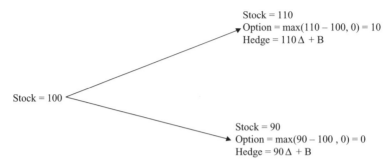

Stock = 110
Option = max(110 – 100, 0) = 10
Hedge = 110 Δ + B

Stock = 100

Stock = 90
Option = max(90 – 100 , 0) = 0
Hedge = 90 Δ + B

Figure 3.5 Hypothetical states of the stock price after 1 month and corresponding option payoffs. Basically, we require that the hedge and option payoffs be the same under both scenarios for the stock price.

The main point is that hedging is supposed to insulate our portfolio from the movements of the underlying. In this sense, a hedger is indifferent to whether the stock will go up or down, when she prices the option. That differentiates an investor from the institution selling the products. **As an investor, you do care about the probabilities of your investment appreciating. As an institution selling derivatives, it is the cost of hedging which determines the sale price.** A lot of opportunities for investment occur because **the sale price (i.e. cost of hedging) does not have to (and indeed often does not) reflect an investor's belief as to the real probabilities of return.**

Rather curiously, as will be seen in Section 3.4, we are interested in the volatility of the underlying when pricing an option.

The Martingale Equation

Any domestic asset with price strictly greater than 0 can be used as a numeraire asset, which is just a unit to measure the value of other assets. The choice of numeraire asset is not unique. For example, the numeraire asset could be the money market account (a fictional deposit of 1 in a bank account which compounds continuously), so that we are measuring value in units of our domestic currency (as we usually do). Or if the numeraire asset is an ounce of gold, we are measuring value in terms of the equivalent in ounces of gold.

No-arbitrage considerations lead to the martingale equation in a complete market. Specifically, if V_t and A_t are **domestic assets**, then

$$\frac{V_t}{A_t} = E^{Q_A}\left[\frac{V_T}{A_T}\right],$$

where Q_A is the measure corresponding to the **numeraire asset** A_t, $E^{Q_A}[\bullet]$ is an expectation with respect to the measure Q_A, and $t < T$ are any two points in time.

A martingale is a process whose expected value at a future time is its value today. The above equation basically says that **the ratio of an asset to a numeraire (i.e. $\frac{V_t}{A_t}$) has expected value equal to its current value.** (Please do not be too bothered about the concept of measure. Our choice of numeraire defines an associated measure, which then determines a set of probabilities. These are not real-world probabilities, but are implied from a hedging analysis. No further explanation is needed for understanding the ideas and themes behind the payoffs.)

The idea is that in a complete market, all payoffs are attainable, and we should be able to replicate relative payoffs (i.e. the ratio of two assets). As such, these relative payoffs must have the same value as the replicating portfolio.

Since the price of V_t is unique,

$$\frac{V_t}{B_t} = E^{Q_B}\left[\frac{V_T}{B_T}\right]$$

for a different numeraire asset B_t under measure Q_B. This gives the relation

$$V_t = B_t E^{Q_B}\left[\frac{V_T}{B_T}\right] = A_t E^{Q_A}\left[\frac{V_T}{A_T}\right].$$

Another note is regarding the emphasis on domestic assets. If V_t or A_t were not domestic assets, the martingale equation does not hold. However, if V_t were foreign and X_t is the spot foreign exchange rate, so that $V_t X_t$ becomes the value in domestic currency of the foreign asset, then the following modified martingale equation holds:

$$\frac{V_t X_t}{A_t} = E^{Q_A}\left[\frac{V_T X_T}{A_T}\right].$$

It is not important for the reader to understand the issues regarding change of measure. The main point to take away is that there is no unique choice of measure in pricing, but the price should be unique. So the framework itself is coherent. And we shall meet both the martingale pricing equation and the version for foreign assets again in subsequent parts of the book.

Key Points

- No-arbitrage considerations mean that if a portfolio replicates a payoff at expiry, it must be worth the same as the payoff today.
- Static replication involves no model assumptions, whereas dynamic replication requires a model to determine how to rebalance the hedging portfolio.
- Having replicated the payoff of an instrument sold, a financial institution does not care about real probabilities, but instead is only interested in the cost of hedging.
- A numeraire is a unit to measure value, and any choice of numeraire must give the same price.

3.4 THE BLACK–SCHOLES MODEL

This section has the most involved mathematical notation in the book outside the appendices (and here and only here have I violated my pledge to avoid obtuse mathematics). If the reader cannot follow the flow, it should not be of undue concern. The main aim is to give an illustration as to how the celebrated Black–Scholes equation for pricing derivatives can be understood intuitively. The main issues are being aware (1) that expected real-world growth of an asset (i.e. the drift) does not affect pricing, (2) that volatility is fundamental to option pricing, and (3) that hedging lies at the heart of derivatives pricing.

Suppose that the stock price process S_t at time t follows a geometric Brownian motion, specifically

$$dS_t = \mu S_t dt + \sigma S_t dW_t,$$

where μ is the real-world drift, σ is volatility, W_t **is a Brownian motion (representing randomness)** and dS_t represents a very small change in S_t. Specifically, the change in S_t is driven by a known dt part and a random dW_t part.

Let $V_t = V(S_t, t)$ be the price of any derivative on S_t (e.g. a call option). Then it can be shown that

$$dV_t = f(S_t, t)\,dt + g(S_t, t)\,dW_t$$

for some functions $f(S_t, t)$ and $g(S_t, t)$ of S_t and t.

Suppose we have sold a call option on S_t. We would like to hedge by buying the appropriate amount $\Delta(S_t, t)$ of stock (generally $0 \le \Delta(S_t, t) \le 1$ and $\Delta(S_t, t)$ varies with both time t and the current stock price S_t). At any given time t, there exists a quantity $\Delta^*(S_t, t)$ of stock, that perfectly cancels our exposure to the option by eliminating the dW_t term (i.e. $g(S_t, t) = \Delta^*(S_t, t)\sigma S_t$). By buying this amount $\Delta^*(S_t, t)$ of stock, we have constructed the portfolio $\Pi_t = -V_t + \Delta^* S_t$ such that the portfolio dynamics are given by

$$
\begin{aligned}
d\Pi_t &= -dV_t + \Delta^* dS_t \\
&= -f(S_t, t)\,dt + \Delta^*\mu S_t dt.
\end{aligned}
$$

Notice that as the random dW_t part is gone, the portfolio is instantaneously risk-free, and must therefore grow at the risk-free rate r.

This is the main idea that leads to the Black–Scholes equation

$$\frac{\partial V}{\partial t} + rS\frac{\partial V}{\partial S} + \frac{1}{2}\sigma^2\frac{\partial^2 S}{\partial S^2} = rV.$$

Specifically, it is worth pointing out that we have constructed a **dynamic hedge** $\Delta^*(S_t, t)$ that changes with time and stock price – i.e. at each point in time, we must maintain a position of $\Delta^*(S_t, t)$ in the stock in order to hedge a short position in the option. This process of hedging eliminates risk (if our process indeed follows a geometric Brownian motion, **which is not true in practice**), so that the **real world drift** μ **of the stock (i.e. by how much the stock is expected to rise or fall) is not relevant** to pricing the option. However, the **volatility** σ **is extremely important in pricing the option**. That should come as no surprise. The cost of a derivative is based on the cost of hedging it. The more volatile the market (i.e. the higher σ is), the more the cost of hedging.

From an investor's perspective, a call option gives her the right but not obligation to buy the stock. If volatility is high, the stock price has a higher probability of rising significantly, as well as of falling significantly. In the event that the stock price increases significantly, the option will have a higher payoff. If the stock price falls below the strike, however, the option just expires worthless.

It is also worth mentioning that $\Delta^*(S_t, t) = \frac{\partial V_t}{\partial S_t}$, i.e. what we refer to as the delta, is the sensitivity of the option price to a unit change in price of the underlying. In practice, traders attempt to hedge by constructing a portfolio where the delta and vega $\frac{\partial V_t}{\partial \sigma}$ (i.e. sensitivity of the option price to a unit change in volatility) are both zero at a given point in time.

Figures 3.6 and 3.7 show the delta profiles of both a call and put option *vis-à-vis* changes in spot. Specifically, we note that they vary smoothly over changes in spot, making hedging not too expensive.

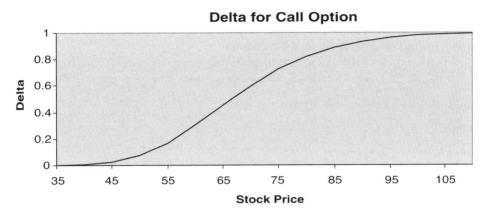

Figure 3.6 Delta of a call option as the stock price varies. Delta tends towards 0 as the stock price falls towards 0, since the option becomes worthless. Delta tends towards 1 as the stock price rises significantly since the option becomes like a forward (with very high probability of exercise).

The price of an option can also be obtained via the martingale equation in Section 3.3. Specifically, for a call option, the price is

$$V_t = B_t E^Q \left[\frac{V_T}{B_T} \right],$$

where our numeraire $B_t = \exp(rt)$ is the money market account, and $V_T = \max(S_T - K, 0)$ is the payoff of our call at expiry T with strike K. The money market account is a fictional deposit in a bank account where interest is compounded continuously (daily compounding is a reasonable approximation in practice).

The point is that both equations are related and both are the result of no-arbitrage considerations. Note that the martingale equation comes from taking an expectation. This expectation with choice of numeraire B_t is under the risk-neutral measure and not the real-world measure.

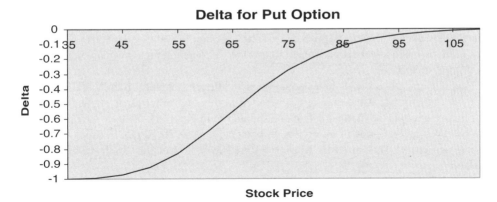

Figure 3.7 Delta of a put option as the stock price varies. Delta tends towards −1 as the stock price falls towards 0, since the option is very likely to be exercised and hence is like a short position in a forward. Delta tends towards 0 as the stock price rises significantly since the option becomes worthless.

This means that the real probability distribution of the stock price is not important. Rather, it is the probability distribution implied by the cost of hedging the option that matters in determining the price of the option.

The Black–Scholes formula comes from evaluating the above equation. For completeness, the formula for the price of a call option with strike K and expiry T is given as follows:

$$V = SN(d_1) - Ke^{-rT}N(d_2),$$

where

$$N(x) = \frac{1}{\sqrt{2\pi}} \int_{-\infty}^{x} \exp\left(-\frac{z^2}{2}\right) dz,$$

$$d_1 = \frac{\log\left(\frac{S}{K}\right) + rT}{\sigma\sqrt{T}} + \frac{\sigma\sqrt{T}}{2},$$

and

$$d_2 = d_1 - \sigma\sqrt{T}$$

and the formula for the price of a put option is

$$V = Ke^{-rT}N(-d_2) - SN(-d_1).$$

(Note that this formula has to be modified slightly if the stock pays dividends.)

Key Points

- The Black–Scholes methodology involves constructing a dynamic portfolio (involving the asset) to match the risky component of a derivative's price process. This requires holding an amount of the asset equal to the derivative's delta.
- Volatility affects the cost of hedging.
- The Black–Scholes formula results from a hedging argument.

3.5   THE VOLATILITY SURFACE

The Black–Scholes framework gives a good starting point for valuing derivatives. However, it would be too much to expect markets to follow the weird geometric Brownian motion process mentioned in Section 3.4.

Nevertheless, the Black–Scholes equation is a sufficiently helpful framework by which to analyse derivatives that the market has resorted to thinking in terms of implied volatilities. Implied volatility is the number σ that one should use in the Black–Scholes formula to match the observed market price of an option. In practice, it is observed that σ varies with option expiry and strike. This gives us what is referred to as a volatility smile in our volatility surface.

Figures 3.8 to 3.12 show examples of volatility smiles for interest rates, equities and foreign exchange.

The volatility smile exists because geometric Brownian motion (also known as the lognormal model) does not correctly depict market variables. But what is the reason for the shape of the smile?

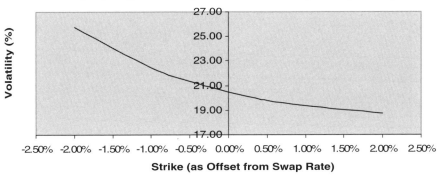

Figure 3.8 Five-year by 10-year swaption (i.e. an option to enter into a 10-year swap with expiry of 5 years) volatility skew (30 September 2008). Typically, in interest rates, volatilities are higher for lower strikes because the absolute magnitude of volatility does not change too much when rates decrease. *Source:* Bloomberg

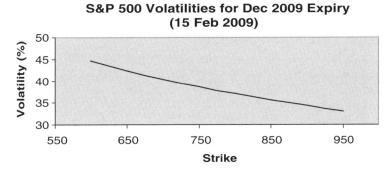

Figure 3.9 S&P 500 volatility skew for December 2009 expiry (15 February 2009). The downward-sloping volatility skew reflects greater investor demand for options at lower strikes, since investors generally tend to own stocks and want protection from a falling market. *Source:* Bloomberg

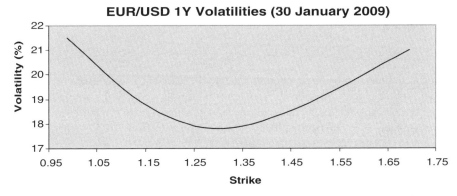

Figure 3.10 EUR/USD 1-year volatility smile as of 30 January 2009. The smile is roughly symmetric as there is no pronounced preference for high or low strikes. Nevertheless, it shows that institutions seek more compensation for selling out-of-the-money options. *Source:* Bloomberg

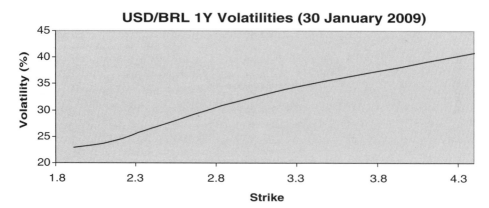

Figure 3.11 USD/BRL 1-year volatility skew as of 30 January 2009. As Brazil is an emerging market, more investors tend to seek protection from a fall in the Brazilian real (i.e. a rise in USD/BRL), so that high strike options are at a premium (i.e. an upward-sloping volatility skew).
Source: Bloomberg

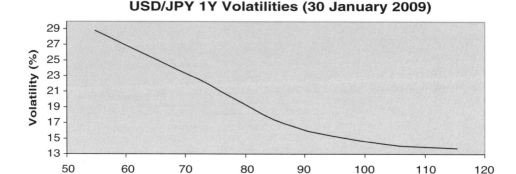

Figure 3.12 USD/JPY 1-year volatility skew as of 30 January 2009. As will be discussed in Chapter 10, the nature of the carry trade and the PRDC market means that many investors are long dollars and short yen and seek protection from a significant appreciation of the yen (i.e. a fall in USD/JPY).
Source: Bloomberg

Even if a continuous process can represent the market variable, a lognormal process may not be the appropriate choice. Specifically, in interest rates, it is said that the absolute magnitude of volatility does not decline as rates fall, at least if interest rates remain between 2% and 6% approximately (i.e. rates are as likely to move up or down by 0.25% whether they are at 2% or 6%). If rates are 5% and lognormal volatility is at 14%, the absolute volatility is $5\% \times 14\% = 0.7\%$. If rates fall to 3.5%, for absolute volatility to stay at 0.7%, the lognormal volatility must rise to $\frac{0.7\%}{3.5\%} = 20\%$. Hence, we get higher volatilities for lower strikes. In this case, a normal process will better describe interest rates. This explains the downward-sloping volatility skew in Figure 3.8.

Alternatively, consider the equity markets. Investors tend to be long stocks and hence generally seek protection from declines in stock prices. Investors tend to buy options (and hence volatility) at lower strikes, and this imbalance leads to a downward-sloping skew, so that equity volatility tends to be higher for lower strikes (see Figure 3.9). The downward-sloping volatility skew can also reflect the fear of a downward jump in stock prices. After all, there is a higher probability of stock prices collapsing due to some firm-specific disaster (e.g. default) than of stock prices going through the roof. (This is true at least for stocks of large corporates.)

From the foreign exchange perspective, for a currency pair involving developed economies (e.g. EUR/USD), a more symmetric smile (see Figure 3.10) can be the result of stochastic volatility. Specifically, periods of high volatility tend to be followed by periods of high volatility and the same for periods of low volatility. This tends to increase the probability of tail events and hence gives rise to higher deep out-of-the-money volatilities. Also, traders would generally want a premium for selling out-of-the-money options since hedging is not risk free in practice and losses from out-of-the-money options can be much bigger than expected gains. They do this by marking up the volatilities for such options.

In FX too, there is a possibility of skew favouring one currency pair. For example, as seen in Figure 3.11, USD/BRL has a positive skew because investors tend to fear more (and hence buy protection against) the weakening of the Brazilian real. Figure 3.12 shows that USD/JPY is the opposite case, where the huge volumes of carry trades (borrowing yen to invest in dollars) and the PRDCs (discussed in Chapter 10) lead to significant fear of substantial yen appreciation if and when the trades get unwound.

Of course, the above phenomena typically require different modelling treatments. Specifically, this supports the case of some form of local volatility in our rates example above, the case of jumps treatment in our equity example, and the case of stochastic volatility in our EUR/USD example. This is not to say that volatility in equities is not stochastic or that local volatility has no role to play in FX, but rather that there are various origins of the volatility smile.

It is worth stressing, however, that whatever the case, the volatility surface significantly affects the prices of options, and is fundamental to derivatives pricing. To the extent that pricing depends on volatility and volatility can vary (nor are we assured of using the correct model or volatility in hedging), it constitutes a significant risk in hedging. This can be partially mitigated by volatility derivatives (e.g. variance swaps).

Key Points

- Implied volatility is the number to put in the Black–Scholes formula to get the quoted market price.
- Implied volatility (lognormal) is usually not constant over expiry or strike.
- In interest rates, absolute volatility tends to change less than lognormal volatility.
- In equities, people seek protection from a stock market crash.
- Low and high volatilities tend to occur in clusters.

3.6   CORRELATION

Correlation is a measure of linear interdependence of two variables. The total volatility of a collection of highly correlated variables is greater than for negatively correlated variables.

The following example will illustrate this. Suppose X and Y are normal variables with 0 mean, standard deviation σ, and correlation ρ. Let $Z = \frac{1}{2}(X + Y)$. Then

$$\text{var}(Z) = \frac{1}{4}\left(\text{var}(X) + \text{var}(Y) + 2\,\text{cov}(X, Y)\right)$$

$$= \frac{1}{4}\left(2\sigma^2 + 2\rho\sigma^2\right)$$

Notice that the variance of Z is the same as that of either X or Y only if $\rho = 1$. For a smaller value of ρ, Z has a smaller variance, and Z has variance 0 if $\rho = -1$. Volatility is the square root of variance, so higher correlation means higher total volatility.

The effect of correlations (less than 1) on reducing variance contributes to the popularity of basket products. Outside the derivatives arena, portfolio diversification (i.e. buying a portfolio of many different stocks rather than concentrating on one or a few) has been touted as a means of eliminating individual stock risk (although it seems that correlations tend to increase dramatically in times of crisis).

In derivatives, it should be pointed out that higher volatility leads to a higher cost of hedging and hence a more expensive product. Consequently, an option on a basket (e.g. the FtSe 100) would be cheaper than options on its constituent stocks.

The Asian Option

An Asian option has a payoff that depends on the average value of an underlying over observation dates. The benign effect of less than perfect correlation also leads to the popularity of Asian options in commodities. The payoff of an average-rate Asian call option at expiry T is

$$\max\left(\bar{S} - K, 0\right),$$

where $\bar{S} = \frac{1}{n}\sum_{i=1}^{n} S_{t_i}$, S_t is the value of the underlying at time t, and $t_1, t_2, \ldots, t_n = T$ are observation dates for the averaging. Typically, averaging is daily, weekly or monthly.

(Note that there is also the average-strike Asian call option whose payoff is $\max\left(S_T - \bar{S}, 0\right)$ at expiry T. We do not consider this payoff in this book, and future references to Asian options should be understood to mean average-rate Asian options.)

Such an option could be of interest for hedging purposes, say, by a manufacturer who is interested in capping the average price she has to pay to buy raw materials. For example, if the manufacturer buys oil weekly, an Asian option with weekly fixings, expiry 3 months and strike 60 can protect her from an increase in her average purchase price over the period. In fact, an Asian option may be more useful to the manufacturer than a single European option as it is more relevant to her than the price of oil on one date 3 months from now. (Of course, the Asian option will only compensate the manufacturer at the end of the 3 months, so there are cashflow mismatches. A strip of European options expiring each week over the 3-month period is a better solution, but that is also much more costly.)

We assume that the log-returns over each observation date are uncorrelated to one another – that is

$$corr\left(\log\left(\frac{S_{t_i}}{S_{t_{i-1}}}\right), \log\left(\frac{S_{t_j}}{S_{t_{j-1}}}\right)\right) = 0 \quad \text{for } i \neq j.$$

This assumption comes from a theory of efficient markets on how the price of an underlying reflects all available market information. (Even if you do not subscribe to this theory, **you most likely agree that the above correlation is less than 1**, in which case the argument on volatility reduction below still holds.) This leads to the volatility of $\overline{S}$ being much less than that of the underlying price S_T at expiry T. In this way, **an Asian option costs less than a comparable European option, since the volatility of the average is lower**.

Figure 3.13 illustrates a path of an underlying S_t and its daily average $\overline{S}_t$. Clearly, we see greater variation in S_t than in $\overline{S}_t$.

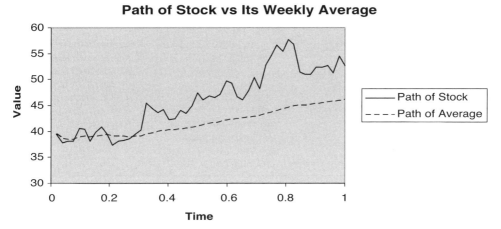

Figure 3.13   A hypothetical path of a stock versus that of its weekly average. Notice how the path of the stock varies much more than the path for its average.

It is instructive to compare the key features of a long position in a forward, a European call option and an Asian call option. This is shown in Table 3.1.

Autocorrelation in Rates

As a final word on correlations, autocorrelation plays a big part in interest rate products. Interest rates are not quite the same as other assets. For example, a 10-year rate becomes a 9-year rate 1 year from now. There is definitely a relation between rates for different expiries and treating them coherently leads to autocorrelation between different parts of the yield curve.

Key Points

- Correlation affects the volatility of a collection of assets (i.e. basket).
- Volatility is less for a basket than the average for its constituents, if correlation is less than 1.
- An Asian option (i.e. where payoff is based on the average of the underlying over time) has lower volatility than a European option.

Table 3.1   Key characteristics of a long position in a forward *vis-à-vis* a European call option and an Asian call option.

Feature	Long forward	European call option	Asian Call option
Cost at Inception	None.	Price of option.	Price of option (less than European).
Potential Upside	Full participation in returns if asset price is above strike.	Full participation in returns if asset price is above strike.	Upside is less because averaging of price over time means smaller returns in rising markets.
Maximum Downside in Falling Market	Equal to strike, since asset price can fall to zero in theory.	Purchase price.	Purchase price.
Sensitive to Final Asset Price	Final asset price completely determines payoff.	Final asset price completely determines payoff.	Less sensitivity because intermediate asset prices are also used to compute average used in payoff.
Potential as Cheap Bet on Unlikely Event	Not applicable. Obligation to enter transaction.	Deep out-of-the-money option is very cheap and has very high strike, so that huge return is possible (with very low probability).	Not ideal, since computed average is less likely to reach extreme values.

3.7   MODELLING CONSIDERATIONS

It is not the purpose of this book to either impart on the reader the basics of financial modelling, or to give insights on the latest advances in derivatives pricing. Such topics would form books in their own right. But an appreciation of how modelling drives product development can be useful.

Firstly, **most linear products (i.e. those with no optionality) do not require a model**. For example, forward contracts (as seen in Section 3.1) or interest rate swaps (more in Chapter 6) can be priced directly by no-arbitrage arguments.

Some products can be **statically replicated in a model-independent** way. An example is the Constant Maturity Swap that can be replicated via cash-settled swaptions (see Chapter 6). And, of course, where models can be avoided, they should be avoided. Typically, margins are much tighter for products that do not require explicit model assumptions as there is more confidence in their hedging strategy (and hence price).

Where specific dynamics exist, a full-blown universal model is not usually the item of choice. For example, swaptions are priced via Black's formula with the appropriate implied volatility. CMS spread options are priced via copulae, having *a priori* obtained the marginal distributions (say by replication). (Chapter 6 will explain these products in some detail.) The **simplified approach is possible because the products only depend on the terminal distribution of the underlying (i.e. the distribution at expiry)**. But when you attach the callable feature on the above, a **full term-structure model for interest rates is unavoidable because the transition probabilities over time matter in deciding if early termination is worthwhile**. It is worth emphasising that the increased dependence of the price of a callable (versus a non-callable) product on the choice of model leads to greater uncertainty, and this will be reflected by the higher margins charged by the issuing institution.

Models often ignore known features to retain simplicity because hedging requires that they be calibrated correctly to price liquid market instruments. Empirically, one can argue that for a particular stock, volatility is stochastic, markets have jumps and volatility need not be constant over time. However, **incorporating all these features makes a model impossible to calibrate**. A realistic compromise is to use stochastic volatility where forward skew is important (e.g. cliquets as Chapter 12 will explain) and jumps where jumps are really important (e.g. short-dated deep out-of-the-money options). Perhaps, however, some allowance for this uncertainty will be made in the bid–offer spread.

And modelling limitations do affect product innovation. For example, PDE methods can only realistically handle three factors, due to computational limitations. Since PDEs tend to produce more stable hedging sensitivities, they are often preferred to Monte Carlo methods where feasible. In particular, Monte Carlo methods for handling callability still leave something to be desired. Thus, callable PRDCs (see Chapter 10) have tended to be treated via PDEs (at least if the institution is not using stochastic volatility in FX which introduces a fourth factor). But when chooser PRDCs were introduced, they required five factors at minimum and hence were outside the scope of PDEs. It is no coincidence then that those chooser PRDCs that are traded tend to be tarns (better handled via Monte Carlo) and not callables (where PDEs are the preferred valuation algorithms).

Key Points

- Static replication, where feasible, is preferred as it does not involve a model.
- It is preferable to use the simplest model that captures the essence of a product's sensitivities.
- It is necessary to keep a model reasonably simple, so that the parameters can be calibrated to market prices, and this calibration produces stable parameters.

4

Barriers

Barriers are instruments where there is an **abrupt change of payoff depending on whether the underlying crosses some specified level**. Barriers have acquired popularity as a way of having a cheaper option. But perhaps the spikes in volatility since mid-2008 have often made them bad investment choices. I shall start with the humble digital option, which can be seen as a combination of two calls of different strikes. I shall then discuss knockouts and reverse knockouts and explain how they can be seen in terms of a portfolio of European options. The chapter then proceeds to one-touches and double barrier options, which are based on similar ideas. It is worth noting that embedded barriers can be used to make a structured note cheaper. In particular, the possibility of early termination of a note when a trigger level is breached can make it less costly to the issuer who then will be willing to provide a higher yield on the note (but that is the province of Chapter 8).

4.1 DIGITALS

A (European) digital call option pays a fixed domestic amount (say $1 for a US stock) if the underlying is above the digital barrier at expiry.

Consider a digital call option that pays you 1p (i.e. pence) if, at the end of 1 year, British Telecommunications (BT) stock is over 150p. (Stocks in UK are quoted in pence rather than pounds.) This is purely a bet. Apart from obvious speculative interest, it can also be useful as part of a package.

Consider now two call options with strikes $K^- = (150 - \delta)\mathrm{p}$ and $K^+ = (150 + \delta)\mathrm{p}$. (Take $\delta = 1$ say.) Suppose we buy $\frac{1}{2\delta}$ of the call with strike K^- and sell $\frac{1}{2\delta}$ of the call with strike K^+.

We note that if BT stock ends below 149p, both options expire worthless. If BT stock ends at S_T above 151p, both stocks will be exercised and you will make a profit of

$$\frac{S_T - 149\mathrm{p}}{2} - \frac{S_T - 151\mathrm{p}}{2} = 1\mathrm{p}.$$

This portfolio of call options (i.e. call spread) produces a payoff that looks remarkably like that for the digital option above, as Figure 4.1 shows.

In fact, as $\delta \to 0$, the payoff of our call spread increasingly resembles that of our digital option. So, one can see that the digital option can be statically replicated via a call spread. If $C(K)$ is the value of a call option with strike K, the value of the digital is

$$\frac{C(K - \delta) - C(K + \delta)}{2\delta}.$$

While pricing a digital option via call spreads (replication) is easy, hedging in this manner can be troublesome as, technically, what we require is a very large quantity of options whose strikes are very close (whereas options with arbitrarily close strikes do not exist). In practice, the institution overhedges (e.g. by buying 1 option with strike 149p and selling 1 option with strike 150p), so that the payoff of the call spread is always above that for the digital sold.

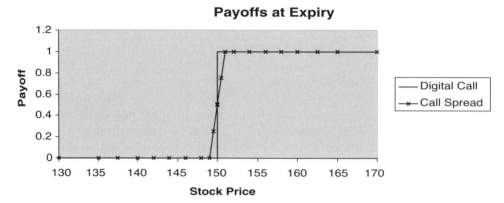

Figure 4.1   Payoffs of a digital call option versus a call spread for different values of spot. Notice how the payoff of the call spread approximates that of the digital call. If we choose strikes closer to 150p, the approximation improves.

If we look at the payoff profile of a digital, we see that it is very discontinuous. If, instead of replication, we delta-hedge by continuously trading in the underlying, it would be very expensive, since the delta changes dramatically as spot changes in the vicinity of the digital barrier (see Figure 4.2).

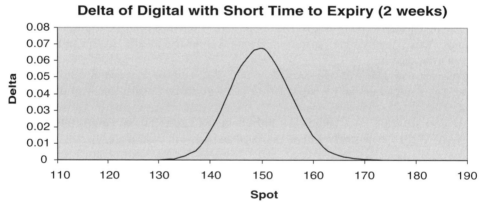

Figure 4.2   For a digital call option with short time to expiry, the delta changes dramatically in the vicinity of the digital barrier, so delta-hedging will be costly.

Similarly, the digital put is an option that pays 1p at expiry if the underlying is below a certain level. Pricing a digital put is similar to pricing a digital call.

Asset-or-Nothing Options

An asset-or-nothing call is an option such that if the underlying trades above a certain level, it pays the value of the underlying. Valuing this is easy since the normal call is the difference between the asset-or-nothing call and the digital call (see Figure 4.3).

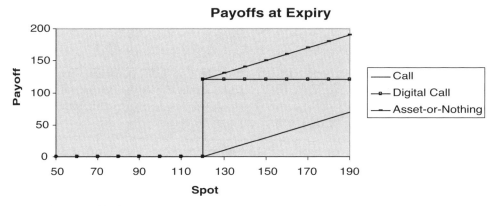

Figure 4.3 Payoffs of a call option, a digital call option and an asset-or-nothing call option. The payoff of a call option is the difference between the payoffs of the asset-or-nothing call and the digital call.

It is worth mentioning that asset-or-nothing options are more popular in foreign exchange. After all, suppose you have a digital in USD/JPY that pays 1 if USD/JPY is over 115 on expiry date in 1 year's time. Should you get paid in yen or dollars?

We note that a USD/JPY option is naturally valued in yen, since it says how much yen it costs to buy 1 dollar. So, a digital option for USD/JPY is naturally payable in yen. Actually, if it is payable in dollars, then it is an asset-or-nothing option, since dollar is like your asset here. (After all, USD/JPY is quoted as the number of yen per dollar. Compare this with the price of a Japanese stock, e.g. number of yen for 1 Toyota share.)

Key Points

- A call spread (i.e. difference between two calls of different strikes) can be used to approximate a digital call option.
- Delta-hedging a digital is expensive since the delta changes dramatically in the vicinity of the barrier.
- An asset-or-nothing option pays the value of the underlying if it trades above the barrier. These are popular in foreign exchange.

4.2   KNOCKOUTS AND REVERSE KNOCKOUTS

You are considering a put option with strike $K = \$5$ on General Motors (GM). Suppose you believe that if GM trades above the barrier $H = \$8$ it is unlikely to fall below strike K by expiry $T = 1y$. Then you could instead go for a **knockout put option** with strike K but which extinguishes if the underlying ever trades above H during the life of the option. Similarly, a knockout call is one where the call option expires worthless if the underlying falls below a barrier $H < K$ during the life of the option.

A knockout call option is like a European call option, but if the underlying ever trades below a barrier, it becomes worthless. A knockout put option is like a European put option, but it is extinguished if the underlying ever trades above the barrier.

The reason for buying a knockout put option as opposed to a regular put option is because it is **cheaper**. This is part of the general theme in this book about **selling optionality for higher yield**. If the option does not cross the barrier H before expiry date T, then the payoff is the same as a normal put option. And you have paid less for it.

Whereas the typical vanilla options buyer is always long volatility (i.e. when volatility rises, the value of the option increases), the holder of a knockout barrier option can sometimes be short volatility in the vicinity of the barrier. Figure 4.4 shows the vega profile for a knockout put option. Notice the negative vega in the vicinity of the barrier.

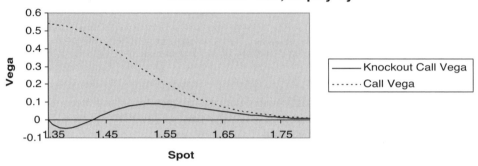

Figure 4.4   Vega profile for a normal call option versus a knockout call option with knockout barrier 1.35. In this example, the vega for the knockout call option is negative in the vicinity of the barrier, since higher volatility increases the chance of the option hitting the barrier and becoming worthless.

(The behaviour of the vega of a knockout option in the vicinity of the knockout barrier is actually more complex. After all, spot would be far below strike when in the vicinity of the barrier, so that a high volatility may be needed for the spot to rise above strike by expiry. The balance of this effect against the probability of the option extinguishing, means that the vega need not always be negative as spot approaches the barrier, but it should fall towards zero to say the least.)

Knockouts have been very popular, especially in foreign exchange prior to mid-2008. Clients have attempted to buy protection (i.e. calls or puts) cheaply with knockouts or even double barriers (covered in a subsequent section) that are not too close to spot. However, the extraordinary volatility spikes that followed the collapse of Lehman Brothers and other financial institutions in September 2008 have wreaked quite extensive havoc on holders of barrier options. In particular, the flight to the dollar has led to a dramatic decline in EUR/USD from 1.45 to 1.25 (see Figure 4.6) and GBP/USD from 1.85 to 1.5 (see Figure 4.5) in the space of 2 months (September to November), following a downward trend since July. Various knockout options have extinguished, leaving the investor with no protection whatsoever as per her initial investment. Figure 4.7 illustrates how this move might have knocked out certain barrier products in GBP/USD. This is a cautionary tale of how selling optionality can be dangerous, and investors should always remember that market conditions can change. Many barrier options were bought before the sharp volatility spikes, in the good old days of "tame" markets.

It is worth mentioning that to price a knockout option, one attempts to replicate the payoff at expiry, as well as for scenarios where realised spot reaches the knockout barrier at various dates prior to expiry (see Figure 4.8).

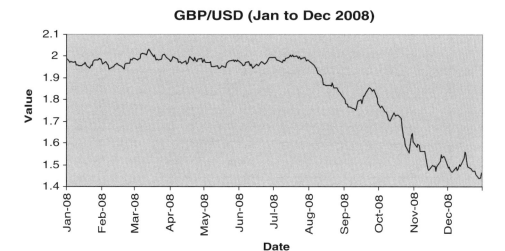

Figure 4.5 Level of GBP/USD from January 2008 to December 2008. Notice how GBP/USD dropped sharply from 1.85 to 1.5 between September 2008 and November 2008.
Source: Bloomberg

The main idea is as follows:

You are wishing to construct a replicating portfolio of vanilla European options and digitals. Going back to the knockout option on GM, the payoff is a European put if it survives until expiry. Consider a time point t_i prior to expiry. If the barrier level H is breached, the knockout option becomes worthless, and you must unwind the replicating portfolio too. For replication to work, you need to determine a quantity of vanilla European options and digitals with strike H and expiry t_i, so that the replicating portfolio has 0 value at barrier H.

Figure 4.6 Level of EUR/USD from January 2008 to December 2008. Notice the drop of EUR/USD from 1.45 to 1.25 between September 2008 and November 2008.
Source: Bloomberg

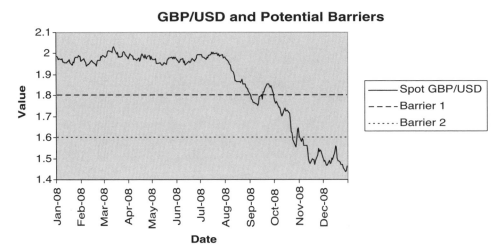

Figure 4.7 Level of GBP/USD from January 2008 to December 2008 (same as Figure 4.5) with some potential barriers superimposed. Notice how both barriers at levels 1.8 and 1.6 would be breached in late 2008. This would extinguish the affected knockout call options, so that they will pay nothing even if GBP/USD subsequently rises above strike by option expiry.

But at t_i, all options with expiry greater than t_i have a value that is based on the implied volatilities corresponding to their times to expiry and strikes. It follows that you need some mechanism to predict forward skew in order to construct your replicating portfolio. In this sense, the **replicating portfolio cannot be said to be static, but merely provides a framework for valuing the barrier option**. In practice, due to the non-static nature of the portfolio and to take account of forward skew, you might want to zero out quantities (e.g. the vega) in addition to the portfolio value at the barrier.

This concept of a **replicating portfolio based on forward skew assumptions can be used to treat any single barrier derivative** (e.g. the one-touch of the next section).

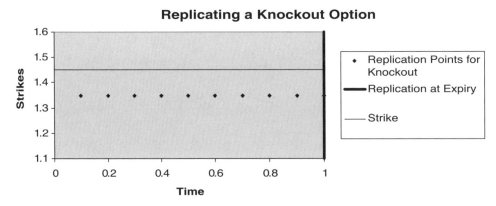

Figure 4.8 Replication points for a knockout option. Replication is aimed at ensuring the combined portfolio has value of zero at expiry (regardless of the spot level) as well as for values of spot at the barrier prior to expiry.

Knockin Options

A knockin option is like a European option but it only comes alive if a barrier is breached prior to the expiry of the option. Suppose we had our GM put option but it only becomes alive if, prior to expiry, GM trades above the knockin barrier $H = \$8$. This is a knockin put option.

Observe that combining the knockin put option and the knockout put option together gives the same payoff under all scenarios as the normal put option. After all, the knockin becomes alive only if the barrier is breached, and this same event extinguishes the knockout. So,

Put = Knockin put + Knockout put

Reverse Knockouts

A reverse knockout is a knockout that extinguishes an in-the-money option. For example, **a reverse knockout put has barrier lower than the strike**.

Suppose you have a 5-month EUR/USD put with strike $K = 1.4$ and barrier $H = 1.35$. Notice that the put initially benefits from falling EUR/USD. However, if EUR/USD trades below 1.35, the put goes from in-the-money to worthless. (See Figure 4.9 for an illustration of the payoff profile at expiry.)

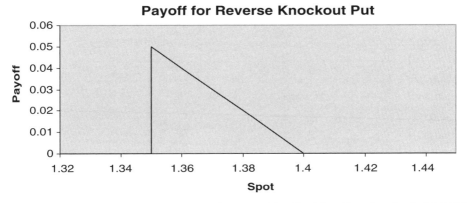

Figure 4.9 Payoff at expiry for a reverse knockout put with strike 1.4 and knockout level of 1.35. The payoff increases as spot FX decreases from 1.4 to 1.35. However, thereafter the payoff drops sharply to 0 when spot falls below 1.35. If FX drops below 1.35 prior to expiry, the payoff will be 0 in any event.

It should come as no surprise that the extinguishment of the payoff at the barrier level leads to a sharp discontinuity that is reflected by the dramatic change in delta as we approach the barrier level, as seen in Figure 4.10. This makes hedging expensive, since, for a small change in the price of the asset, hedging might require the institution to go from being short the asset to being long the asset.

Figure 4.11 also shows how the vega drops below 0 close to the barrier level, since the higher volatility increases the chance of an in-the-money option being rendered worthless if spot breaches the knockout barrier.

For the reverse knockout, you do not need a high volatility to ensure that the option expires in-the-money, since the knockout occurs when the option is already deep in-the-money! In this sense, higher volatility in the vicinity of the barrier is always bad for a reverse knockout option.

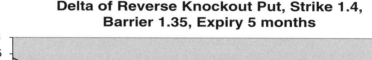

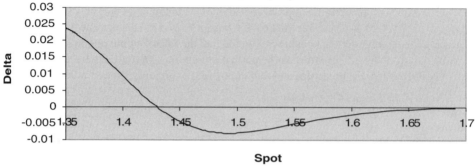

Figure 4.10   Delta profile of a reverse knockout put with strike 1.4 and knockout level of 1.35. Notice how the delta of the reverse knockout put is initially negative (as expected for a put) but then increases to above zero as we approach the knockout barrier of 1.35, since knockout extinguishes an in-the-money option.

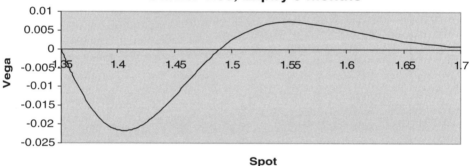

Figure 4.11   Vega profile of a reverse knockout put with strike 1.4 and knockout level of 1.35. The vega drops below zero in the vicinity of the knockout barrier of 1.35, since a higher volatility increases the probability of knockout, which extinguishes the option.

Similar to reverse knockout puts, there are reverse knockout calls where the extinguishing barrier is higher than the strike, i.e. $H > K$.

It is not common for an investor to want to suffer such risk of a deep in-the-money option becoming worthless. So, usually reverse knockouts are packaged together with one-touches (see next section), which provide some rebate if the barrier is breached.

Key Points

- A knockout option is extinguished if the barrier is breached any time prior to expiry. This makes it cheaper than a normal option.
- A buyer of a knockout option can be short volatility in the vicinity of the barrier. The volatility spikes in late 2008 have extinguished many knockouts in FX.

- A barrier option can be approximately "replicated" by a portfolio of vanilla European options and digitals, but this depends on model assumptions.
- A knockin option comes alive when the barrier is breached (i.e. when a knockout with the same barrier is extinguished).
- A reverse knockout is extinguished by a barrier that is in-the-money, so this leads to a sharp discontinuity if the barrier is breached.

4.3   ONE-TOUCHES AND NO-TOUCHES

A digital call option pays 1 if the underlying is above a certain level H on the expiry date. But this is very arbitrary. What if the underlying goes up prior to expiry and then falls below H on the expiry date itself? Perhaps we could have an option that pays 1 at expiry if the underlying goes above H at any time during the life of the option. This is the upside one-touch (also the American digital call option). Figure 4.12 shows the hypothetical path of spot FX and how this leads to a payoff of 1 for a one-touch but not a digital.

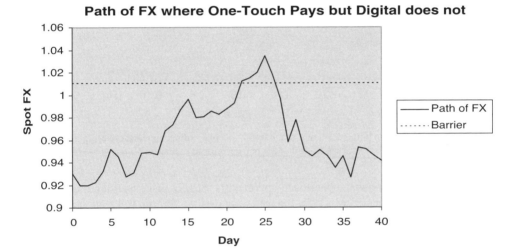

Figure 4.12   Hypothetical path of spot FX versus the barrier of a one-touch. The one-touch pays 1 but the digital does not since spot FX is under the barrier at expiry.

Apart from the speculative value of a bet that pays if the underlying exceeds some level over the life of the option, a one-touch can form part of a package. Recall our example in the previous section, where we have a reverse knockout put that extinguishes at a level H, which is less than the strike K. It is not common for an investor to want her in-the-money put option to be valueless if the underlying drops below H, but she may well accept a certain fixed rebate should H be breached (since this would make the package cheaper than a normal put option). Hence, a downside one-touch added to a reverse knockout put will satisfy this investor.

Specifically, consider our earlier example of a reverse knockout put on EUR/USD with strike $K = 1.4$ and barrier $H = 1.35$. We could add a one-touch to the package with level $H = 1.35$ and notional $1.4 - 1.35 = 0.05$ to fully compensate the investor if the barrier is breached. Notice that this structure is more valuable than a capped put (i.e. where you have bought a put with strike 1.4 and sold a put with strike 1.35). After all, if 1.35 is breached at any point prior to expiry, this structure pays the investor $0.05 regardless of the value of EUR/USD at expiry. As such, for cost reason, the notional of the rebate might be less than the 0.05 required to fully compensate the investor. In this sense, the investor in the reverse knockout put (with rebate) is better off with EUR/USD trading in the tight range of between 1.35 and 1.4.

From a pricing perspective, a one-touch option could be treated via the replication approach in the previous section. Specifically, depending on model assumptions, you hedge an upside one-touch with a certain quantity of digitals exercisable above a barrier level H, and choose these quantities in order to ensure a payoff of 1 should this barrier be breached prior to and including expiry (see Figure 4.13).

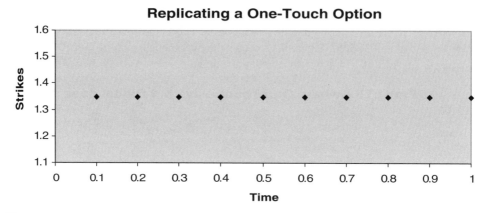

Figure 4.13 Replication points for a one-touch option. Replication is aimed at ensuring the combined portfolio has value of zero for values of spot at the barrier prior to expiry.

It is worth mentioning that a one-touch option costs roughly twice that of a normal digital option (with the same barrier level) for the following reason: You can sell a one-touch option and buy two digital options to hedge. If the one-touch does not breach the barrier level prior to and including expiry, then neither will the digitals and therefore they are all worthless. If, however, the one-touch hits the barrier at a time τ prior to expiry, then the digitals become roughly at-the-money since spot is at the barrier level. Ignoring discounting (justifiable if expiry is not too distant), at-the-money digitals have a value of about 0.5, whereas the one-touch pays off 1 and hence has a value of 1. So, they should be roughly of the same value today.

Table 4.1 compares certain features of a digital call option versus an upside one-touch.

Table 4.1 Features of digital call option versus upside one-touch.

Feature	Digital call	Upside one-touch
Price	Moderate.	Much higher than a digital.
Sensitive to Final Asset Price	Final asset price completely determines payoff.	Much less sensitive since payoff at expiry is assured if asset price breaches barrier during life of option.
Benefits from High Asset Price during Life	No.	Yes, because payoff at expiry is assured if asset price breaches barrier.

A no-touch option pays 1 at expiry provided the underlying never breaches the barrier prior to and including the expiry date. A no-touch option is thus equal to a discount bond minus a one-touch option.

Key Points

- A one-touch pays 1 at expiry if the underlying breaches the barrier at any time prior to expiry.
- A one-touch can be useful as part of a package with a reverse knockout option.
- A one-touch costs roughly twice what a digital costs.
- A no-touch pays 1 at expiry if the barrier is never breached.

4.4   DOUBLE BARRIERS AND MORE

A double barrier knockout has two barriers (one above and one below spot at deal inception). If the underlying breaches either barrier, the option extinguishes. Adding a barrier makes an option cheaper, so adding 2 barriers must make it even cheaper. In this case, there will be one barrier H_U above the spot at deal inception and one H_L below. Also, the investor takes the view that the underlying will stay between H_L and H_U during the life of the option.

Table 4.2   A comparison of key characteristics of barrier options versus a European call option. Note that barrier options become worthless when the barrier(s) is breached.

Feature	European call	Knockout call	Reverse knockout call	Double knockout call
Price	Moderate.	Cheaper than European call.	Cheaper than European call.	Cheapest of the above.
Benefits from High Final Asset Price	Yes.	Yes.	Yes provided final asset price less than high barrier; otherwise, payoff $= 0$.	Yes provided final asset price less than high barrier; otherwise, payoff $= 0$.
Sensitive to Temporary Asset Price Rises during Life	No.	No.	Yes, since option becomes worthless if high barrier is breached during life.	Yes, since option becomes worthless if high barrier is breached during life.
Sensitive to Temporary Asset Price Declines during Life	No.	Yes, since option becomes worthless if low barrier is breached during life.	No.	Yes, since option becomes worthless if low barrier is breached during life.
Benefits from Rising Volatility	Yes.	Can suffer if asset price is close to barrier; otherwise, benefits.	Suffers badly if asset price is close to barrier; otherwise, benefits.	Suffers badly if asset price is close to either barrier; otherwise, benefits.

To take a concrete example, consider a 6-month put option on EUR/USD with strike 1.5 and barriers at 1.3 and 1.7. Provided EUR/USD does not trade below 1.3 or above 1.7 during the life of the option, the investor would be paid max $(1.5 - S_T, 0)$, where S_T is the value of EUR/USD at expiry. So the investor is hoping that EUR/USD will decline, but not below 1.3. The package could come with a downside one-touch to pay the investor $1.5 - 1.3 = 0.2$ (or a smaller amount) at expiry if the option breaches the lower level.

As noted in Section 4.2, high volatility does not favour knockouts if spot is trading close to the barriers. And the decline of EUR/USD from 1.6 to 1.25 from July to November 2008 has wiped out lots of double barrier options, since the lower barriers were typically around 1.35 or even 1.4 for EUR/USD (especially when EUR/USD spot was 1.6). Should there be no rebate (via the one-touch), the investor would have ended up with no put option protection. Hence, it is worth bearing in mind that **the investor is selling valuable optionality when going for barriers (or double barriers)**.

It is worth mentioning that the replication approach to pricing single barriers does not fit as nicely for double barriers because, in the construction of the replicating portfolio at dates prior to expiry, we would have to take account of both the up barrier and the down barrier. However, breach of one barrier requires liquidation of the replicating portfolio and cancels any dynamics assumed regarding breach of the other barrier, so they cannot be treated independently.

Partial barriers are barriers that operate over certain periods only (e.g. the barrier is effective only during the first 6 months of a 1-year option). Such barriers can be part of a package of exotic products, tailored to a specific investment strategy.

Finally, in Table 4.2 we summarise the key characteristics of a European call option versus knockout call options of various flavours.

5

Quantoes

Quantoes are products that are paid in a **non-natural currency without foreign exchange conversion**. In this chapter, I shall explain what quantoes really are, and why they are not so unnatural. In particular, a multi-currency basket is quite likely to involve the concept of quantoes (or self-quantoes at the very least). We shall also see how self-quanto and quanto payoffs relate to normal payoffs.

5.1 SOME MOTIVATION

As an example, British Petroleum (BP) stock is denominated in pence. Consider a call option to buy BP stock at 700 pence (i.e. £7) with expiry 1 year from today. If you were an American investor, the value to you would be the pound value converted into dollars at the appropriate exchange rate on expiry. Suppose you do not want to take a foreign exchange risk. If, instead, you buy an option that would **pay you the difference between BP stock and 700 pence but in dollars**, you have just bought yourself a quanto.

This product depends on the correlation between the BP stock price and the GBP/USD FX rate. Suppose the BP stock price is positively correlated with GBP/USD. Consider the two scenarios: (1) when BP stock is higher in value, a US dollar investor in an ordinary option would further benefit from a stronger pound; (2) when BP stock is lower in value, the dollar investor would also benefit because his pound loss is not as much as it would be in dollars (since the pound is weaker). Figures 5.1 and 5.2 show hypothetical paths of the domestic value of a foreign stock (i.e. product of stock price and foreign exchange rate) in conjunction with the stock price and the FX rate.

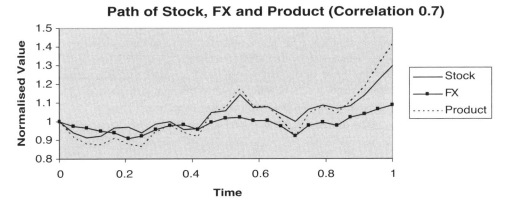

Figure 5.1   Hypothetical paths of a stock, the spot FX and their product for high correlation (0.7). For ease of comparison, time 0 values are normalised to 1. When the stock and spot FX move in the same direction, the variation in the product tends to be more pronounced than the stock.

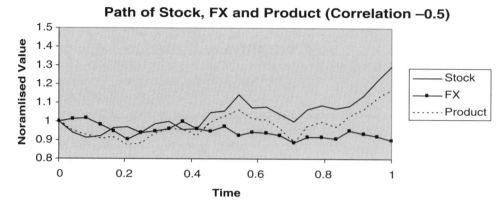

Figure 5.2 Hypothetical paths of a stock, the spot FX and their product for high negative correlation (−0.5). For ease of comparison, time 0 values are normalised to 1. Where the stock and spot FX move in opposite directions, the product tends to show a less pronounced variation than the stock.

In a quanto option, there is no foreign exchange aspect, hence it must cost a dollar investor less to buy the quanto call option than the normal call option if correlation is positive. A similar argument would show how negative correlation increases the price of a quanto call option *vis-à-vis* the normal call option. **Correlation is therefore extremely important in quantoes**.

Of course, one can naturally ask why an investor needs a BP option that has a US dollar payoff. Well, if you want to hedge, it does not seem to be very useful, but a US investor who seeks higher yield by international diversification may not be interested in exchange rate vagaries. In fact, quantoes are in sufficient demand that there are exchange-traded quantoes. For example, the Nikkei 225 futures contract (based on the Japanese stock market index) on the CME Group is settled in US dollars.

Subsequent sections will also show why quantoes need to be treated differently from a mathematical perspective.

Key Points

- A quanto is a product that has a reference underlying in one currency but settles numerically in a different currency, without FX conversion.
- Correlation affects the price of a quanto because if an asset and FX are positively correlated, a foreign investor would benefit from them rising together or the value (in his currency) falling less. A quanto product removes this aspect.
- Quantoes allow foreign investment without FX risk.

5.2 MULTI-CURRENCY PRODUCTS

However, in case you think that quantoes are unusual products for niche investors, I shall remark that quantoes are actually quite natural if you have derivatives on multi-currency baskets. Suppose you have a structured note that pays you, in 2 years' time, 40% of the best return of the S&P 500 index, the STOXX 50 index and the Nikkei 225 index. Clearly, the

S&P 500 index is naturally settled in dollars, the STOXX 50 index is settled in euros, while the Nikkei 225 index is settled in yen. Assuming that the investor wants payment in only one currency rather than dollars, euros or yen (depending on the best performer), or their equivalents after (uncertain) FX conversion, then you cannot escape quantoes.

Consider the example above about multiple stock indices in possibly different currencies. We could generalise to a basket of stocks, stock indices or commodities in different currencies.

Specifically, let's assume that we have $X_1, X_2, \ldots, X_n$ in our basket, and suppose we pay out in currency A. Each X_i is then naturally denominated in currency A, or it has to be quantoed. In fact, apart from correlations, quantoeing is possibly the only added complexity versus single-currency products.

Foreign exchange quantoes also exist. Suppose you have a basket that pays the best performance of EUR/CHF, AUD/JPY, USD/CHF and EUR/GBP, and say it is paid in dollars. You then basically have to quanto each non-dollar currency pair against the dollar. In particular, for purposes of pricing, you would have to introduce USD/JPY and GBP/USD to respectively quanto AUD/JPY and EUR/GBP. Moreover, you would have to self-quanto USD/CHF as USD/CHF naturally pays in Swiss francs and not dollars. (Self-quantoes will be discussed further in Section 5.4.) You may ask why such strange baskets exist. Yield investors might be interested, but, more pragmatically, a hedge can involve a basket against the domestic currency of the company, say everything *vis-à-vis* dollars. So EUR/USD, USD/JPY, GBP/USD and AUD/USD would be fair game. And self-quantoes then become unavoidable.

Interest rate quantoes also exist: perhaps a bunch of different interest rates or their differentials paid in a different currency. For example, we can have a contract that pays in euros the spread between 3-month Polish Libor versus 3-month Euribor (e.g. bets on the convergence of interest rates of Eastern European economies to those of the Eurozone countries). Similar concepts apply, except that interest rates are not assets. Quantoeing here will be with regard to the process driving the rates.

Key Points

- Multi-currency baskets that pay the best returns typically involve quantoes.
- FX quantoes also exist, since USD/JPY is naturally payable in yen and no other currency.

5.3 NON-DELIVERABLE PRODUCTS

A non-deliverable contract is not necessarily a quanto. For example, suppose you have a forward contract to sell the Chinese yuan at a strike of USD/CNY 6.5. Normally, you would pay ¥6.5 and receive \$1 at maturity. Also, the cash value of that would be (in Chinese yuan)

$$X_T - K,$$

where X_T is the USD/CNY exchange rate at maturity T, and $K = 6.5$.

But the Chinese yuan is not freely convertible, so you may wish to settle in dollars instead. You settle by being paid

$$\frac{X_T - K}{X_T}$$

in dollars.

A non-deliverable product is one that is settled in a foreign currency, with conversion at the appropriate FX rate. The above contract is non-deliverable since payment is not actually made in Chinese yuan. But there is no quanto, because if you were paid the original amount of $X_T - K$ in Chinese yuan, the value after conversion to US dollars would be $\frac{X_T - K}{X_T}$. Clearly, **the value of a contract should not matter whether or not you convert into a particular currency, provided you do so at the prevailing FX rate**.

If, however, the contract was settled in dollars, based on the payoff $X_T - K$ without conversion, it then becomes a quanto. We shall cover this issue in Section 5.5.

Key Point

- A non-deliverable product need not be a quanto, since you can convert by the appropriate FX rate before settlement.

5.4 SELF-QUANTOES (AUTO-QUANTOES)

Self-quantoes are not uncommon to foreign exchange. Let's say you are long a forward on EUR/USD with strike 1.2. This is naturally settled in dollars. Suppose, however, you want to be paid the numerical difference in euros. That is a self-quanto (also termed "auto-quanto") forward.

Let X_T be the EUR/USD exchange rate at expiry T, and let $K = 1.2$ be the strike. If the option is settled in dollars, the payoff at expiry is

$$X_T - K.$$

If, however, it is settled in euros, what is its **dollar value** at expiry? I claim it should be

$$X_T(X_T - K).$$

We multiply by X_T because our payoff is in euros, and, to get a dollar value, we should multiply by the EUR/USD exchange rate at expiry. (The value today of the payoff thus defined is computed in dollars. To obtain the value in euros, we then divide the computed dollar value by the current EUR/USD exchange rate X_0.)

This is why a **squared payoff** (X_T^2 here) is not so unusual. It is merely the result of converting to comparable quantities.

A word of explanation is due on why we need to **value the euro-paying contract as a dollar payoff**. If you recall Chapter 3 on derivatives valuation, it is the ratio of **domestic** assets that is a martingale (i.e. the expected future value is the present value) under the measure associated with the numeraire.

In this case, let $V_T = X_T - K$. Suppose our numeraire can be any asset in dollars (say the money market account B_t). If V_t pays in dollars, it is a domestic asset. If it pays in euros, it is not. Hence,

$$\frac{V_t}{B_t} \neq E^Q\left[\frac{V_T}{B_T}\right].$$

On the other hand, $X_T V_T = X_T(X_T - K)$ is the value of a domestic (dollar) asset. Hence,

$$\frac{X_t V_t}{B_t} = E^Q\left[\frac{X_T V_T}{B_T}\right]$$

gives us a valuation equation.

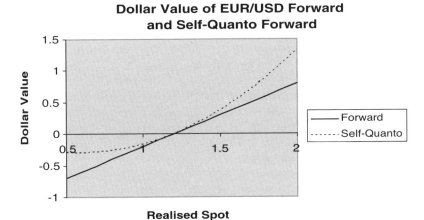

Figure 5.3   Dollar value at maturity of 1 unit of the EUR/USD forward versus $1/K$ units (for comparability) of the self-quanto forward on EUR/USD. Notice how the self-quanto forward gives a higher profit when spot is above the strike $K = 1.2$, whereas the loss is less than the forward when the spot falls below the strike. This means a self-quanto forward must be worth more than a normal forward with the same strike.

Figure 5.3 compares the dollar values at expiry of a unit of the EUR/USD forward with strike K versus $\frac{1}{K}$ units of the self-quanto with the same strike. (The choice of $\frac{1}{K}$ units for the self-quanto is somewhat arbitrary, but allows us to have comparable values at expiry. The payoff of the self-quanto therefore looks like $\frac{X_T}{K}(X_T - K)$.) Intuitively, in the self-quanto, if EUR/USD rises, your euros received can be converted to more dollars. If EUR/USD falls, the euros payable cost less in dollars (i.e. less loss).

But why should we use a dollar numeraire? Alternatively, we could change to measure R where the numeraire (say money-market account B_t^f) is based on a euro asset. This involves a change in drift. And it is this change of numeraire that gives us our **self-quanto correction**. Specifically, we have

$$\frac{V_t}{B_t^f} = E^R\left[\frac{\max(X_T - K, 0)}{B_T^f}\right].$$

Notice how we now obtain V_t by evaluating an expectation that does not involve X_T^2. Solving for the drift is done by equating V_t from both equations.

Key Points

- Self-quantoes are the result of a contract in a currency like EUR/USD being paid in euros rather than dollars, since to get the equivalent dollar value, we have to multiply by EUR/USD.
- Self-quantoes lead to squared payoffs.
- When EUR/USD rises, a euro payoff is worth more than a dollar payoff since it is worth more in dollars after conversion.

5.5   QUANTOES

You could have a stock or commodity paid in an unnatural currency. You could also have an interest rate paid in a different currency (e.g. dollar Libor paid in yen). You could further have an exchange rate contract settled in a different currency (e.g. USD/JPY contract settled in euros).

The nature of foreign exchange quotation (e.g. the exchange rate between dollars and yen, USD/JPY, is always quoted as yen per dollar) means that there are two cases as regards quantoes. For example, if you have a dollar amount and want a yen equivalent, you multiply by USD/JPY. Conversely, if you have a yen amount and want a dollar equivalent, you divide by USD/JPY. We shall look at both cases.

Stock/Commodity Quantoes

Consider an option on Walmart stock X_T, denominated in currency A (dollar), with strike K and expiry T. This option is, however, paid in currency B (yen). Conversion from dollars to yen is by multiplication by the USD/JPY exchange rate Y_T.

If we think with respect to a currency B (yen) numeraire, the payoff is

$$\max\left(X_T - K, 0\right).$$

With respect to a currency A (dollar) numeraire, the payoff is

$$\max\left(\frac{X_T - K}{Y_T}, 0\right).$$

Notice that we divide by Y_T here, because we have a yen amount and need to divide by USD/JPY to convert to a dollar amount. Evaluating this payoff gives us the current dollar value of the contract. (Once we have computed the current price of the contract in dollars, we can get the value in yen simply by multiplying by the current value of USD/JPY, Y_0.)

Now consider an option on Toyota stock X_T^* (denominated in yen), with strike K^* and paid in dollars. Conversion of yen to dollars is by division by USD/JPY.

Now, the payoff with respect to a currency A (dollar) numeraire is

$$\max\left(X_T^* - K^*, 0\right).$$

With respect to a currency B (yen) numeraire, the payoff is now

$$\max\left(Y_T\left(X_T^* - K^*\right), 0\right),$$

where Y_T is the USD/JPY rate at expiry T.

Now we multiply by Y_T, because we have a dollar amount and need to multiply by USD/JPY to convert to a yen amount for valuation. This payoff can be evaluated to give the current yen value of the contract.

Foreign Exchange Quantoes

These are harder to visualise but are otherwise very similar to stock/commodity quantoes. In place of the examples of multiplying and dividing above, let us consider the following cases.

Suppose we have a EUR/USD contract and wish to settle in yen. Since the natural payment currency for the FX rate is the dollar, this is like a dollar asset paid in yen. Dollars are converted into yen by multiplying by USD/JPY. This is the same as the above example on Walmart stock paid in yen.

Suppose, instead, we have a EUR/USD contract and wish to settle in pounds. Now the natural payment currency for the FX rate is dollars. However, to convert from dollars to pounds, you have to divide by GBP/USD. This is similar to the above example in which Toyota stock was paid in dollars (and conversion from yen to dollars involves division by USD/JPY).

Interest Rate Quantoes

The principles are very similar but now you cannot really think of quanto-adjusting the Libor rate or swap rate (at least beyond usage as an approximation), except in special cases of modelling one rate at expiry.

Quanto Adjustment in Practice

However, people have applied quanto-adjustments to interest rates. Furthermore, assuming a Black–Scholes world, quanto-adjustment is just adding a term $\pm\rho\sigma_A\sigma_X$ to the drift, where σ_A is the asset volatility, σ_X is the FX volatility and ρ is the correlation between them. The sign depends on whether conversion is by multiplication or division. This is perhaps an oversimplistic view, but quantoeing a product generally introduces at least an extra dimension if the volatilities are dependent on spot – and that can be computationally expensive. Besides, lots of simplifications are made where acceptable (e.g. in modelling interest rates, the full-term structure is rarely applied if only the terminal distribution is required, such as in a European CMS spread option).

Correlation is particularly crucial to quantoes. In fact, the quanto-adjustment can be shown to be $\pm\rho\,(\ldots)\,\sigma_A\,(\ldots)\,\sigma_X\,(\ldots)$ for a general diffusive process, so that no correlation means no quanto-adjustment. Since correlation estimates are notoriously unstable, one might wonder about how much effort to spend in getting the quanto-adjustment correct. (Self-quantoeing is, however, always very important as the appropriate correlation there has to be 1.)

Table 5.1 Main features of a quanto forward versus a normal forward.

Feature	Normal forward	Quanto forward
Value Depends on FX Rate	Yes, if you want the domestic value of a foreign asset.	No, unless the underlying asset is an FX rate.
Payoff Profile	Profit if asset price at maturity is above strike; loss if below.	For a self-quanto forward, profit is more than a normal forward with the same strike; loss is less than a normal forward. For full quantoes, this depends on the correlation of the asset with the FX rate.
Correlation With FX Rate Affects Price	No.	Yes for all quantoes. (For self-quantoes, the correlation is 1.)

Intuitively, it is not difficult to see the quanto-adjustment as being due to correlation. See, for example, the earlier explanations regarding the behaviour of normal options and quanto options in Section 5.1.

Table 5.1 presents a summary of the main differences between a quanto forward and a normal forward.

Key Points

- Quantoes in stocks, commodities, FX and interest rates exist.
- The basic intuition in valuing a quanto is to convert to an equivalent payoff in the domestic currency, by using the appropriate FX rate.
- In practice, a Black–Scholes style quanto-adjustment is often used for simplicity.

6

Swaps, Constant Maturity Swaps and Spreads

Most of the time, it can be observed that short-term interest rates (e.g. 1-year rates) are lower than long-term interest rates (e.g. 30-year rates). The constant maturity swap is an instrument designed to allow an investor to benefit from an upward-sloping yield curve. But to meaningfully explain the constant maturity swap, it is necessary to go through more fundamental interest rate instruments.

We shall start with the humble swap, which represents an exchange of fixed for floating cashflows. This is an extremely important instrument and among the most liquid in the interest rates derivatives market. We shall next see how interest rates have a natural payment time and how the Libor-in-Arrears has to be treated differently because the natural payment time is not applied. The swaption (i.e. option on a swap) is then examined. This forms the basis of understanding the constant maturity swap, which shall be shown to be a portfolio of cash-settled swaptions. We shall next explain how the upward-sloping yield curve can be taken advantage of in the CMS spread, i.e. an instrument that pays on the basis of the difference between two rates (e.g. 10-year vs 2-year). Callable CMS products are then briefly touched upon, and the reader will be shown how callability greatly increases the complexity of pricing such products. (Callability is properly covered in Chapter 8 on early termination.)

6.1 THE SWAP

Swaps are among the most liquid of interest rate derivatives. They form the basis of understanding many interest rate instruments.

The interbank interest rates market is normally very liquid for most developed economies. (The turmoil in the aftermath of Lehman Brothers' bankruptcy on 15 September 2008 has certainly led to a dislocation of the interbank markets, but it is hoped that there will be an eventual recovery.) Based on liquidly-traded instruments (mainly deposits, forward rate agreements, interest rate futures and swaps), it is generally possible to accurately determine the value of a zero-coupon bond for any maturity. A zero-coupon bond pays 1 at maturity, and since we all prefer to be paid sooner rather than later, the longer the maturity, the lesser the value. Knowing the value of zero-coupon bonds for all maturities gives us the discount curve. (The value of a zero-coupon bond for a maturity is termed the discount factor for that maturity.) An example is seen in Figure 6.1.

Given a discount factor (of 0.964 say) for a maturity (say 9 months, i.e. accrual fraction of 0.75), we can back out a simple interest rate as follows. Specifically, we seek r such that

$$\frac{1}{1 + r \times 0.75} = 0.964.$$

This gives a 9-month rate of $r = \left(\frac{1}{0.964} - 1\right)/0.75 = 4.98\ \%$ per annum.

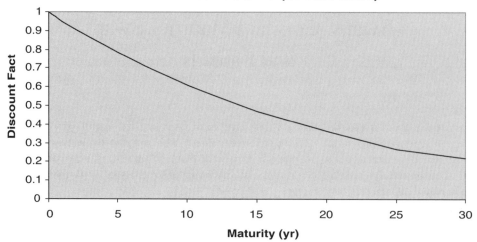

Figure 6.1 The US discount curve as of 30 November 2006. Notice how the discount factor decreases monotonically as maturity increases.
Source: Bloomberg

We also have periodically compounded rates. For example, if a rate $\hat{r}$ is quarterly compounded, then over a period of 3 years, the total value (including interest) is $(1 + \hat{r} \times 0.25)^{4 \times 3}$, where the 0.25 is an accrual fraction since interest is paid 4 times a year.

The Forward Rate

NB It is not essential to the flow of the material for the reader to be able to follow forward rate or swap rate calculations. Understanding the main ideas may be helpful though, especially the appreciation that such calculations are model independent.

Note that if the discount factor for maturity T is Z_T, then $\frac{\$1}{Z_T}$ gives the value (including interest earned) of a deposit of $1 today after time T. Suppose the zero-coupon bonds with maturities $t = 0.4y$ and $t + \tau = 0.6y$ have values $Z_t = 0.98$ and $Z_{t+\tau} = 0.97$ respectively. This means that $1 deposited for 0.4y will be worth $\frac{\$1}{0.98} = \$1.02$ at maturity (including interest earned), while $1 deposited for 0.6y will be worth $\frac{\$1}{0.97} = \$1.03$.

A forward rate is the rate at which one can earn interest on a deposit in the period between two future dates. We would like to know the forward rate between times t and $t + \tau$. This happens to be

$$f_{t,t+\tau} = \left(\frac{Z_t}{Z_{t+\tau}} - 1 \right) / \tau = \left(\frac{0.98}{0.97} - 1 \right) / (0.6 - 0.4) = 5.15\%.$$

The logic is as follows: Suppose I have $0.97 today. I can deposit it for 0.4y and get $0.97 \times \frac{1}{0.98} = \$0.99$ at the end of it or for 0.6y and get $0.97 \times \frac{1}{0.97} = \$1$ at the end of it.

Suppose I deposit it for 0.4y and do a forward rate agreement to deposit between times 0.4y and 0.6y. I expect the same result. In fact, what I end up with is

$$\frac{\$0.97}{0.98}\left(1 + f_{t,t+\tau}\tau\right) = \frac{\$0.97}{0.98}\left(1 + \left(\frac{Z_t}{Z_{t+\tau}} - 1\right)\right) = \frac{\$0.97}{0.98}\frac{Z_t}{Z_{t+\tau}} = \frac{\$0.97}{0.98} \times \frac{0.98}{0.97} = \$1.$$

So, this is all consistent. Any other choice of $f_{t,t+\tau}$ will allow for arbitrage.

Strictly speaking, there is a rather large set of conventions to determine accrual fractions given period dates (e.g. Act/360 takes the number of days in the period divided by 360). The conventions differ for different markets and instruments. However, the exact accrual fraction computed does not affect the ideas presented. As such, we will ignore these conventions in this book (and assume the accrual fraction for 6 months is 0.5, etc.).

The Swap Contract

Now that I have explained how forward rates are calculated, I can proceed to swaps. A swap is an instrument which involves exchanges of cashflows on a series of coupon dates. At each coupon date, one party pays a fixed rate (termed the swap rate) agreed at deal inception, and another pays a floating rate typically based on Libor or Euribor. (Libor is the average of interbank offered rates for lending in London but applies to various currencies, e.g. US dollars and Japanese yen. Euribor is the main euro interbank lending benchmark rate.) Figure 6.2 illustrates the cashflows of a swap. The floating rates are determined based on the discussion on forward rate calculations above.

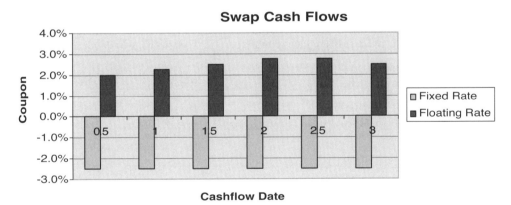

Figure 6.2   Fixed versus floating cash flows on a swap. The floating rates tend to be based on Libor or Euribor and set at the beginning of each period.

Typically, dollar Libor has quarterly fixings, whereas Euribor has semi-annual fixings. In contrast, the fixed leg for dollar swaps typically pays coupons semi-annually and the fixed leg for euro swaps typically pays annually. In that sense, there will be coupon dates where the floating leg pays but the fixed leg does not. (These conventions do not really affect the essence of our discussions so we will not bother too much about them in the rest of the chapter.)

Valuing a Swap

Let Z_t be the value of a zero-coupon bond maturing at time t. Then the value of the fixed leg is

$$R \sum_{i=1}^{n} \tau_i Z_{t_i} = R\tau_1 Z_{t_1} + R\tau_2 Z_{t_2} + \ldots + R\tau_n Z_{t_n},$$

where R is the fixed rate, τ_i are accrual fractions (e.g. 0.5 if the coupons are paid semi-annually), t_i are cashflow dates, and n is the number of coupons.

The value of the floating leg is

$$F = \sum_{i=1}^{n} f_{t_{i-1},t_i} \tau_i Z_{t_i},$$

where $f_{t,T} = \left(\frac{Z_t}{Z_T} - 1 \right) / (T - t)$. Thus,

$$F = \sum_{i=1}^{n} \tau_i Z_{t_i} \left(\frac{Z_{t_{i-1}}}{Z_{t_i}} - 1 \right) / \tau_i$$

$$= \sum_{i=1}^{n} \left(Z_{t_{i-1}} - Z_{t_i} \right)$$

$$= \left(Z_{t_0} - Z_{t_1} \right) + \left(Z_{t_1} - Z_{t_2} \right) + \ldots + \left(Z_{t_{n-1}} - Z_{t_n} \right)$$

$$= Z_{t_0} - Z_{t_n}$$

Most swaps are designed so that at inception, both legs are equal in value, so that it costs zero to enter into the swap. (This reduces counterparty risk.) For this, we require

$$R \sum_{i=1}^{n} \tau_i Z_{t_i} = Z_{t_0} - Z_{t_n}.$$

This gives the fair value fixed swap rate as

$$R = \frac{Z_{t_0} - Z_{t_n}}{\sum_{i=1}^{n} \tau_i Z_{t_i}}.$$

It is worth mentioning that in a normal swap (as opposed to a cross currency swap), there is no exchange of notional. For a bond, in the event of default, you could lose big time because the notional is at risk. For a swap, all you could lose in the event of default is based on the extent to which the instrument acquires value due to market conditions moving in your favour (typically much less than the swap's notional).

For example, if you are paying the fixed rate (and receiving floating coupons) and overall interest rates (hence the floating coupons) go up, then the swap is in your favour, so that its present value is positive. If the counterparty defaults, the present value reflects the extent of your possible loss. If, however, interest rates go down, the swap has a negative present value, so that you incur no loss from the counterparty's default.

Contingent Liability

Similar to the forward contract discussed in Section 3.1, the swap is a contingent liability instrument, since it costs zero to enter into a swap. This means that the potential losses in a swap (due to market moves) are not limited to the initial investment.

Historical Behaviour of Interest Rates

Historically, the yield curve has typically been upward sloping in most major economies. So, short-term interest rates have usually been lower than long-term interest rates (see Figure 6.3).

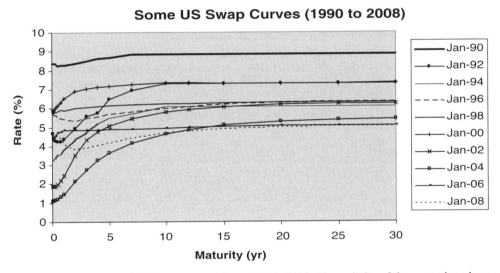

Figure 6.3   Some sample US swap curves from 1990 to 2008. The majority of the curves have been upward sloping, if only mildly in some cases.
Source: Bloomberg

So, usually, it is a good strategy to receive the fixed leg and pay the floating leg. This is effectively betting that future interest rates will be less than implied by forward rates. After all, consider the case where the 1-year rate is 4% and the 2-year rate is 5%, then the forward rate between years 1 and 2 would be

$$\left(\frac{Z_{1y}}{Z_{2y}} - 1\right)/1 = \left(\frac{1/(1+0.04)}{1/(1+0.05)^2} - 1\right) = 6.01\%.$$

But it is quite likely the 1-year rate 1 year from now is only 4% again. Figures 6.4 and 6.5 illustrate a hypothetical upward sloping curve, the projected 1-year forward curve, and how the actual curve 1 year in the future might appear.

However, there have been times of an inverted curve, especially when interest rates are high. This is usually when the central bank attempts to raise rates to stoke out inflation at the end of a cycle of growth. (Central banks typically have much more control over short-term interest rates.) This can lead to significant losses for people who bet on upward sloping yield curves. Figure 6.6 on the dollar yield curve in the early 1980s should serve as a good illustration.

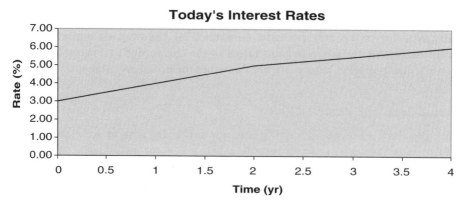

Figure 6.4 Hypothetical upward sloping interest rate curve.

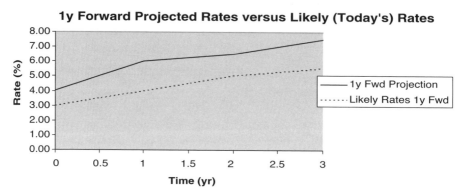

Figure 6.5 One-year forward curve based on upward sloping interest rate curve in Figure 6.4. This is about 1% higher overall than the curve in Figure 6.4. The likely curve 1 year in the future is also shown. This looks more like the curve in Figure 6.4.

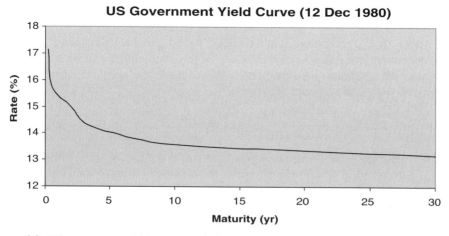

Figure 6.6 US government yield curve as of 12 December 1980. This inverted curve had sky-high short-term rates of over 17% and long-term rates around 13%.
Source: Bloomberg

Commercial banks traditionally lent money via mortgages funded by deposits. In the US, most mortgages used to be 30-year fixed rate instruments, whereas bank deposits tended to be much shorter term (e.g. with maturities less than 2 years). In the early 1980s, the Federal Reserve raised interest rates substantially to fight soaring inflation. This led to short-term interest rates going to over 16%, and an inversion of the yield curve. Many savings-and-loans institutions found themselves holding mortgage assets from a low interest period (e.g. the 1960s to mid 1970s) paying coupons under 10% and having to instead borrow at much higher rates. Only government assistance via generous tax breaks (and refunds) in the 1980s averted a collapse of many of these institutions.

Key Points

- A zero-coupon bond pays no coupon but only the principal at maturity. A discount curve shows the values of zero-coupon bonds with different maturities.
- A forward rate between two maturities can be computed from the prices of zero-coupon bonds. After all, you can buy the longer bond. Alternatively, you can buy the shorter bond and agree in advance the rate of deposit interest between the two maturities.
- A normal swap comprises a leg that pays a fixed rate and another that pays a floating rate (typically based on the Libor or Euribor benchmark rates). Its fair value can be computed from a discount curve.
- A swap is a contingent liability instrument, i.e. potential losses are not limited to one's initial investment.
- Historically, the yield curve in most developed economies has typically been upward sloping. So, it often makes sense to borrow via a floating rate.
- Central banks raise rates to control inflation at the end of a cycle of growth. This can lead to an inversion of the yield curve, hurting fixed rate investors.

6.2 NATURAL PAYMENT TIME AND THE LIBOR-IN-ARREARS

This section introduces the Libor-in-Arrears (LIA). It is the easiest instrument which illustrates non-natural payment times and how they are treated. The ideas would be helpful in understanding the Constant Maturity Swap in Section 6.4.

Consider a 3-month Libor rate. You observe the rate $f_{t,t+\tau}$ at the beginning of the period t and pay at the end of the period $t + \tau$. This is the **natural payment time**. After all, our earlier financing argument suggests that this nicely fits in with our zero-coupon bond prices. Suppose however I want to have the rate $f_{t,t+\tau}$ paid at time t instead (say I prefer not to trust the credit-worthiness of the institution any more than I need to). This is in essence the principle of a Libor-in-Arrears (LIA). A Libor-in-Arrears is an instrument where the fixing and payment dates of the Libor rate are the same.

(Strictly an LIA involves observing at the end of the period and paying at the end of the period. The "in-arrears" means that the fixing is at the end of the period. But that is like our case of fixing and paying at the start of the period, if we start from the next period. We shall ignore this distinction as it makes no difference conceptually.) Figure 6.7 illustrates the fixing and payment dates for an LIA versus a normal Libor.

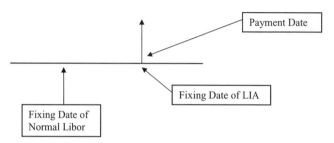

Figure 6.7 Fixing and payment dates for an LIA versus a normal Libor coupon. The fixing and payment dates for an LIA are the same.

Suppose I am due to receive the floating coupons in an LIA and pay a fixed strike of K. The observation date is t, the accrual end date is $t + \tau$, and the accrual period is τ. Then if Libor is L_t at time t, my payoff is

$$(L_t - K)\tau.$$

A forward rate agreement (FRA) is an agreement that fixes the rate of borrowing or lending for the period between two future dates. For a normal FRA that pays the fixed rate, I would get paid the same quantity at time $t + \tau$, which is equivalent to being paid

$$\frac{(L_t - K)\tau}{1 + L_t\tau}$$

at time t (where the division by $1 + L_t\tau$ is to discount the cashflow back to time t).

Alternatively, we note that the normal FRA pays $(L_t - K)\tau$ at time $t + \tau$ and the LIA pays the equivalent of $(L_t - K)\tau(1 + L_t\tau)$ at time $t + \tau$ (where we have multiplied by $1 + L_t\tau$ to grow our cashflow in time). Notice that we have an L_t^2 term (similar to self-quantoes), so actually squared payoffs are not some fancy quirks but the result of just paying at a non-natural time.

It is worth looking at this intuitively too. For our Libor-in-Arrears, if Libor is above strike, we get the payoff at time t and hence can invest at the higher Libor rate. If Libor is below strike, we lose money but have to finance it at the lower Libor rate. It follows that the fair value for the LIA rate must be higher than the normal Libor rate. This is incidentally a consequence of the L_t^2 term from earlier.

Option Replication

An LIA caplet pays $\max(L_T - K, 0)\tau$ at expiry time T if strike is K. It turns out that we can statically replicate an LIA caplet with a bunch of caplets of different strikes.

A caplet is a call option on interest rates, which turns out to be an option on a forward rate agreement paying the fixed rate. A caplet with strike K and expiry T has payoff given by $\max\left(\frac{L_T - K}{1 + L_T\tau}, 0\right)\tau$. It can be shown that Black's formula can be used to price caplets and we have an equation similar to Section 3.4. There is no issue with using Black's model since the implied volatility is a number that can be used to obtain whatever caplet price is observed. So, basically, caplet prices can be treated as market data.

Let me explain replication in more detail. Suppose we are at expiry T. Consider $K = K_0 < K_1 < K_2 < \ldots < K_n$. We want to set up a replicating portfolio with strikes at $K, K_1, K_2, \ldots, K_{n-1}$. We shall solve for the appropriate weights $w_0, w_1, w_2, \ldots, w_{n-1}$.

Basically, we want to ensure that if realised Libor at expiry is $K, K_1, K_2, \ldots, K_{n-1}$, the replicating portfolio has payoff that agrees with the LIA caplet. This is illustrated in Figure 6.8 below. We assume quite reasonably that if $K, K_1, K_2, \ldots, K_{n-1}$ are sufficiently close to each other, the replication errors for values of realised Libor in between will be acceptably small.

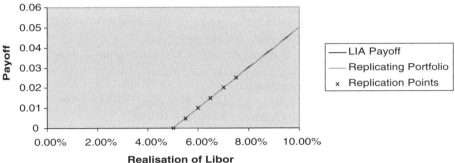

Figure 6.8 Payoffs of Libor-in-arrears versus replicating portfolio for different realised Libor rates. They should agree for values of realised Libor of $K_1, K_2, \ldots, K_n$.

Suppose $L_T = K_1$. Then only the caplet with strike K is in-the-money. We have from the payoffs of our LIA caplet and our replicating portfolio:

$$(K_1 - K)\tau = w_0 \frac{(K_1 - K)\tau}{1 + K_1 \tau},$$

from which we find w_0.

Suppose now $L_T = K_2$. Then only the caplets with strikes K and K_1 are in-the-money. We have from the payoffs of the LIA caplet and our replicating portfolio:

$$(K_2 - K)\tau = w_0 \frac{(K_2 - K)\tau}{1 + K_2 \tau} + w_1 \frac{(K_2 - K_1)\tau}{1 + K_2 \tau}.$$

But we know w_0 already, so the equation uniquely determines w_1.

We can continue in the same manner to solve for w_i, $i = 2, \ldots, n - 1$, and we can stop at an n for which we are satisfied that we have covered a sufficiently large set of strikes (say until $K_n = 100\%$). In that case, our LIA caplet is approximately worth $\sum_{i=0}^{n-1} w_i C(K_i, T)$, where $C(K, T)$ is the value of a caplet with strike K and expiry T.

The Fair Value LIA Rate

Similarly, we can replicate an LIA floorlet which pays $\max(K - L_T, 0)\tau$ at expiry time T, using a portfolio of ordinary floorlets with payoff $\max\left(\frac{K - L_T}{1 + L_T \tau}, 0\right)\tau$. We can then use put–call parity (as per Section 3.2) to establish the fair value of the LIA rate as

$$L_t = \frac{C_t - P_t}{\tau Z_{t.T}} + K,$$

where C_t is the price of a LIA caplet with expiry T and strike K as seen at time t, P_t is the price of the corresponding LIA floorlet, and $Z_{t,T}$ is the value of a zero-coupon bond with maturity T as seen at time t.

It is worth highlighting that there is no model involved in this replication. This leads to high confidence, in so far as any errors are only due to volatility interpolation (since clearly options do not trade over continuous strikes). The high confidence means spreads for LIA products tend to be very tight.

Key Points

- A normal floating rate coupon fixes at the start of the period and pays at the end.
- A Libor-in-Arrears has the same fixing and payment dates.
- For comparison with a normal floating rate coupon, we have to grow the Libor rate in an LIA until the end of the period, giving a squared payoff. An LIA coupon has to be worth more than a normal floating rate coupon.
- We can replicate an LIA caplet using a portfolio of ordinary caplets. Similarly, we can replicate an LIA floorlet using a portfolio of ordinary floorlets.
- Put–call parity using an LIA caplet and floorlet give the fair value LIA rate.

6.3 THE SWAPTION

Swaptions are interesting in their own right, being options to enter into swaps (Section 6.1). Furthermore, it is necessary to introduce them as you will see in the next section how a portfolio of swaptions can be used to replicate a Constant Maturity Swap.

A swaption is an option to enter into a swap. Suppose you have an option to enter into a swap where you pay the fixed rate K. Then the value at expiry $T = t_0$ is

$$\max\left(R_T - K, 0\right) \sum_{i=1}^{n} \tau_i Z_{T,t_i},$$

where $Z_{t,T}$ is the value of a zero-coupon bond maturing at time T as seen at time t, with $Z_{t,t} = 1$, and $R_t = \frac{Z_{t,t_0} - Z_{t,t_n}}{\sum_{i=1}^{n} \tau_i Z_{t,t_i}}$ is the swap rate.

It turns out that Black's formula can be used to price swaptions if the annuity $\sum_{i=1}^{n} \tau_i Z_{t,t_i}$ (i.e. sum of zero-coupon bonds weighted by accrual) is used as numeraire. Black's formula (compare Section 3.4) gives the value of a swaption that pays the fixed rate as

$$V = A\left(RN\left(d_1\right) - KN\left(d_2\right)\right),$$

where

$$N(x) = \frac{1}{\sqrt{2\pi}} \int_{-\infty}^{x} \exp\left(-\frac{z^2}{2}\right) dz,$$

$$d_1 = \frac{\log\left(\frac{R}{K}\right)}{\sigma\sqrt{T}} + \frac{\sigma\sqrt{T}}{2},$$

$$d_2 = d_1 - \sigma\sqrt{T},$$

and

$$A = \sum_{i=1}^{n} \tau_i Z_{0,t_i}.$$

(If this formula troubles you, please do not mind it. It is not crucial to the flow of the chapter.)

In practical terms, this means that **a single number (i.e. implied volatility) for each strike, option expiry and swap maturity,** fully specifies the price of a swaption. This constitutes the swaption volatility surface and is regarded as market data. Figures 6.9 and 6.10 show two US swaption volatility surfaces as seen at different points in time.

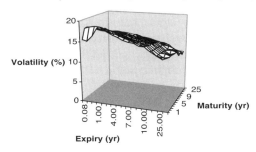

Figure 6.9 US swaption at-the-money volatility surface as of 31 July 2007. Notice the humped shape where volatility increases as expiry increases up to around 1 year and then falls. This is because there is little uncertainty for interest rates in the very short-term, whereas long-term rates do not move too much. *Source:* Bloomberg

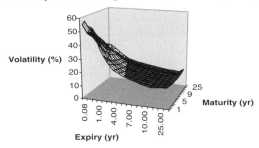

Figure 6.10 US swaption at-the-money volatility surface as of 31 January 2008. This downward sloping volatility surface represents the heightened uncertainty in the short-term as a result of the credit crunch. The interest rate volatility surface under normal conditions is humped, as seen in Figure 6.9. *Source:* Bloomberg

Cash-Settled Swaptions

The above discussion holds only for swaptions which exercise into an underlying swap. Strictly speaking, if we settled the option in cash, this should also be the valuation approach. However, the term "cash-settled swaption" is used to refer to a slightly different type of instrument. And unfortunately, this is the normal type of swaption traded in euros and pounds.

Specifically, the payoff of a cash-settled swaption at expiry is

$$\max\left(R_T - K, 0\right) \Lambda\left(R_T\right),$$

where $\Lambda\left(R_T\right) = \sum_{i=1}^{n} \frac{\tau_i}{(1+R_T \tau_i)^{t_i/\tau_i}}$ is the internal rate of return (IRR).

The rationale for using this weird $\Lambda\left(R_T\right)$ function is that it depends only on the swap rate R_T at time T, and so for settlement purposes, it is only necessary for the relevant banks to agree on one reference swap rate, rather than a whole bunch of discount factors used in computing the annuity for a normal swap. Furthermore, $\Lambda\left(R_T\right)$ gives a value reasonably close to the value of the annuity $\sum_{i=1}^{n} \tau_i Z_{T,t_i}$ under most normal market conditions.

But it is worth mentioning that the internal rate of return does not form a proper numeraire so that strictly Black's formula cannot be consistently used to value cash-settled swaptions. Nevertheless, Black's formula is used in practice and the errors from the inconsistency are generally tolerable. Specifically, the formula used is

$$V = \Lambda\left(R\right)\left(RN\left(d_1\right) - KN\left(d_2\right)\right),$$

where A earlier is replaced by $\Lambda\left(R\right)$ (i.e. the value of the IRR with the swap rate as seen on valuation date is used as a pseudo-numeraire).

The nice thing about the IRR being only a function of R_T at time T is that it makes the cash-settled swaption a perfect candidate to replicate the payoff of a CMS caplet. This we cover in the next section.

It is useful to compare a caplet *vis-à-vis* a swaption (paying the fixed rate), and this is shown in Table 6.1.

Table 6.1 Comparison between a swaption and a caplet.

Feature	Caplet	Swaption (paying fixed)
Amount At Risk	Price of option.	Price of option.
Benefits from Rising Short-Term Rates	Yes.	Yes, but much less than caplet because effect on swap rate is more limited.
Benefits from Overall Rise in Rates Across Maturities	Yes.	Benefits more than caplet, in that coupons affected cover a longer period.
Sensitive to Correlation between Rates	No.	Yes, since that affects the volatility of the swaption.

Key Points

- A swaption is an option to enter into a swap.
- Black's formula, with the appropriate implied volatility (as a market quote), is used to value it.
- A "cash-settled swaption" does not refer to a swaption settled in cash. Instead, the term refers to a different payoff, which depends only on the swap rate.
- Using Black's formula to value a cash-settled swaption is strictly incorrect, but it is good enough as an approximation and universally used in practice.

6.4 THE CONSTANT MATURITY SWAP

This section discusses the Constant Maturity Swap (CMS), which involves receiving coupons based on a floating long-term (e.g. 10-year) swap rate, reset at the end of each coupon period (e.g. every 6 months). Before we look into the CMS, it is worth providing some historical context on the economic environment favouring its growth.

Historically, the yield curves in the US, the Eurozone countries and Japan have been upward sloping much of the time. Naturally, this leads to people preferring to be paid coupons based on the long end of the curve, and to borrow money based on the short end of the curve. On a cursory view, this suggests that a fixed rate bond is a better asset to hold than a floating rate note.

However, what if you think interest rates are too low and are on their way up? In that case, fixed rate bonds will prove disastrous. After all, you will receive the low fixed rate over the life of the bond (e.g. 10 years), even when interest rates go up. Perhaps it would be better to borrow at a fixed rate under such circumstances.

It is worth telling this story regarding choosing to borrow at a floating rate versus fixed rate. The period between 2001 and 2004 saw significant declines in US interest rates. Figures 6.11 to 6.13 show sample US swap curves from 2002 to 2007. With US interest rates at decades-low levels of about 1% to 2%, many borrowers in the USA opted for adjustable (floating) rate mortgages (ARM), with floating interest set at 2.5% to 3% over the benchmark 1-year government rate after a (typically 2-year) teaser period of even lower rates. Instead, they could have locked in their borrowing via traditional fixed rate mortgages for 30 years with the fixed rate at a near historic low (of about 6%). In a similar vein, some borrowers of poor credit standing (i.e. sub-prime) took out mortgages (at 5% over the benchmark 1-year rate) which they could only afford if short-term rates remain ultra-low. However, in 2007 the Federal Reserve raised interest rates to contain inflation following a spike in commodity prices and to tame the excesses of the easy-credit era. This led to the ARM borrowers having to pay rates of 7.5% or more (and even worse for sub-prime borrowers). Opting to borrow via

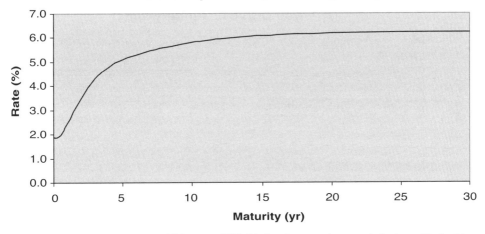

Figure 6.11 US swap curve as of 2 January 2002. Notice the curve is upward sloping with short-term rates of 2% much lower than long-term rates of 6%.
Source: Bloomberg

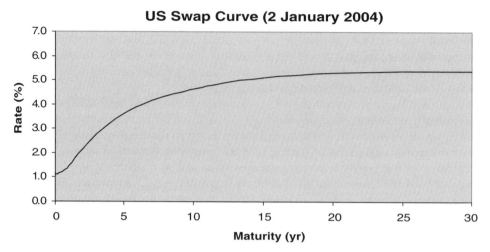

Figure 6.12 US swap curve as of 2 January 2004. The curve is quite steeply upward sloping with short-term rates just over 1% and long-term rates at 5%.
Source: Bloomberg

floating rates versus fixed rates can be a very risky thing indeed. Some (mainly sub-prime) homeowners basically found themselves delinquent on their mortgages and had their properties foreclosed.

As luck would have it, in late 2008, the Federal Reserve cut rates aggressively to stimulate the economy as the full effect of the credit crunch and a potentially devastating recession in the US became apparent, leading to a discount rate target at historic lows of between 0 to 0.25%. So, those ARM borrowers not forced by rising rates to sell their properties in 2007 might not

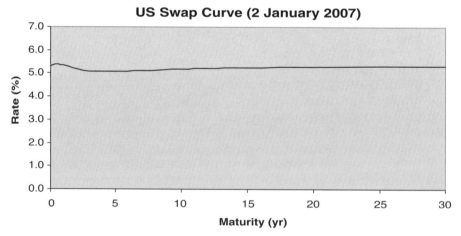

Figure 6.13 US swap curve as of 2 January 2007. The curve has flattened significantly with rates uniformly just over 5%.
Source: Bloomberg

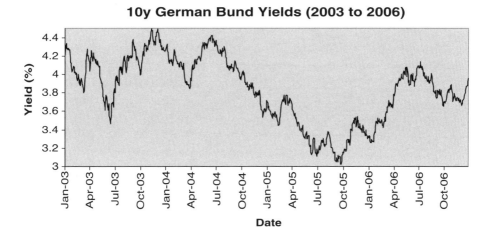

Figure 6.14   Yields for 10-year German government bunds from 2003 to 2006. They have ranged from just over 3% to just below 4.5% over the period.
Source: Bloomberg

have done so badly by choosing to go with floating rates after all. ARM borrowers indexed to short-term rates might be paying just over 3% in early 2009.[1]

However, consider the situation in the Eurozone countries between 2003 to 2005, when 10-year German bunds (i.e. government bonds) were yielding under 4.5% (see Figure 6.14), and the benchmark short-term rate was about 2.2% (from 2004 to 2005). Figures 6.15 to 6.18 show sample euro swap curves from 2003 to 2006. People felt that 10-year German bund yields had to rise. And more sinister was the fact that a yield of 4.5% would cause problems

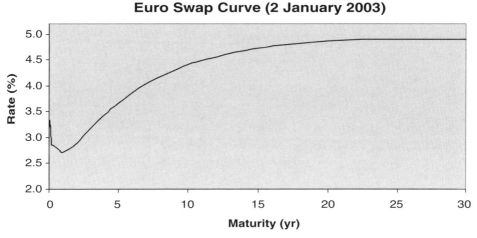

Figure 6.15   Euro swap curve as of 2 January 2003. The curve is upward sloping with short-term rates around 3% and long-term rates almost 5%.
Source: Bloomberg

---

[1] A useful source for mortgage rates data is www.mortgage-x.com/general/mortgage_indexes.asp.

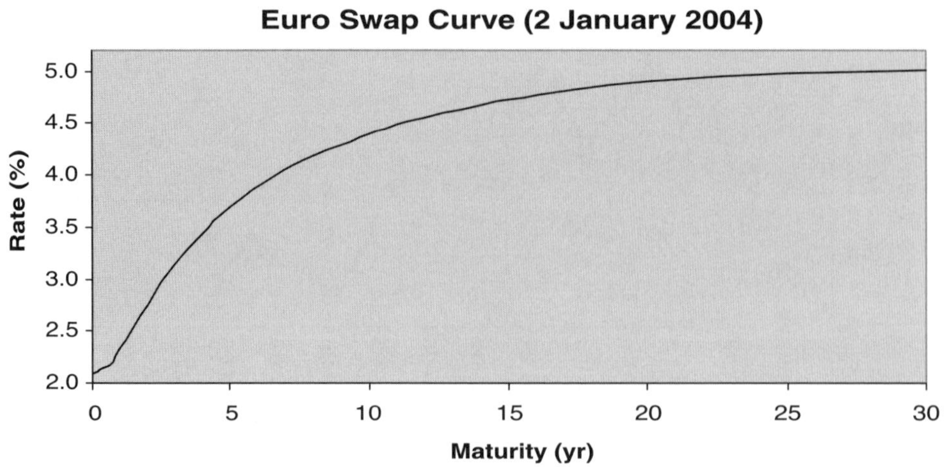

Euro Swap Curve (2 January 2004)

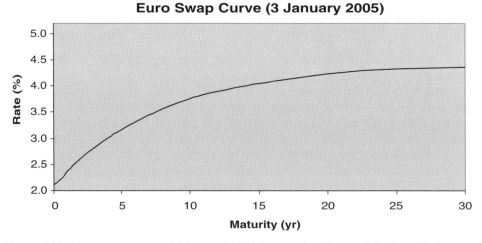

Figure 6.16 Euro swap curve as of 2 January 2004. The curve has got even more upward sloping with short-term rates just over 2% and long-term rates about 5%.
Source: Bloomberg

for many pension funds in terms of their required rates of return for meeting future liabilities. Many pension funds in Eurozone countries have statutory limits to their equity investments (and equities were not doing too well anyway in the years just after 2001).

Suppose you were such an investor who saw an upward sloping curve, but felt that overall interest rates would rise. You want to be paid based on the long end of the curve, but still benefit if the yield curve rises. The answer is a **product that pays you the (floating) 10-year swap rate but reset on each coupon date (e.g. every 6 months say). That is what a Constant Maturity Swap (CMS) is.** Notice that the CMS has not been popular in the UK as the interest

Euro Swap Curve (3 January 2005)

Figure 6.17 Euro swap curve as of 3 January 2005. The curve is still upward sloping with short-term rates just over 2% although long-term rates have dropped to about 4%.
Source: Bloomberg

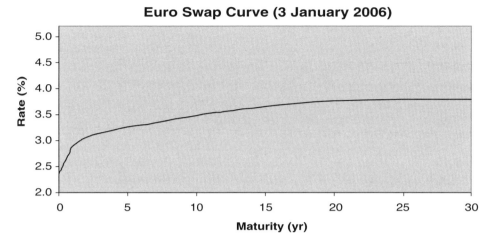

Figure 6.18 Euro swap curve as of 3 January 2006. The curve has flattened somewhat (but remains upward sloping). Apart from very short-term (under 1 year) rates of 2.5%, rates for other expiries range from 3% to 3.8%.
Source: Bloomberg

rate curve has historically been quite flat, so that betting on an upward sloping curve does not make sense. Figure 6.19 shows sample UK swap curves from 2003 to 2006.

It is worth stressing that CMS products in themselves are not particularly dangerous. At its most basic, the investor gives up the low coupons on the bond (e.g. 4.5% above) and instead gets coupons linked to the swap rate, e.g. 0.8 times the 10-year swap rate. At worst, he loses his coupon. But his principal is no more at risk than if he invested in a normal fixed rate bond.

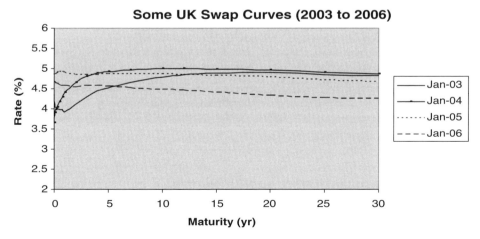

Figure 6.19 Some sample UK swap curves from 2003 to 2006. The curves are at most mildly upward sloping (short-term rates up to 1% less than long-term rates) or even mildly inverted. This is not conducive to the growth of CMS products, since there is no incentive to receive a long-term floating rate.
Source: Bloomberg

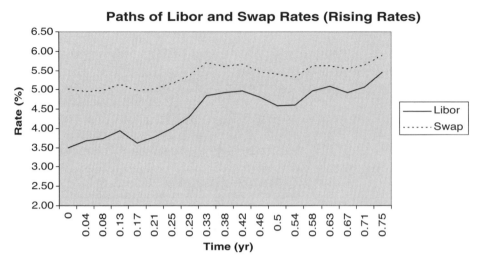

Figure 6.20 Hypothetical path of Libor and swap rates in rising rates environment. Both Libor and swap rates tend to rise together, if not to the same extent.

Intuition behind Convexity Adjustment

You see now that the period for which interest is accrued (e.g. every 6 months) does not determine the reference rate to pay your interest (e.g. 10-year rate here) in a CMS product. This is unnatural and will require a convexity adjustment.

We can approach this intuitively as follows: Let's assume that you buy a CMS bond and finance it with fixed rate borrowing. If swap rates go up, you make money; if they go down, you lose money.

If interest rates have risen across all maturities, then the (floating) swap rate would increase, giving you a profit. Figures 6.20 and 6.21 show hypothetical paths of Libor rates in conjunction with swap rates. For a CMS bond, since you receive the higher coupon after 6 months, you can invest your profit at the higher prevailing interest rates until maturity.

If, instead, interest rates have decreased, you would make a loss since the swap rate has decreased. However, you can borrow more cheaply to fund the loss. So, actually you benefit more from rising rates and suffer less from falling rates with your CMS. This must be worth something. Specifically, it means that the CMS rate must be higher than the swap rate for the equivalent maturity.

CMS Replication

Actually, CMS products can be rather accurately priced, since they can be replicated via a portfolio of cash-settled swaptions. This means that they are not model dependent.

Suppose we have a CMS caplet based on the 10-year rate R_T observed and payable at time T. Specifically, the payoff at time T is

$$\max\left(R_T - K, 0\right) \tau,$$

where K is the strike and τ is the accrual period.

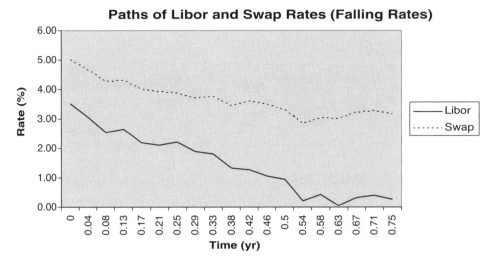

Figure 6.21 Hypothetical path of Libor and swap rates in falling rates environment. Both Libor and swap rates tend to decline together, although Libor rates can be more volatile.

Recall that the payoff of a cash-settled swaption (paying the fixed rate) with strike K at expiry T is

$$\max\left(R_T - K, 0\right) \Lambda\left(R_T\right),$$

where $\Lambda\left(R_T\right) = \sum_{i=1}^{n} \frac{\tau_i}{(1+R_T \tau_i)^{t_i/\tau_i}}$ is the IRR.

We want to set up a replicating portfolio of cash-settled swaptions with strikes at

$$K = K_0 < K_1 < K_2 < \ldots < K_n.$$

We shall solve for the appropriate weights $w_0, w_1, w_2, \ldots, w_{n-1}$. The logic is very similar to the replication of LIA caplets.

Suppose $R_T = K_1$. Then only the swaption with strike K is in-the-money. We have from the payoffs of our CMS caplet and our replicating portfolio:

$$\left(K_1 - K\right)\tau = w_0 \left(K_1 - K\right) \Lambda\left(K_1\right),$$

from which we find w_0.

Suppose now $R_T = K_2$. Then only the swaptions with strikes K and K_1 are in-the-money. We have from the payoffs of the CMS caplet and our replicating portfolio:

$$\left(K_2 - K\right)\tau = w_0 \left(K_2 - K\right) \Lambda\left(K_2\right) + w_1 \left(K_2 - K_1\right) \Lambda\left(K_2\right)$$

But we know w_0 already, so the equation uniquely determines w_1.

We can continue in the same manner to solve for w_i, $i = 2, \ldots, n - 1$, and we can stop at an n for which we are satisfied that we have covered a sufficiently large set of strikes.

In that case, our CMS caplet is worth $\sum_{i=0}^{n-1} w_i S\left(K_i, T\right)$, where $S\left(K, T\right)$ is the value of a swaption with strike K and expiry T.

Similarly, we can use replication to value a CMS floorlet that pays

$$\max\left(K - R_T, 0\right)\tau$$

at time T.

Put–call parity in Section 3.2 then gives the fair value of the CMS rate as

$$R_t = \frac{C_t - P_t}{\tau Z_{t,T}} + K,$$

where C_t is the price of a CMS caplet with expiry T and strike K as seen at time t; P_t is the price of the corresponding CMS floorlet; and $Z_{t,T}$ is the value of a zero-coupon bond with maturity T as seen at time t (say today).

Time Lag

It is worth mentioning that our replication approach for CMS assumes that the observed swap rate is paid immediately. Normally, however, the swap rate is paid at the end of the period (e.g. after 6 months). This, of course, affects our convexity adjustment (i.e. reduces the rate) since we do not benefit from being able to invest our coupon in a high-rate environment immediately but only at the end of the period (e.g. 6 months later).

At this stage, it is useful to contrast the key features between standard fixed income instruments (e.g. the fixed rate bond and floating rate note) and, for example, the Libor-in-Arrears note and the Constant Maturity Swap. Table 6.2 provides a summary.

Table 6.2 Summary of key features of floating rate note, fixed rate bond, LIA note and Constant Maturity Swap. Basically, a CMS is best when the curve is upward sloping and rates are expected to rise.

Feature	Floating Rate Note (FRN)	Fixed Rate Bond	Libor-in-Arrears (LIA) Note	Constant Maturity Swap (CMS)
Benefits from Overall Rise in Interest Rates	Yes.	No. Suffers to the extent that new bond can be obtained with higher coupon.	Yes.	Yes.
Appropriate for Upward Sloping Yield Curve	No. Floating short-term rates are lower than long-term rates.	Yes, since fixed rate is based on long-term rates.	No. Same problem as floating rate note.	Yes. Same reason as fixed rate bond.
Affected by Interest Rate Volatilities	No.	No.	Yes, since options are used to replicate. More expensive when vols are higher.	Yes. Same reason as LIA.
Payoff Profile	Payoff grows with rising short-term rates.	Fixed payoff.	Payoff grows faster than FRN when short-term rates rise.	Payoff grows, based on long-term rates rise.

Key Points

- Short-term US interest rates were at decades lows shortly after 2001. Lots of adjustable rate mortgages (that pay a floating rate) were taken out and these suffered briefly when interest rates rose in 2007 until the sharp rate cuts of 2008.
- The euro yield curve was upward sloping just after 2001, but rates were too low (e.g. 4.5% yield on 10-year bunds).
- CMS products allow you to receive a floating long-term (e.g. 10-year) rate reset at each period (e.g. every 6 months).
- The fair value CMS rate should be higher than the swap rate because you receive money immediately and can invest at higher rates (assuming rates rise together).
- A CMS caplet can be replicated by a portfolio of cash-settled swaptions. Similarly for a CMS floorlet. Put–call parity can be used to find the fair value CMS rate.
- Usually, the CMS rate is fixed at the beginning of the period and paid at the end.

6.5   SPREAD BETWEEN TWO CMS RATES

A CMS spread is the difference between two CMS rates. We shall see in this section why the CMS spread is of interest to a yield investor.

As discussed earlier, the main driver for the CMS market is that yield curves in the USA, Japan and the Eurozone countries have tended to be upward sloping much of the time. If we observe carefully, however, we can see that they are not just upward sloping but tend to flatten as maturity increases. (See Figures 6.22 and 6.23.)

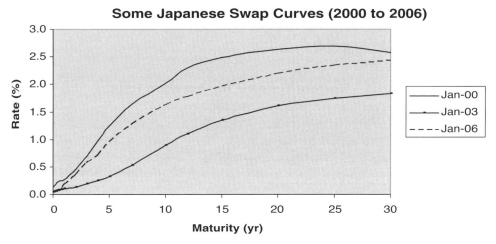

Figure 6.22   Some sample Japanese swap curves from 2000 to 2006. They tend to be upward sloping; however, they also flatten with increasing maturity.
Source: Bloomberg

Let us examine the euro 10-year vs 2-year spread (i.e. difference between the 10-year rate and the 2-year rate). It is quite steep, with a greater than 1% interest rate differential. Now, from the flattening of the yield curve, it would appear that the forward 10-year and 2-year rates as seen 10 years hence, are about the same. Figure 6.24 illustrates this phenomenon. If

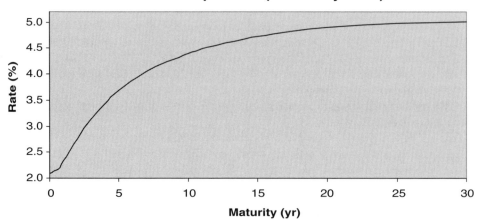

Figure 6.23 Euro swap curve as of 2 January 2004. The curve is upward sloping, although the gradient is much steeper at the short end (e.g. rise of 2.3% over the first 10 years versus 0.6% over the next 20 years). (Same as Figure 6.16.)
Source: Bloomberg

we believe that future yield curves are going to be upward sloping like the one in 2004, can we take advantage of this in a product? Specifically, we could have a **product that pays the difference between the 10-year and 2-year rates. This is a CMS spread.**

Again, this need not be a dangerous product. You could have a 10-year bond but rather than get coupons of 4.5%, you get a payoff every 6 months, based on

$$3 \times \max\left(10y\text{Rate} - 2y\text{Rate}, 0\right) \times 0.5$$

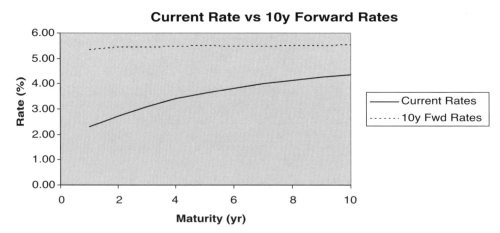

Figure 6.24 Hypothetical 10-year forward curve versus current curve. The current curve is much steeper than the projected 10-year forward curve. This means that the current spread between the 10-year and 2-year rates is much bigger than the spread on the projected curve. Investors usually do not believe that the future curve will be as flat as the projected curve.

(where the 0.5 is because coupons are paid semi-annually), and your principal is no more at risk than for a normal bond.

More interestingly, a theme emphasised in this book is how selling optionality can lead to higher yields. Perhaps if you feel that the curve will remain upward sloping and you think the flatness at the long end will not be realised, you could have a payoff conditional on the spread being above some level.

Specifically, our earlier CMS bond would pay

$$0.8 \times 10y\text{Rate} \times 0.5.$$

If, however, you are prepared to receive the coupon only if the 10-year vs 2-year spread is above some level, you might be able to get the following payoff

$$
\begin{array}{ll}
1.3 \times 10y\text{Rate} \times 0.5 & \text{if} \quad 10y\text{Rate} - 2y\text{Rate} > 0.6\% \\
0 \text{ coupon} & \text{otherwise}
\end{array}
$$

This theme of conditional payoffs that could lead to higher yields is developed in Chapter 7 on Range Accruals.

It is worth mentioning that since CMS products are very liquid and can be priced with no model assumptions, there is a liquid market for European options on the CMS spread, i.e. with payoff

$$\max\left(R_T^1 - R_T^2 - K, 0\right),$$

where R_T^1 and R_T^2 are the values of swap rates for different maturities (e.g. 5-year versus 20-year) at expiry T and strike K.

The main consideration for pricing is the correlation between the two rates involved. Specifically, the higher the correlation, the less is the volatility of the spread (i.e. difference) and hence the less is the optionality value. (The spread option could still be worth a lot because it could be in-the-money.)

It is worth concluding the section by comparing the characteristics of a CMS rate with a CMS spread product, as shown in Table 6.3.

Table 6.3   Comparison of the features of a CMS rate vs a CMS spread payoff.

Feature	CMS rate	CMS spread
Benefits from Upward-Sloping Yield Curve	Yes.	Benefits even more than CMS, since you are paid the difference between a long-term rate and a short-term rate.
Benefits from Rising Interest Rates	Yes.	May not benefit, since typically short-term rates rise more than long-term rates, so that the spread decreases.
Sensitive to Interest Rate Volatilities	Yes.	Yes.
Sensitive to the Correlation between Interest Rates	No.	Very, since higher correlation means curve steepening is unlikely (i.e. less chance of increase in spread).

Key Points

- The swap curve tends to flatten for long maturities.
- If you believe that the curve will remain upward sloping, you can buy a spread (e.g. 10y–2y rate) to bet that future rates 10 years from now are not as flat as the forward predicts.
- You can also have coupons conditional on the spread being above some level, so as to make the product cheaper.
- The value of a spread depends on correlation.

6.6   CALLABLE CMS

What if our investor is not happy with getting 0.8 times the 10-year swap rate, or even 1.3 times the 10-year swap rate (provided 10-year vs 2-year spread is above 0.6%)? How can our investor get more yield? To build on earlier themes of selling optionality, let us introduce callable CMS products.

Specifically, the investor gets a bond that pays a CMS-linked coupon. However, at each coupon date, the issuer is given the right to repay the principal and stop further coupon payments. The issuer will call when it is optimal from her point of view and suboptimal from the investor's point of view. So, the investor is giving up a valuable right and expects to be compensated via a higher yield, e.g. 0.95 times the 10-year swap rate. The same callability feature can be applied to our bond with CMS coupons conditional on the spread. (A more detailed analysis of early termination features, including callability, is presented in Chapter 8.)

It is worth mentioning that callability is much harder to price for the issuer, as the evolution of rates over time has to be modelled to decide if it is optimal to call. It is no longer possible to set up a simple replication portfolio of cash-settled swaptions. There are significant model risks involved in the selection of and calibration to a full-term structure model, and this is, of course, reflected by a higher profit margin tagged on to the product.

Many CMS structures are long-dated (up to 30 years) and there is not always sufficient liquidity for a full hedge. Hedging correlation risk (across rates of different expiries) can also be difficult. Typically, hedging is based on certain assumptions of the macro-economic environment, but this can sometimes lead to grief. For example, in early 2008, when the European Central Bank unexpectedly raised interest rates, many banks lost significant sums of money in hedging CMS products, since their position was based on an upward-sloping curve. It is a cautionary tale of how hedging of exotics is often far from perfect.

Key Points

- Callability allows the issuer to repay the structured note when it is to his advantage, and hence makes the note cheaper.
- Callability requires significant model assumptions in pricing.
- Lack of liquidity in hedging long-dated CMS products (up to 30 years) can mean significant losses for institutions who position their hedges wrongly.

7

Range Accruals

Range accruals are instruments that have **payoffs based on the number of days an underlying either stays in or out (dependent on investor preference) of a range**. The idea is quite simple. As compared with a digital where too much emphasis is on whether the underlying is above some level at expiry, a range accrual averages out the risk. We start with some basic motivations for the different types of range accruals. Then we go on to examine single reference accruals and multiple reference accruals in more detail.

7.1 MOTIVATION

Consider a European digital call option that pays 1 if at expiry date 6 months from today EUR/GBP is above 0.81. It is plain and simple a bet on the EUR/GBP exchange rate. But what if EUR/GBP remains above 0.81 for much of the time and then disappointingly drops to 0.795 one day prior to the expiry date. Our unlucky investor gets nothing. Of course, our investor could opt for a one-touch that pays 1 (at expiry) if at any time during the 6 months EUR/GBP is above 0.81. But if EUR/GBP is at 0.82 today, this is a meaningless bet. Basically, it would cost the same as a zero-coupon bond that pays 1 after 6 months. (Even if EUR/GBP is under 0.81, a one-touch may be a more expensive bet than you would like!)

What about a product that pays the notional multiplied by

$$\frac{n}{N},$$

where n is the number of business days in the 6-month period where EUR/GBP is above 0.81 and $N = 132$ is the total number of business days in the 6-month period?

This is a **range accrual** at its simplest – **an instrument that pays out proportional to the number of days in a period for which the underlying satisfies certain conditions** (e.g. stays

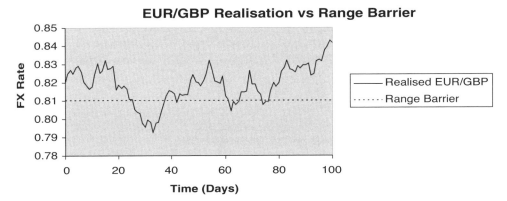

Figure 7.1 Hypothetical path of FX versus barrier. FX is above barrier for 80 out of 100 days in range, giving an accrual multiplier of $80/100 = 0.8$.

above some level). Figure 7.1 shows a hypothetical path of EUR/GBP versus the range barrier of a range accrual. If our investor is interested in getting protection whenever EUR/GBP is above 0.81 (e.g. because it costs him more to import goods from Eurozone countries and he does his imports daily), then this product might to a certain extent satisfy his needs.

A Fader

Let's consider another case. We have an investor who would like to have protection against a falling value of euros. Specifically, she wants put options on EUR/USD say at strike 1.25 but thinks they are too expensive. She could go for a knockout put with knockout level 1.35 (i.e. the put option extinguishes if EUR/USD rises above 1.35). However, the rather huge volatilities since late 2008 may make one uncomfortable. Specifically, even if the investor feels that EUR/USD is on a downward trend, it might not be wise to expose herself to the risk of the option becoming worthless if during a single day in the life of the option demand for euros pushes EUR/USD above 1.35. Can the investor have a cheaper put option that does not becomes a total bet on EUR/USD never going above the barrier level during the life of the option? The answer is again a range accrual type structure (referred to as a Fader here). Basically the payoff is

$$\frac{n}{N} \times \max\left(1.25 - S_T, 0\right),$$

where S_T is the value of EUR/USD at expiry time $T = 0.5y$, n is the number of business days in the 6-month period where EUR/USD is below 1.35 and $N = 132$ is the total number of business days in the 6-month period.

Figure 7.2 shows how the Fader might perform based on a hypothetical path of spot FX.

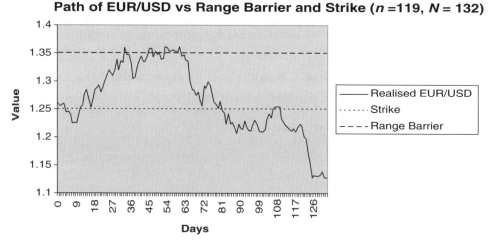

Figure 7.2 Hypothetical path of FX versus barrier and strike. FX is below barrier for 119 out of 132 days in range. This leads to an accrual multiplier of $119/132 = 0.90$, which is multiplied onto the put payoff of $1.25 - 1.128 = 0.122$ at expiry. In contrast, a knockout put will pay 0 since the barrier of 1.35 has been breached.

Spread Accruals in Rates

One last example on range accruals will illustrate their full power. Recall our discussion in Chapter 6 on the upward-sloping yield curve and how an investor might be happy to bet on the curve remaining upward sloping as well as on the spread between the 10-year and 2-year swap rates being above some level. We had discussed a payoff as follows:

$$1.3 \times 10y\text{Rate} \times 0.5 \quad \text{if} \quad 10y\text{Rate} - 2y\text{Rate} > 0.6\%$$
$$0 \text{ coupon} \qquad\qquad \text{otherwise}$$

But perhaps the investor may not like to subject her entire coupon to a bet that the 10y–2y rate is above 0.6% on one particular date. Maybe it is more acceptable to have a coupon that is

$$1.3 \times 10y\text{Rate} \times 0.5 \times \frac{n}{N},$$

where n is the number of business days in the 6-month period where the 10y–2y rate is above 0.6% and $N = 132$ is the total number of business days in the 6-month period. (Actually, the multiplier appropriate to such a structure may not be 1.3 however. It might instead be 1.15 for example.)

In any case, having illustrated how range accruals could help to achieve certain investor payoff objectives, let's look further into them.

Key Points

- A range accrual pays based on the number of days an observable (e.g. spot FX) stays in some range. This is safer than betting on the value of the observable on one date (e.g. digital option).
- A Fader has a vanilla-like payoff multiplied by the number of days an observable stays in some range. This is less volatile than a knockout.
- A spread accrual is where the observable is a spread. These are popular in rates.

7.2 SINGLE REFERENCE ACCRUALS

Recall our product that pays

$$\frac{n}{N},$$

where n is the number of business days in the 6-month period in which EUR/GBP is above 0.81.

This is a single reference range accrual in a sense that it pays out on the basis of one-reference entity, namely EUR/GBP. Actually, notwithstanding appearances, it turns out to be merely a portfolio of digital call options with the same barrier level 0.81 each with notional $\frac{1}{N}$, and each expiring on a different business day during the 6-month period (**but with payment delayed until the end of the period**).

This can be seen since, if EUR/GBP is above 0.81 on each business day, the relevant digital call pays $\frac{1}{N}$ and 0 otherwise. Adding up all payoffs gives us the $\frac{n}{N}$ of the range accrual. Figure 7.3 shows a hypothetical path of EUR/GBP versus the range barrier and how a single digital fits into the picture.

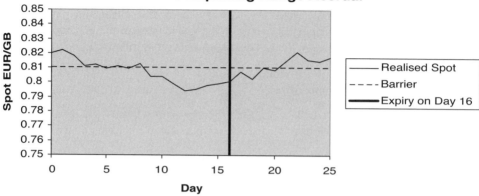

Figure 7.3 Hypothetical path of spot versus barrier level. Also shown is the expiry date of one digital (i.e. 16 days) as part of the range accrual package. Since spot is below 0.81 on this day, this digital expires worthless.

Table 7.1 illustrates how a simple range accrual compares with a digital or one-touch. What about our second (Fader) example? The payoff is

$$\frac{n}{N} \times \max\left(1.25 - S_T, 0\right),$$

Table 7.1 Comparison of range accrual *vis-à-vis* digital option and one-touch.

Feature	Digital	One-touch	Range accrual
Price	Moderate.	Most expensive.	Can be cheaper than normal digital if barrier level is out-of-the-money, since the structure comprises a portfolio of digitals, the majority of which have shorter expiries.
Sensitive to Final Asset Price	Final asset price completely determines payoff.	Much less sensitive than digital since payoff at expiry is assured if asset price breaches barrier during life of option.	Much less sensitive to final asset price, since on each observation date for which asset price satisfies condition, accrual occurs.
Upside Potential	Moderate probability of payoff of 1. (Only other possible payoff is 0.)	Higher probability of payoff of 1 than digital.	Lower probability of achieving maximum payoff of 1, since each accrual fraction is based on asset price satisfying condition on that observation date. Similarly, less likely for payoff to be 0.

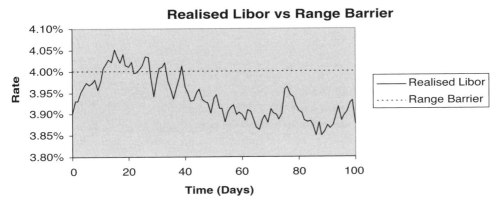

Figure 7.4 Hypothetical path of Libor versus range barrier. Libor fixes at 3.9% at the start of the period but is still above the 4% barrier for 19 days out of 100 in the range, giving an accrual multiplier of $19/100 = 0.19$ to apply to the 3.9% rate.

where S_T is the value of EUR/USD at expiry time $T = 0.5y$, and n is the number of business days in the 6-month period where EUR/USD is below 1.35.

If we decompose it conceptually, we have a bunch of partial barrier options. Specifically, we have a bunch of put options expiring after 6 months with strike 1.25 and notional $\frac{1}{N}$, but each is **subject to a partial barrier with level 1.35 that is effective only on one business day**.

A further example is where the payoff is

$$\frac{n}{N} \times L_T,$$

where L_T is the Libor rate at fixing date T (start of period), and n is the number of business days in the period (from T to $T + \tau$) where the Libor rate L_t is above 4%. This looks like a portfolio of asset-or-nothing options. However, it should be observed that the Libor rate paid is not the same as that determining whether we accrue. For example, if Libor fixes at 3.9%, it is still possible that for some business days in the whole period Libor is above 4%. (See Figure 7.4 for an illustration.) In fact, we need to know how the Libor rate at time T is correlated with the Libor rate at time t (such that $T \leq t < T + \tau$).

Key Points

- At its simplest, a single reference accrual is a portfolio of digitals, with payment delayed until the end of the period.
- A Fader can be thought of as a portfolio of partial barrier options (with each barrier lasting one business day).
- Suppose a range accrual pays on the basis of an observable (e.g. Libor) on one date, and accrues on the basis of the same observable over the period. Then it is possible for payments to be due even if the fixing value is outside the range for accruing.

7.3   MULTIPLE REFERENCE ACCRUALS

Our third example in Section 7.1 is

$$1.3 \times 10y\text{Rate}_T \times 0.5 \times \frac{n}{N},$$

where n is the number of business days in the 6-month period (from T to $T + \tau$) where the 10 year–2 year spread at time t is above 0.6%. This is a multiple reference accrual.

The principle of decomposition into a portfolio of options each with notional $\frac{1}{N}$ still holds. However, each of these options is now no longer a simple option. Specifically, we have a bunch of options that pay the 10-year rate as observed at time T, if at a future time t (such that $T < t < T + \tau$) the 10 year–2 year rate stays above 0.6%. This involves treatment of the correlations of the 10-year and 2-year rates and even the correlation of the 10-year rate at time T versus that at a future time t.

While we are on the topic of multiple reference accruals, we can afford to be creative. Arguably all we are doing is selling optionality (a familiar theme). Versus a straight payoff with no accrual features, we could get a higher yield if the payoff accrual is based on the number of days a certain condition is satisfied. For example, we could have a payoff based on the STOXX 50 index times $\frac{n}{N}$, where n is the number of business days where EUR/USD remains in the range 1.2 to 1.3, and 6-month Euribor stays under 3%.

Accruals of Other Fixing Periods

We are not restricted to daily observations on our range accruals. Perhaps we could have a payoff of $\frac{n}{N}$, where n is the number of weeks (based on a weekly observation on Friday at 12 noon, say) that a certain condition is satisfied. Monthly observation range accruals are also not uncommon.

Accruals with Early Termination

Finally, it is worth mentioning that adding early termination features (e.g. callability) can significantly complicate our range accruals, as we can no longer treat the range accrual as a separate portfolio of options, but instead have to treat them together to decide if early termination is worthwhile. This requires a much more involved modelling effort, and margins for products will correspondingly increase.

Key Points

- Multiple reference accruals have fixings based on a different observable from that used to determine accruals. These can be popular in hybrids due to higher yields.
- Accrual periods need not be daily. Weekly or monthly accruals exist.
- Early termination features complicate the pricing of range accruals.

8

Early Termination

It cannot be overemphasised that investors are always seeking higher yields. And selling optionality is an effective way to obtain higher yields. **A common means of selling optionality is by attaching a feature to an instrument that would make it terminate early and repay the principal** (usually when it would be better for the investor if the instrument continues paying coupons).

This can be achieved by making the instrument callable, i.e. giving the issuer the right to repay the principal at any time at his sole discretion, so that he no longer has to pay coupons. We start by examining this feature. The next feature we examine is the trigger, where repayment of principal occurs automatically if the underlying satisfies certain conditions (e.g. spot FX is above some level). Then we consider the tarn feature, which causes repayment to occur if the total coupons paid out to the investor exceed a certain amount.

The flipside of callability is puttability, i.e. where the investor has the discretion to demand repayment of the note. This is a valuable feature and will be examined. Finally, we consider how early termination might be modified where cashflows are of a contingent liability nature.

8.1 THE MINDSET OF A BENCHMARK INVESTOR

It should be stated that since early termination typically works to the disadvantage of the investor, **the investor would be forced to retain an instrument when it is unfavourable for him to keep it. This is however not usually a concern**. For example, consider a fixed rate bond paying 4% coupon per annum. If interest rates go up, the investor is stuck with a below market coupon; but if interest rates go down, he is happy with his above market coupon.

If this bond were callable, perhaps the investor could get a 5% coupon instead. If interest rates go up, he is cushioned by that extra 1% but otherwise no worse off than the investor in a normal bond. If rates go down, the bond would be called and he would get back his principal, which he admittedly would have to invest at the lower prevailing rate of interest (so worse off than a normal bond investor). But this would not make our investor worse off than the holder of a floating rate note, who would always get the prevailing rate of interest. Figure 8.1 illustrates the yields of a callable bond versus a normal bond and a floating rate note. Thus, our callable bond investor might not have trouble beating his benchmark (if he is a portfolio manager) in any case.

Often, the investor actually prefers early termination, so that after getting a juicy coupon initially, he is free to re-invest as he pleases. This is so especially if the early termination feature produced a coupon that was good enough that the investor would be happy to have it, even if only for a short period. Typically, for an investor whose mandate is to beat a benchmark, a 1% yield pickup can be very attractive.

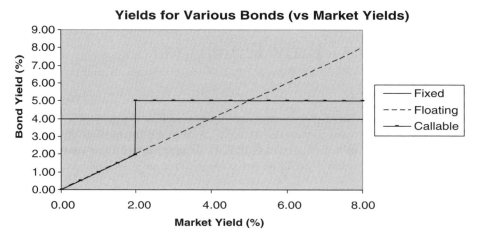

Figure 8.1   The fixed rate bond always yields 4%. The floating rate note has yield that corresponds to the market yield. The callable bond has yield that is 5% (i.e. higher than the fixed rate bond) provided it is not called; it would be called when the market yield drops significantly, say, to 2%.

Key Points

- Early termination features mean that an investor is unlikely to continue receiving above-market coupons for too long (since the note would be repaid), whereas he would be stuck with the instrument when coupons are unfavourable.
- A normal bond investor is also stuck with fixed coupons when rates are high, but continues to receive these fixed coupons if rates fall.
- If a deal has initial above-market coupons, an investor may prefer early termination so that he is free to re-invest his principal.

8.2   CALLABLES

If a note is callable, the issuer has full discretion to repay the principal, so that no future coupons are payable.

A typical callable structured note is designed as follows. **There is one or more "attractive" fixed initial coupons** (e.g. 8%). Thereafter, coupons are linked to some market variable. For example, an inverse floater of notional $100 has payoff

$$\$100 \times G \max (K - L_T, 0) \, \tau,$$

where $G = 2$ is a gearing factor, $K = 5\%$ is the strike, $\tau = 0.25$ is the accrual fraction for 3 months, and L_T is the 3-month Libor rate at time T.

Typically, **there is a period where the note cannot be called**, e.g. the first 2 years in a 20-year note. Thereafter, on each coupon payment date, the issuer has to pay the coupon due, but is then **free to also repay the principal, so that there will be no liability to pay any future coupons**. (NB Usually a note is only callable on coupon dates after payment of the coupon for that period. This prevents the obvious possibility of the issuer calling a note just before the coupon date to avoid paying the coupon accrued for that period.)

Our inverse floater pays the investor more if interest rates remain low. In fact, for high interest rates, the coupon is 0. It follows that the issuer will only call if interest rates drop further, e.g. if they drop to 1.8% per annum, giving an annualised coupon of $2 \times \max(0.05 - 0.018, 0) = 6.4\ \%$.

We can see in Figure 8.2 how the value increases as interest rates decrease but then flattens, showing how callability limits the potential upside.

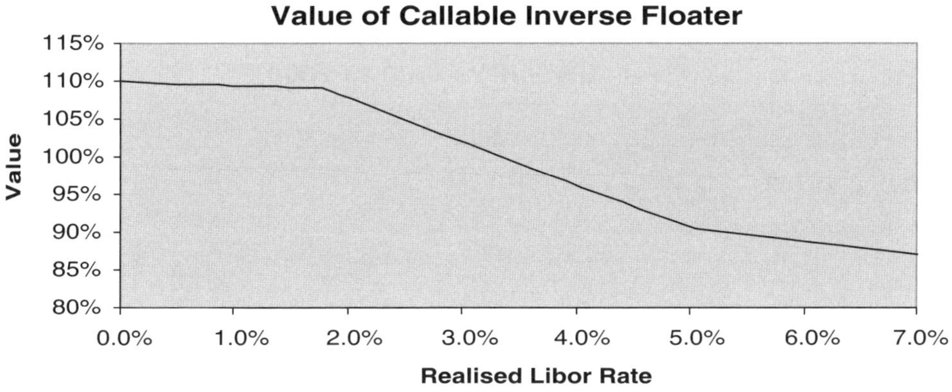

Figure 8.2 Value of callable inverse floater for different realised Libor rates. As Libor rates decrease, the inverse floater would have a higher payoff. However, beyond a certain point, say 2%, the issuer will find it optimal to call the note, thus capping the upside.

It should be mentioned, however, that typically it is only optimal to call when the note is sufficiently out-of-the-money (i.e. paying much higher coupons than market) from the issuer's perspective. For example, where prevailing interest rates are 3.5%, they may have to drop to below 2% for callability to be worthwhile.

Table 8.1 illustrates the features of a callable note versus a non-callable one.

Table 8.1 The features of a callable note

Feature	Non-callable	Callable
Coupons	As per payoff type.	Higher than coupon for non-callable note.
Potential Upside	Depends on the payoff type.	Limited since issuer will repay the principal if in her advantage (typically to the disadvantage of the investor).
Downside	Depends on the payoff type.	Similar downside as non-callable note, except that the higher coupon provides some cushion.

As another example, consider a 30-year note that, on quarterly coupon dates, pays

$$0.0016 \times \max(S_T - 80, 0) \times 0.25,$$

where S_T is the spot USD/JPY rate at time T, and the 0.25 reflects the quarterly coupons. These are power reverse dual currency (PRDC) deals (covered in Chapter 10).

Typically, these parameters applied where the deal was done when spot USD/JPY was 115, and it would be optimal to call the deal in its early years only if spot rose to 135! (Although in subsequent years, as the time to maturity decreases, calling the deal for a lower value of spot might be warranted.)

These PRDC deals present a cautionary tale, however. Many were done in the final years of the 1990s or early years of this decade at somewhat high strikes (e.g. 90 or above), and when USD/JPY dropped (back towards 100 around 2005), many investors found that their bets on big juicy coupons followed by quick repayment of the principal did not materialise. Basically, coupons were small, and it was not optimal to call the notes. (Admittedly, since PRDCs tend to be 30-year deals, a lot can change prior to maturity of the notes. But 2008 saw sharp declines of USD/JPY towards 90, so the prospect of the notes being called is now even more distant.) Figure 8.3 shows the fluctuations in spot USD/JPY from 2000 to 2008.

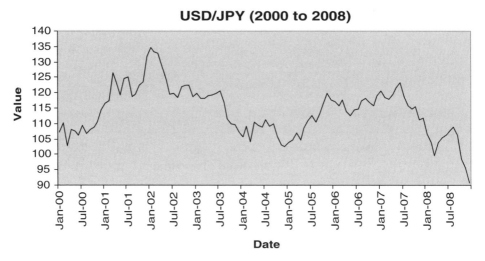

Figure 8.3   Value of spot USD/JPY from 2000 to 2008. Deals were often done when USD/JPY was around 115 at correspondingly higher strikes. This proved frustrating to investors when USD/JPY dropped to 100 or even 90.
Source: Bloomberg

As mentioned earlier, if the investor is happy to invest in a deal (e.g. fixed rate bond) regardless of whether it is called, callability can sweeten things somewhat. **But for an investor to do a deal with which she is comfortable only if it gets called, is usually not a good idea**.

It should be mentioned that callability introduces significant modelling challenges in that the decision of whether to call a deal requires computation of transition probabilities. For interest rate instruments, non-callable deals usually require us to model only the terminal distribution, whereas callable deals require the evolution of the entire curve over time to be modelled. Full-term structure models are also harder to fit to available market data. The increased model risks engendered obviously imply that bigger margins are applied when callable deals are sold to investors. Such modelling issues also apply to trigger deals and tarn deals (covered in subsequent sections).

Key Points

- A callable deal can be repaid at the discretion of the issuer, who will do so when coupons are high relative to the market. Callability, therefore, cheapens a structure.
- An inverse floater has a payoff based on strike minus Libor.
- It is usually not optimal to call unless a deal is sufficiently in-the-money.

- Many PRDCs were done in the early years of this decade when USD/JPY was 115. They would have been worth calling if USD/JPY had reached 135, but that did not happen.
- Callability introduces modelling challenges.

8.3 TRIGGERS (AUTOCALLS)

There is something inherently unsatisfying about callable products. Basically, the issuer has full discretion to call, and could choose not to do so even if it is optimal or could choose to call when it is suboptimal (e.g. a trader might call a deal so that reserves get released in time for bonuses to be paid). If, from the investor's perspective, she would first like a juicy coupon and then get her principal repaid, this lack of certainty about the conditions that would cause the note to be called is not ideal.

Perhaps it is better to have the **note automatically repaid** (hence the alternative term "autocall") **under certain conditions (albeit favourable to the issuer and unfavourable to the investor**, in order to cheapen the note). **The trigger or autocall feature is a good way to achieve it**. This basically stipulates that on each coupon date the note will be repaid if a certain condition occurs (e.g. if 3-month Libor is below 2% on coupon date). Figure 8.4 illustrates this for a hypothetical path of 3-month Libor. Note that the coupon for that period is still due. Also, as in callables, it is possible and often the case that the trigger condition applies only after a certain time, e.g. after the first year.

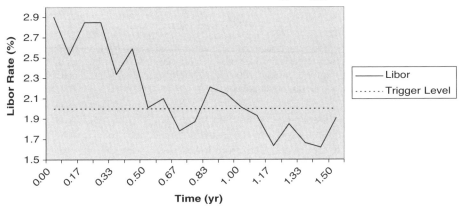

Figure 8.4 Hypothetical path of 3-month Libor versus trigger level of 2%. Deal is triggered at time 8 months, when Libor falls below 2%.

There is no limit to the type of conditions that can be stipulated. Indeed, developing further the theme of selling optionality for yield, perhaps you could have a structured note linked to the STOXX 50 index that is repaid based on a trigger condition of either EUR/USD rising above 1.3 or euro interest rates rising above 2.5%.

However, to illustrate the features of a trigger, it is perhaps best to look at our inverse floater again with payoff

$$\$100 \times 2 \times \max(0.05 - L_T, 0) \times 0.25,$$

where L_T is the 3-month Libor rate at time T.

Suppose now that the trigger condition is 3-month Libor falling below 1.8%. If, on our observation date, 3-month Libor happens to be 1.75% per annum, the appropriate coupon is

$$\$100 \times 2 \times \max{(0.05 - 0.0175, 0)} \times 0.25 = \$1.625,$$

and the note gets repaid, so that no further coupons are payable. However, if 3-month Libor were 1.81%, then the appropriate coupon is

$$\$100 \times 2 \times \max{(0.05 - 0.01810)} \times 0.25 = \$1.595$$

(not too different from before), but the note is not repaid, and further coupons are still due. This demonstrates the digital nature of the risk (which is not really desirable). Figure 8.5 shows how the payoff changes abruptly as the underlying crosses the trigger level.

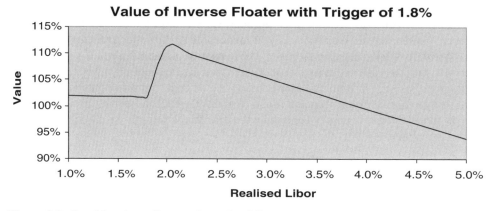

Figure 8.5 Possible values of inverse floater for different realised Libor. Notice how above the 1.8% trigger level, the value rises for decreasing values of realised Libor (as expected for an inverse floater). However, the value drops abruptly to around 100% when the trigger level is breached since the deal terminates and future cashflows are no longer payable.

It is worth highlighting that in a deal with many coupons, it is possible that a trigger could be activated when it is suboptimal (from the issuer's perspective) for the deal as a whole. For example, our inverse floater may benefit from lower rates. However, interest rates are not sufficiently low for repayment of the principal to be optimal. In this case, the trigger feature works against the issuer (and in the favour of the investor). Figure 8.6 shows how the payoff to the investor benefits from the trigger.

We should further note that termination may be subject to different trigger conditions at different times. For example, if the forward of the underlying is increasing with maturity, it is only sensible to have trigger conditions requiring the spot level to be above a barrier that increases over coupon dates as per Figure 8.7. (The forward of an asset increases if the interest rate is greater than the asset yield.) Similarly, if the forward decreases with increasing maturity, step-down triggers are the logical choice (see Figure 8.8). (For an FX perspective on decreasing forwards, Chapter 10 on PRDCs offers a much clearer illustration.)

It is worth repeating how early termination via triggers is a more transparent approach than by allowing the issuer to call a note at her discretion, as the condition for repayment is externally observable and early termination is not subject to the whim of the issuer. However, the digital nature of the payoff when a trigger level is crossed is not ideal, and perhaps this has led to some interest in an alternative, namely the tarn feature, described in the next section.

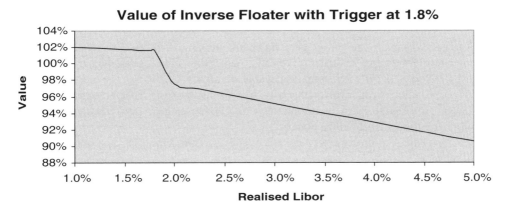

Figure 8.6 Other possible values of inverse floater for different realised Libor. Whereas the value increases for decreasing values of realised Libor, it stays stubbornly below 100% prior to breaching the trigger level. When the trigger level is breached however, suboptimal termination (from the issuer's perspective) of the deal occurs and the value is about 100%.

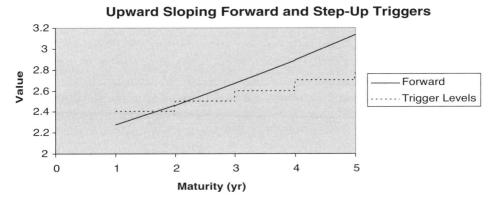

Figure 8.7   Step-up triggers in the presence of an upward-sloping forward curve.

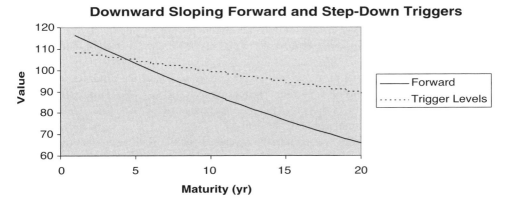

Figure 8.8   Step-down triggers in the presence of a downward-sloping forward curve.

Key Points

- A trigger terminates the note if a certain condition is satisfied (e.g. Libor falling below some level for an inverse floater). Typically, such termination is favourable to the issuer as it is likely to occur when coupons payable are high.
- Trigger conditions can involve other asset classes distinct from those in the payoff.
- Triggers can lead to sharp discontinuities with a huge change in exposure depending on whether a trigger level will be breached.
- We often have step-up triggers (if the asset's forward is increasing) or step-down triggers (if the asset's forward is decreasing).

8.4   THE TARGET REDEMPTION NOTE

Consider our inverse floater from earlier with payoff

$$2 \times \max(0.05 - L_T, 0) \times 0.25,$$

where L_T is the 3-month Libor rate at time T.

Suppose that interest rates continued to fall; specifically, consider the realised interest rates and the associated coupons shown in Table 8.2.

Table 8.2   Hypothetical accumulated coupons on an inverse floater tarn deal. Based on a tarn level of 4%, the note terminates at the end of 1 year when accumulated coupons at 4.4% exceed this level.

Fixing time T (years)	Payment time $T + \tau$ (years)	Libor L_T (per annum) (%)	Coupon payable (%)	Accumulated coupons (%)
0	0.25	3.4	$2 \times \max(5.0 - 3.4, 0)$ $\times 0.25 = 0.8$	0.8
0.25	0.5	3.0	1.0	1.8
0.5	0.75	2.6	1.2	3.0
0.75	1	2.2	1.4	4.4
1	1.25	1.7	1.65	6.05
1.25	1.5	1.8	1.6	7.65

If the note were callable, perhaps it would be called at time 1 year when rates fell below 2%. Or if the trigger level was at 1.8%, it would be automatically repaid after 1 year 3 months (assuming the trigger condition is applied at the end of the period) since the Libor fixing at time 1 year was 1.7%.

An alternative feature that promotes early termination is to have the **note automatically repaid when total accumulated coupons reach some level**, say 4%. **This is the target redemption note (or tarn)**. In this case, the note is repaid after 1 year, since the last 1.4% coupon takes the total accumulated coupons over 4%.

The payoff profile of a tarn is such that the investor benefits from the market moving his way (in this case lower rates) but this is (loosely) **capped by a certain target return**. There is some discontinuity however. Suppose in our earlier example, the observed Libor rate at fixing time 9 months was 3.01% (instead of 2.2%), the investor would have had a smaller coupon of

$$2 \times \max(0.05 - 0.0301, 0) \times 0.25 = 0.995\%$$

as opposed to 1.4% after 1 year. But the note will not be repaid, since accumulated coupons at
$3\% + 0.995\% = 3.995\%$ are less than the 4% level.

So the note survives into the next coupon period, and the investor will be eligible for the
above-market 1.65% coupon at that point (if the rest of the rates remained unchanged). This
discontinuity is, however, not as severe as a trigger where early termination is totally dependent
on an arbitrary level. This is illustrated in Figure 8.9.

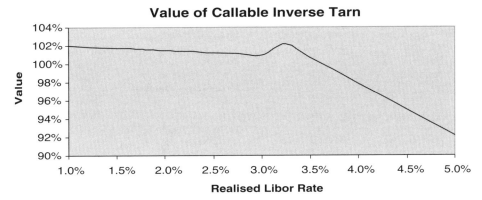

Figure 8.9   Hypothetical values of tarn for different realised Libor rates. Notice how there is a slight
drop in value of the note to about 100% when realised Libor falls to about 3%, since the deal tarns out.

Whereas a tarn is a means of selling optionality (via early termination for higher yield),
an investor will be stuck with an underperforming note if the market moves contrary to his
expectations. For example, consider the Libor rates and coupons illustrated in Table 8.3.

Table 8.3   Another set of hypothetical accumulated coupons on an inverse floater tarn deal. No
coupons are paid from 6 months and beyond. Obviously, the note does not tarn out, so that the investor
is stuck with this. (Admittedly, the speed of rate rises is higher than typical.)

Fixing time T (years)	Payment time $T + \tau$ (years)	Libor L_T (per annum) (%)	Coupon payable (%)	Accumulated coupons (%)
0	0.25	3.4	$2 \times \max(5.0 - 3.4, 0)$ $\times 0.25 = 0.8$	0.8
0.25	0.5	4.2	0.4	1.2
0.5	0.75	5.0	0	1.2
0.75	1	5.2	0	1.2
1	1.25	5.3	0	1.2
1.25	1.5	5.4	0	1.2

Our investor receives no coupons after 6 months, as Libor has reached 5% and the accumulated coupons do not increase (and so remain below the 4% tarn level). Unless market conditions
improve over the life of the deal, the investor will be stuck with no coupons, and neither will
there be an early termination.

At least in a tarn deal, the reward and penalty profile seems quite clear. **Either you get paid
enough above-market coupons to reach the target level to be repaid principal (early), or
you get stuck with low or zero coupons over the life of the deal.**

At this stage, it is worth contrasting the characteristics of early termination via callability,
triggers or tarns. This is shown in Table 8.4.

Table 8.4 Comparison of the characteristics of the three main early termination methods: callability, triggers and tarns. Note that here we are using early termination to cheapen the structure, so that early termination has to be designed to occur when such termination is unfavourable to the investor.

Feature	Callability	Trigger	Tarn
Transparent Termination Criteria	No. Termination at the discretion of the issuer.	Yes.	Yes.
Change in Market Variable can Cause Abrupt Change in Note Value (due to Termination)	Least so in comparison with other two.	Yes. Termination depends on a market variable satisfying trigger condition, which may not always correspond too closely with note value.	Yes, but less so than for trigger. Abruptness is because marginally higher coupon can lead to tarn level being reached, and hence termination.
Can Terminate in Favour of Investor	Unlikely (but possible since issuer has full discretion).	Yes, since termination condition is independent of (although related to) note value.	No.
Cumulative Coupons Paid in Event of Termination Predictable	Least so, since issuer has full discretion.	Less predictable than tarn, but likely that deal terminates only if continuation favourable to investor, i.e. substantial coupons have been paid.	Yes.

It is possible to combine features of callability, triggers and tarns together to achieve higher yields. But things get messy quickly and banks might not be sufficiently confident to price such deals competitively. Furthermore, the added benefit of having such features combined is not high, since they all typically lead to early termination when circumstances make it favourable for the issuer to do so. It is not clear if having many different possibilities of early termination may make such a big difference from the issuer's perspective.

Key Points

- A target redemption note (tarn) is repaid if total accumulated coupons exceed a target level.
- Either an investor gets above-market coupons and the deal terminates early, or she could be stuck with low or zero coupons in a deal that will not terminate soon.
- A tarn has discontinuities in its payoff profile, but this is milder than for a trigger.
- It is possible but not usually of much benefit to combine features of callability, triggers and tarns.

8.5 PUTTABLES

As discussed in Section 8.2, a callable note is one where the issuer has the discretion to repay the note early, so as to end any obligation to pay future cashflows. In a similar vein, **a puttable**

note is one where the investor has the discretion to demand repayment of the note early.
(Typically, the note is puttable only on coupon payment dates.) In this case, the investor will
demand repayment when it is no longer favourable to receive cashflows under the note. Thus,
puttability is a valuable feature, and makes the note more expensive.

A Puttable Bond

Let us consider a puttable bond to illustrate how things work. Consider a bond of notional
€100 with maturity 5 years that pays 4% coupon annually. If interest rates remain at 4%, then
the bond will be worth €100. If interest rates rise to 5%, then it would be worth less than
€100 since, if the investor had not bought the bond, she could have now bought one with a
5% coupon instead. Similarly, if interest rates fell to 3%, the bond would be worth more than
€100.

For a puttable bond, the investor has the right to seek repayment of the bond. Suppose the
bond is puttable for €100. In that case, the investor would "put" the bond back to the issuer
if interest rates rise. This means that the bond has to be worth at least €100. Notice, however,
that the investor is able to benefit if interest rates fall, and the 4% coupon turns out to be above
market value. This is a valuable feature of the note, and hence will incur a cost. Specifically, if
the non-puttable note yielded a 4% coupon, a puttable bond might only yield a 3.5% coupon.
Figure 8.10 shows the values of a normal bond and a puttable bond for varying interest
rates.

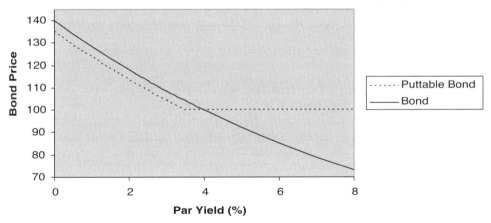

Prices of Bond and Puttable Bond for Varying Rates

Figure 8.10 Prices of normal and puttable bonds for different interest rates. Both benefit from falling
interest rates (although the puttable bond has a lower value). However, as rates rise, the puttable bond is
worth at least 100 since the investor can seek redemption of the bond.

Note that puttability is not common for most structured notes. After all, it involves buying
optionality, which increases the cost of the note. On the other hand, a typical investor since
2001 (or even earlier) tended to utilise structured notes to seek higher yields. Such investors
preferred to sell optionality rather than buy more optionality. Thus, puttability is included
partly for completeness of exposition.

Corporate Bonds

For corporate bonds however, puttability is more sensible. Having existed for a while, puttable bonds were in vogue especially in the 1980s when the memory of high interest rates (from 1980 to 1982 in the USA) was fresh, and investors would have been more afraid of a potential return to high inflation and high rates. More importantly, for corporate bonds, the credit risk of the issuer is often worth paying attention to. Companies experience changes to their fortunes, and can find their market positions collapsing for unexpected reasons. A puttable bond allows an investor to seek repayment from a company, and thus get protection against imminent default in a company whose situation is deteriorating. In the same token, a puttable bond can exacerbate the situation of a company in a precarious position, as the drain on cash required to repay the bond can potentially tip it into default.

In the realm of structured notes, puttability can be useful. Whereas prior to the credit crisis of 2008, banks were generally seen as credit-worthy, this has become less clear since that time. The right to terminate a structured note early, at the discretion of the investor can thus be very valuable. In fact, even the right to terminate at a loss can be valuable. Suppose you have the right to terminate a note for 70% of your principal. If you have good reason to believe that the issuer is imminently going to default and you are unlikely to recover 70% of the principal, then it might be worth "putting" the note to cut your losses!

Other Forms of Early Termination

Other early termination features favourable to the investor can also exist. For example, for a note that benefits from rising stock indices, a low trigger level could be set, so that if stocks fall below a certain level, the note terminates. Again, such features are not popular on structured notes, as they reduce the coupon yield, which is contrary to the desires of many investors.

Key Points

- Puttability gives the investor the discretion to seek repayment when in her interest, and so makes a note expensive. Thus it is not a popular feature in structured notes.
- Puttability is more popular in corporate bonds, where default is a serious possibility, in addition to potential rises in rates. It offers protection from a deterioration in an issuer's credit worthiness.

8.6 EARLY TERMINATION AND CONTINGENT CASHFLOWS

Another curious issue is regarding early termination for cashflows where the payment can be negative, i.e. the investor can be obliged to pay the issuer instead under certain market conditions. (Section 6.1 briefly touched on contingent liability, and mentioned how a certain level of sophistication is required for involvement in such products.)

But suppose you have a total return swap. This is similar to synthetically buying an asset. In period (t_{i-1} to t_i), you receive $\frac{S_{t_i}}{S_{t_{i-1}}} - 1$, where S_t is the value of the asset at time t. (Notice that if the asset drops in value over the period, $\frac{S_{t_i}}{S_{t_{i-1}}} < 1$ and you actually have to make a payment instead.) Another possibility is where in each period you receive $S_t - K$, where K is some strike. Notice that if $S_t < K$, you are obliged to make a payment instead. There is no optionality involved in the coupon! (This is why an investor should be very careful of such products.)

For purposes of early termination, a contingent liability cashflow introduces no real complications for callability or triggers. For tarns, it gets interesting. Suppose your tarn level is 10%, and your coupons over the period are 4%, −3%, 6.2%, 2.1%, −2.5%, 5%. Then you tarn out only after the sixth period. Notice how the negative returns prolong the time it takes to tarn out.

One way for the issuer to ensure a quicker termination is to take account of positive coupons only (see Table 8.5). In this case, you tarn out after the third coupon. It is worth stressing that tarns are designed to terminate a note whose coupons are in the investor's favour, and in this sense make the note cheaper. A condition that takes account of only positive coupons (where cashflows are contingent liability) in determining the tarn condition is even more to the investor's disadvantage, insofar as the investor is likely to forgo coupons in her favour after having endured unfavourable coupon conditions.

Table 8.5 Hypothetical cashflows in a "positive-only" tarn where cashflows are contingent liability. Tarning out occurs faster than if the normal tarn condition applies.

Period	Coupon (%)	Cumulative (%)	Positive cumulative (%)
1	4	4	4
2	−3	4 − 3 = 1	4 + max(−3, 0) = 4
3	6.2	7.2	10.2
4	2.1	9.3	Tarned out
5	−2.5	6.8	. . .
6	5	11.8	. . .
7	N/A	Tarned out	. . .

An investor deciding to go ahead with such structures should fully consider what circumstances could potentially be of concern to her, rather than just be drawn by potentially attractive initial coupons.

Key Points

- Contingent liability cashflows may require a payment from the investor at times.
- You can have a tarn that is based on the accumulation of positive coupons only. This is much cheaper since it quickly stops an investor from getting good coupons even if she had endured bad ones earlier.

9

Pathwise Accumulators

This chapter will cover some rather unusual and extremely complex products. It takes a rather confident investor to want to bet on the path of certain market variables. I cannot say such products are the mainstream, nor can I assume that they would be popular in the new deleveraged world post-2008. In any case, the material should make interesting reading.

We start our discussion with the definition of a one-way floater. Each coupon is based on market interest rates, but is contractually guaranteed not to be less than the previous coupon. This is a safe (and actually very expensive) product, but its introduction helps us to have a first glimpse at strongly path-dependent products generally.

We then discuss the rather more exotic skylines and snowballs. Each coupon on these instruments is dependent on a market variable, which could turn out to be zero. Furthermore, **each coupon is linked to the previous coupon, so that if a previous coupon were zero, the pain would be felt for a long time**. Of course, getting the path right will be much more rewarding in yield (than a normal instrument), but getting it wrong can also be much more painful. Recall the discussion on barriers in Chapter 4 and triggers in Chapter 8, and how much was at stake based on the behaviour of the underlying *vis-à-vis* some arbitrary trigger level. You will see how the **skylines and snowballs have a lot of leverage riding on previous coupons**, and the interested investor should be aware of the real danger of adverse market scenarios badly affecting all future coupons. However, many of these deals are at least principal protected.

9.1 THE ONE-WAY FLOATER

The one-way floater is an instrument where coupons increase as interest rates rise, but do not decrease as interest rates fall. Let us start by considering when this product might appeal most to an investor.

It appears that the the economy faces boom and bust cycles that last about 7 years on average. During periods of low inflation and weak growth, central banks cut interest rates to stimulate demand, and when the economy overheats, they increase rates rapidly to try to control inflation. Table 9.1 and Figure 9.1 show interest rate decisions by the Federal Reserve over the last decade.

Let's assume that you are an investor who feels that a boom cycle is nearing its end, i.e. currently rates are expected to rise to cool the economy but, say, in 1 or 2 years they are likely to fall to prevent a recession. An example of just such a scenario can be found in 1999 to 2000, just before the burst of the dotcom bubble. Could you invest in an instrument that allows you to lock-in growing interest rates but not expose you to declines?

One possibility (not popular in practice because of its cost) is the one-way floater. The payoff on each coupon date is

$$\left(\max\left(L_i, L_{i-1}^*\right) + s\right) \times 0.25,$$

Table 9.1 Federal Reserve rate decisions from 1999 to 2008.

Date	Change (%)	Level (%)
16-Dec-08	−1 to −0.75	0 to 0.25
29-Oct-08	−0.5	1
08-Oct-08	−0.5	1.5
30-Apr-08	−0.25	2
18-Mar-08	−0.75	2.25
30-Jan-08	−0.5	3
22-Jan-08	−0.75	35
11-Dec-07	−0.25	4.25
31-Oct-07	−0.25	4.5
18-Sep-07	−0.5	4.75
29-Jun-06	0.25	5.25
10-May-06	0.25	5
28-Mar-06	0.25	4.75
31-Jan-06	0.25	4.5
13-Dec-05	0.25	4.25
01-Nov-05	0.25	4
20-Sep-05	0.25	3.75
09-Aug-05	0.25	3.5
30-Jun-05	0.25	3.25
03-May-05	0.25	3
22-Mar-05	0.25	2.75
02-Feb-05	0.25	2.5
14-Dec-04	0.25	2.25
10-Nov-04	0.25	2
21-Sep-04	0.25	1.75
10-Aug-04	0.25	1.5
30-Jun-04	0.25	1.25
25-Jun-03	−0.25	1
06-Nov-02	−0.5	1.25
11-Dec-01	−0.25	1.75
06-Nov-01	−0.5	2
02-Oct-01	−0.5	2.5
17-Sep-01	−0.5	3
21-Aug-01	−0.25	3.5
27-Jun-01	−0.25	3.75
15-May-01	−0.5	4
18-Apr-01	−0.5	4.5
20-Mar-01	−0.5	5
31-Jan-01	−0.5	5.5
03-Jan-01	−0.5	6
16-May-00	0.5	6.5
21-Mar-00	0.25	6
02-Feb-00	0.25	5.75
16-Nov-99	0.25	5.5
24-Aug-99	0.25	5.25
30-Jun-99	0.25	5

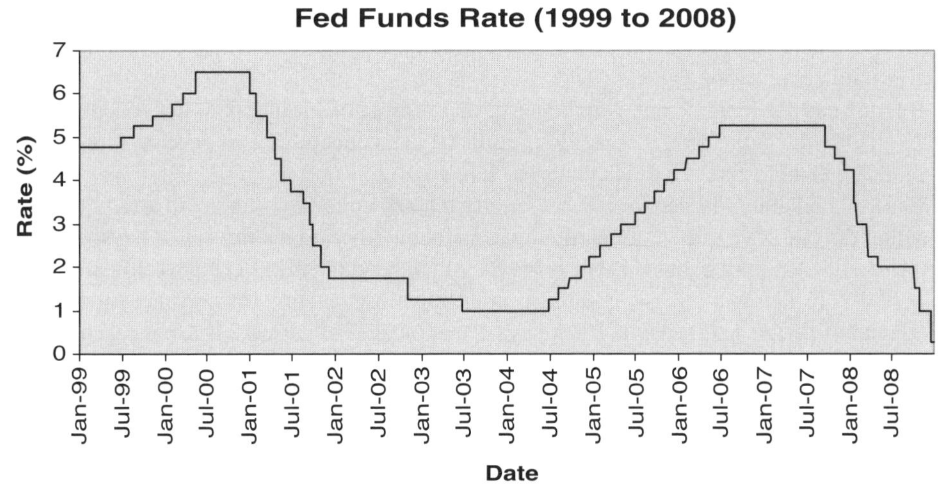

Fed Funds Rate (1999 to 2008)

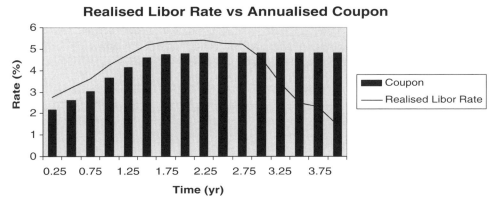

Figure 9.1 Federal Funds Rate from 1999 to 2008. We can see rising rates peaking at 6.5% in May 2000; thereafter, a series of rate cuts followed to stave off the recession from the bursting of the dot-com bubble and the September 2001 terrorist attacks, taking the Fed Funds rate to a decades-low of 1%. As the economy picked up and grew strongly, rate rises started in June 2004 and reached 5.25%. From September 2007, rate cuts followed in quick succession as the severe fallout of the credit crunch became apparent, reaching a historic low of 0 to 25bps in December 2008.
Source: Bloomberg

where L_i is the 3-month Libor rate at fixing time t_i; L^*_{i-1} is the highest Libor rate fixing from start of deal to previous time t_{i-1}; $s = -0.6\%$ is a negative spread to compensate the issuer for this optionality; and 0.25 represents the 3-month accrual fraction.

Figure 9.2 shows a possible evolution of the 3-month Libor rates (based on this boom–bust discussion) and the corresponding payoff of the one-way floater. As the 3-month Libor rate increases, so does the coupon. As the 3-month Libor rate declines, the coupon is based on the highest Libor rate observed thus far. Thus, the coupons never go down.

Realised Libor Rate vs Annualised Coupon

Figure 9.2 Annualised coupons of a one-way floater versus the hypothetical path of Libor rates. The coupon of this instrument increases as the Libor rate rises, and remains at this highest level as the Libor rate declines.

Of course, such a feature as in the one-way floater is not cheap. In fact, if it were, the lookback, where payment is based on the maximum of a market variable over the life of the deal, would be quite popular.

But one can see how the one-way floater is an example of a rather path-dependent product. In particular, the dependence on previous coupons is a concept we can develop much further to produce a whole zoo of exotic creatures. A few will follow.

Before I conclude this section, let me briefly remark on the relevance of barriers to understanding the one-way floater.[1] In particular, consider a 2-period instrument. It pays you Libor at the end of each period, but if Libor is over 4% at the end of period 1, it pays you at least 4% in period 2. Notice that this is a combination of three instruments: (1) a normal Libor payout at the end of period 1; (2) a digital that pays 4% at the end of period 2 if Libor reaches 4% at the end of period 1; and (3) a knockin call option that pays $\max(\text{Libor} - 4\%, 0)$ at the end of period 2, where the knockin is only possible based on Libor observed at the end of period 1. Imagine a whole set of strikes for knockins and digitals and you can see that actually barriers are a conceptual building block to something as complex as a one-way floater.

Key Points

- Central banks raise rates towards the end of a business cycle to control inflation, and cut rates in a recession to stimulate the economy.
- A one-way floater pays based on the higher of the current interest rate (e.g. Libor) and its maximum for each period since the start of the deal. It is expensive.
- The coupon on a one-way floater has strong dependence on previous coupons.
- The one-way floater can be thought of as a portfolio of digitals and knockin barriers.

9.2 SKYLINES

Imagine the aftermath of 11 September 2001. The US equity markets had taken a beating, and the economy had already been reeling earlier in the year from the burst of the dotcom bubble. The Federal Reserve had been cutting the Fed funds rate from 6% at the beginning of 2001 to 3% by 17 September, and was likely to continue doing so to insulate the economy from the effects of the terrorist attacks.

You are an investor seeking a high yield, in an environment of low rates and weak equity markets. Suppose you are highly confident that 3-month Libor will stay under 3% for the next few years, notwithstanding forward rates projecting 3-month Libor at 4% to 5% within 2 years (see Figure 9.3). Then perhaps a skyline will interest you. (And it did indeed interest some investors of that period.)

The skyline payout is based on the previous coupon plus an increment if the market variable stays below some level. Otherwise, the coupon is zero, and future accumulation starts from this zero coupon level.

The payoff of a skyline is as follows. Suppose you have a 10-year note with quarterly coupons. At the first two coupon dates, your payoff is fixed at 5% per annum, giving coupons of

---

[1] The ideas in this paragraph were inspired by de Weert (2008), especially Chapters 12 and 13 in his treatment of Ladder Options and Lookback Options.

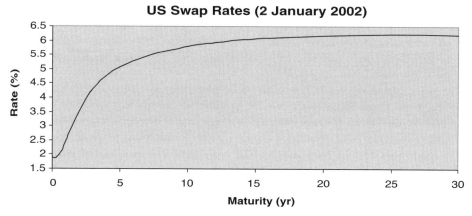

Figure 9.3   US swap rates as of 2 January 2002. 3-month Libor rates are around 2%. The 1-year swap rate is 2.46% whereas the 2-year swap rate is over 3.514%, so that the 1-year forward curve will have a 3-month rate over 4%. The 2-year forward curve will have an even higher 3-month rate.
Source: Bloomberg

$0.05 \times 0.25 = 1.25\%$ (where the 0.25 represents the 3-month accrual period). On subsequent coupon dates, the payoff is

$$\begin{array}{ll} \text{PrevCoupon} + 0.25\% & \text{if Libor} < 3\% \\ 0 & \text{otherwise} \end{array}$$

(Actually, since we have an upward-sloping yield curve, it is quite likely that the barrier would be increasing for future maturities, e.g. 3% barrier in year 1, 3.2% in year 2, 3.4% in year 3, etc. Such a step-up barrier feature does not affect the main ideas in our discussion, so we shall ignore it.)

Let us consider what coupons you would get as interest rates evolved over time. An illustration is found in Table 9.2 based on a hypothetical path of Libor rates.

Table 9.2   Hypothetical coupons of skyline. Due to Libor rates remaining below 3% until $2\frac{1}{2}$y, the coupon payable keeps rising by 0.25% each period. This leads to a very high annualised coupon of 13% by $2\frac{1}{2}$y. However, the moment the Libor rate breaches the 3% level, the coupon payable drops sharply to 0.

Fixing time T (y)	Payment time $T + \tau$ (y)	Realised Libor L_T (%)	Coupon at $T + \tau$ (%)	Annualised coupon (%)	Accumulated coupons (%)
0	0.25	2	1.25	5	1.25
0.25	0.5	1.75	1.25	5	2.5
0.5	0.75	1.7	$1.25 + 0.25 = 1.5$	6	4
0.75	1	1.51	1.75	7	5.75
1	1.25	1.25	2	8	7.75
1.25	1.5	1.5	2.25	9	10
1.5	1.75	1.92	2.5	10	12.5
1.75	2	2.28	2.75	11	15.25
2	2.25	2.7	3	12	18.25
2.25	2.5	2.9	3.25	13	21.5
2.5	2.75	3.2	0	0	21.5
2.75	3	3.1	0	0	21.5

We see that over the course of 3 years, total accumulated coupons of 21.5% have been paid, which is quite nice. Remember we are betting against forwards here and forwards suggest that our Libor rates should actually rise. So, we are benefiting from this bet. Also, note that coupons have continued to increase notwithstanding rising Libor rates, and then dramatically dropped to 0% when Libor reached 3%.

This suggests that we would not want this deal to continue indefinitely. After all, based on the economic cycle, if rates were lowered to stimulate growth, they would be raised after some years to cool down the economy. So, why not have a tarn feature, so that the note is automatically repaid when accumulated coupons reach 15% for example? In this case, the note will be repaid after 2 years, and achieving total coupons of 15% in a low-rate environment is not bad at all.

However, notice the dramatic drop to a coupon of 0 when Libor reaches 3%. Let me continue Table 9.2 in Table 9.3.

Table 9.3 Hypothetical coupons of skyline over next period of time (after 3% barrier has been breached). The 3% level was breached at $T = 2.5$y. Thereafter, the coupon starts accumulating from 0%, so that after 3 periods of below 3% Libor rates, we still have merely an annualised coupon of 3%.

Fixing time T (y)	Payment time $T + \tau$ (y)	Realised Libor L_T (%)	Coupon at $T + \tau$ (%)	Annualised coupon (%)
2.25	2.5	2.9	3.25	13
2.5	2.75	3.2	0	0
2.75	3	3.1	0	0
3	3.25	2.9	$0 + 0.25 = 0.25$	1
3.25	3.5	2.95	0.5	2
3.5	3.75	2.87	0.75	3
3.75	4	3.02	0	0

Since rates have risen to 3.2% at time $2\frac{1}{2}$ years, our reference coupon is 0. But the skyline is defined on the basis of the previous coupon. We see that when rates drop below 3% again (at time 3 years), we however start with a measly annualised 1% coupon, and then have to accumulate from there. Figure 9.4 illustrates this graphically. This **huge dependence of future coupons on previous coupons, especially if we are close to the barrier level**, is something to be careful about. Effectively, there is a highly leveraged bet on Libor not crossing 3% when it is close, **especially if the current coupon is substantial**. An investor should make sure he is comfortable with such a risk.

For what it is worth (since the differences seem obvious), Table 9.4 displays the features of a skyline along those of a note whose coupons are digital (say the note pays an annualised coupon of 4% for each period if Libor is under 3%).

If, as a point of curiosity, we plot the coupons received over time (see Figure 9.5), we see what appears to be skyscrapers. This is how the name "skyline" occurred – it looked like the skyline of a North American city.

Finally, a skyline is nice if you think market variables will be below (or above) some level but are not sure by how much, so that your investment of choice is a digital. If, however, you believe that market variables will be significantly above or below some level – maybe you want something that rewards you for the extent of the difference – and for that you might want to turn to the snowball (covered below).

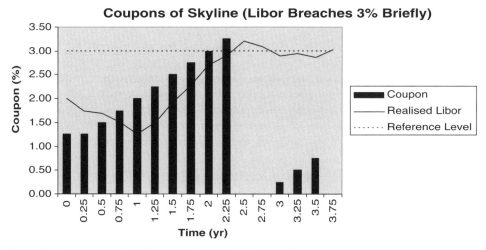

Figure 9.4 Coupons of skyline versus hypothetical path of Libor rates. See how the coupons drop dramatically to zero when Libor breaches the 3% level. Since these coupons are quarterly, the annualised rates are 4 times as high, but to fit on the same scale, we show period rates (i.e. for the quarter).

Table 9.4 How the coupons of a skyline compare *vis-à-vis* digital options.

Feature	Skyline	Digital
Potential Upside	Very high, since coupons increase over each period if Libor remains under 3% for the entire life of the note.	Moderate. Coupon in each period is limited to 4%.
Sensitivity to Previous Coupon	Very high. If previous coupon is zero, all subsequent coupons accumulate from zero.	None.
Potential for Low Coupons	Very high. If barrier is breached in one period, it would take a lot for future coupons to recover to a decent level.	Moderate. Condition on each coupon is based on Libor for that period.

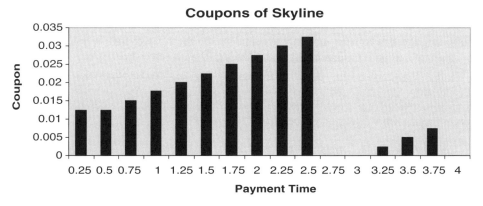

Figure 9.5 Pictorial representation of skyline, depicting skyscrapers in a city.

Key Points

- A skyline pays out on the basis of the previous coupon plus an increment, provided that Libor stays under some level.
- If Libor breaches the barrier, the coupon is zero, and future accumulation starts from zero. So, there is a very strong bet that Libor remains below the barrier.
- The breaching of the barrier can be especially expensive, if the current coupon is really high.

9.3 SNOWBALLS

Imagine a ball of snow rolling down a mountain. It starts quite small, but gathers mass and grows as it picks up momentum. Eventually, it could become an avalanche. Or perhaps it smashes into a huge tree early enough and breaks into small pieces or even ceases to exist. Figure 9.6 illustrates this pictorially. Fanciful as it sounds, such a tale is quite fitting for our financial snowball.

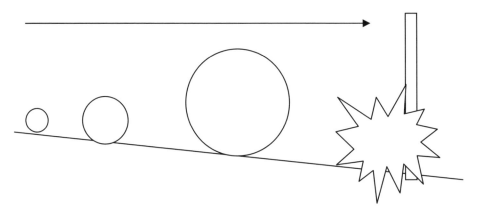

Figure 9.6   Snowball growing with time before imploding when it hits a tree.

Put yourself in the shoes of the investor above in the aftermath of 11 September 2001, but this time assume that you feel strongly that rates will go down and not just remain below 3%. You would like a payoff that not only accumulates on the basis of the previous coupon but also takes into account the amount by which rates are below 3%.

The payoff of a snowball (as below) caters to this market view: Suppose you have a 10-year note with quarterly coupons. At the first two coupon dates, your payoff is fixed at 5% per annum, giving coupons of $0.05 \times 0.25 = 1.25\%$ (where the 0.25 represents the 3-month accrual period). On subsequent coupon dates, the payoff is

$$\max\left(\text{PrevCoupon} + 0.25 \times 0.4 \times (3\% - L_T), 0\right),$$

where L_T is 3-month Libor as seen at time T, the 0.25 is due to the 3-month accrual period, and 0.4 is a leverage factor that the investment bank can give while still making its desired profit on the deal.

(In practice, since our yield curve is upward sloping, we are likely to have a reference strike that increases with maturity, e.g. the payoff for year 2 may be

$$\max\left(\text{PrevCoupon} + 0.25 \times 0.4 \times (3.2\% - L_T), 0\right) \text{ instead.}$$

Again, we shall ignore this and stick to a constant reference strike in our discussion for the sake of simplicity.)

Notice that if 3-month Libor is high enough, the coupon will be 0, and the accumulation starts from 0.

Let us consider the interest rate scenario as before in Table 9.5. (I have not solved for the appropriate prices of the snowball and skyline, so the scenarios are not strictly comparable. But they should illustrate some points of interest.)

Table 9.5 Hypothetical coupons of snowball where rates stay generally low.

Fixing time T (y)	Payment time $T + \tau$ (y)	Realised Libor L_T (%)	Coupon at $T + \tau$ (%)	Annualised coupons (%)	Accumulated Coupon (%)
0	0.25	2	1.25	5	1.25
0.25	0.5	1.75	1.25	5	2.5
0.5	0.75	1.7	$\max(1.25 + 0.1$ $\times(3.0 - 1.7), 0)$ $= 1.38$	5.52	3.88
0.75	1	1.51	1.529	6.116	5.409
1	1.25	1.25	1.704	6.816	7.113
1.25	1.5	1.5	1.854	7.416	8.967
1.5	1.75	1.92	1.962	7.848	10.929
1.75	2	2.28	2.034	8.136	12.963
2	2.25	2.7	2.064	8.256	15.027
2.25	2.5	2.9	2.074	8.296	17.101
2.5	2.75	3.2	2.054	8.216	19.155
2.75	3	3.1	2.044	8.176	21.199
3	3.25	2.9	2.054	8.216	23.253
3.25	3.5	2.95	2.059	8.236	25.312
3.5	3.75	2.87	2.072	8.288	27.384
3.75	4	3.02	2.07	8.28	29.454

Figure 9.7 depicts the coupons of a snowball as per Table 9.5. Notice first that the snowball allows for more coupon pickup the further rates are below 3%. Furthermore, even when rates go above the 3% level after $2\frac{1}{2}$ years, the coupon decreases but does not drop to 0. This is much preferable as there is less leverage on the bet of remaining below the magical 3% barrier. (The lower leverage of the snowball *vis-à-vis* the skyline means that it generally pays smaller coupons for comparable scenarios where rates remain below the barrier.)

However, the snowball is still a highly leveraged bet and if rates were rising, **the decrease in coupon that results as rates go over 3% is reflected in all subsequent coupons.** The different interest rate scenario in Table 9.6 will demonstrate this.

Figure 9.8 illustrates how the coupons of a snowball appear in a period when rates rise and then fall sharply. I admit the scenario is not the most common, as rates often take much longer to rise and seldom fall quite so rapidly. (The drastic rate cuts following the collapse of the dotcom bubble and the terrorist attacks of 2001, and those following the collapse of Lehman Brothers in 2008, should not be seen as typical.) However, notice how when rates fall back (under 3%) to 2.5% after 3.25 years, we are still getting really paltry coupons (under 1%),

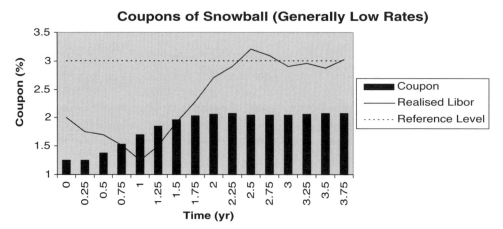

Figure 9.7 Coupons of snowball given hypothetical path where realised Libor stays generally low. The coupon pickup is greater as rates decrease. Furthermore, the coupon does not fall to zero immediately when the 3% level is breached. However, the pickup decreases the closer Libor gets to 3%.

since we are starting from a previous coupon of zero. The bottom line is that **an investor who buys a snowball should be aware of this leverage effect of previous coupons and its implications for future coupons**, if her view proves wrong.

It should be clear that for a snowball to pay attractive coupons, interest rates must continue to stay low. But rates are unlikely to stay low forever, since central banks tend to raise rates to control inflation after several years of growth. Hence, some form of early termination feature like the tarn would be ideal for this product. In fact, the snowball tarn is sufficiently popular a combination that it has its own name – the snowblade. In contrast, callability may not be ideal

Table 9.6 Hypothetical coupons of snowball where rates rise and then fall sharply.

Fixing time T (y)	Payment time $T + \tau$ (y)	Realised Libor L_T (%)	Coupon at $T + \tau$ (%)	Annualised coupon (%)
0	0.25	2	1.25	5
0.25	0.5	2.5	1.25	5
0.5	0.75	3	$\max(1.25 + 0.1$ $\times(3.0 - 3.0), 0)$ $= 1.25$	5
0.75	1	3.4	1.21	4.84
1	1.25	4	1.11	4.44
1.25	1.5	4.8	0.93	3.72
1.5	1.75	5.5	0.68	2.72
1.75	2	6	0.38	1.52
2	2.25	6	0.08	0.32
2.25	2.5	5.5	0	0
2.5	2.75	5	0	0
2.75	3	4	0	0
3	3.25	3	0	0
3.25	3.5	2.5	0.05	0.2
3.5	3.75	2.3	0.12	0.48
3.75	4	2	0.22	0.88

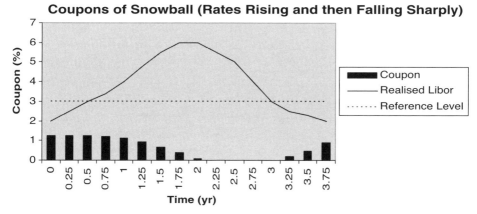

Figure 9.8 Coupons of snowball given hypothetical path where the realised Libor rises and then falls sharply. Since rates rise above 3%, the coupon decreases with each period. At some point, they reach 0. When rates subsequently fall below 3% (even quite substantially by 3.25 years), the coupon is measly (reaching a mere 0.88% at 3.75 years), since the accumulation starts from 0 at time 3.25 years.

on a snowball, since for a structure with such leveraged coupons, it is not ideal to leave the decision to terminate at the whim of the issuer.

Snow Bear

I should like to end by remarking that there is also the possibility of betting on rising rates as opposed to falling rates. In this case, you could instead have the payoff

$$\max\left(\text{PrevCoupon} + 0.25 \times 0.4 \times (L_T - 3\%), 0\right),$$

where L_T is 3-month Libor as seen at time T.

This instrument is rather curiously referred to as a snow bear (presumably since rising rates is the precursor to a bear market in stocks and bonds).

Other bets involving the market variable staying within some range also exist. (These are snow rangers.)

It is worth remarking that apart from possible principal protection features, skylines and snowballs are highly leveraged notes and the investor should be aware that scenarios can exist where she will lose all future coupons. As such, **apart from sophisticated investors who, in addition, have a very strong view as to the path of the market variable of interest, they are not generally suitable investments**.

Key Points

- A snowball pays out on the basis of the previous coupon plus strike minus Libor, if positive.
- If the coupon is zero due to high Libor rates, then future coupons start accumulating from zero.
- The snowball is a highly leveraged bet on rates staying low, but less so than the skyline. If rates rise sharply and then fall, total coupons will be very low.
- A snow bear is like a snowball, except that the bet is instead on rising rates.

10
Power Reverse Dual Currencies

Power Reverse Dual Currencies (PRDCs) are Japanese products that essentially involve betting that the spot USD/JPY (or AUD/JPY) FX rate will be higher than the forward suggests. In this chapter we shall explain how the **low interest rates in yen** (versus the US dollar or the Australian dollar, at least prior to 2008) coupled with the Japanese government's preference to have no significant yen appreciation, have led to a **flourishing carry trade** in the last decade. The PRDC is the solution to retail investors trying to earn higher coupons by betting against appreciation of the yen, much akin to the carry trade, but in such a way that only the (sacrificed) low coupons of a bond are at risk. However, yield-hungry investors have then agreed to forgo principal protection in their willingness to be repaid in dollar notional (at a strike higher than the forward). Chooser PRDCs are finally covered as an extension to normal PRDCs.

10.1 THE CARRY TRADE

The carry trade involves borrowing in a currency where interest rates are low, and converting this to a currency that attracts high interest. This is how it began.

Japan has seen near zero interest rates for much of the last decade. Figure 10.1 shows how low the Bank of Japan uncollateralised overnight call rate target has been. Even 5-year yen

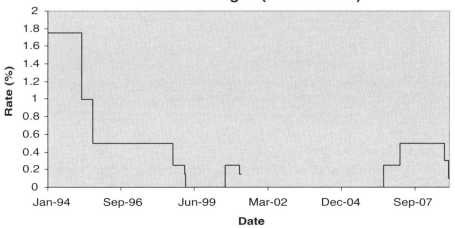

Figure 10.1 Bank of Japan Uncollateralised Overnight Call Rate Target from 1994 to 2008. Between 19 March 2001 and 8 March 2006, the Bank of Japan operated a policy of monetary easing instead (i.e. it targeted the outstanding balance of current accounts at the Bank).This effectively meant near zero interest rates.
Source: Bloomberg

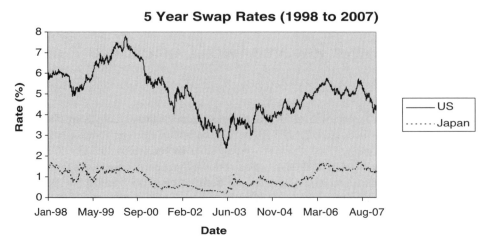

Figure 10.2 US and Japanese 5-year swap rates from 1998 to 2007. Notice how 5-year Japanese swap rates have remained below 2% and at times hovered around 0. In contrast, US rates have tended to be around 4% to 5% except for a brief period around 2003.
Source: Bloomberg

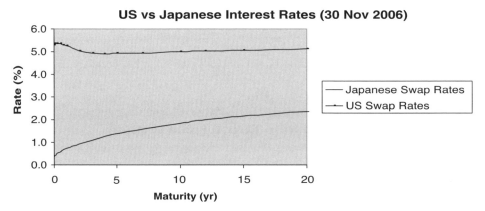

Figure 10.3 US and Japanese swap curves as of 30 November 2006. Japanese interest rates are much lower (a few percent) than US interest rates across all maturities.
Source: Bloomberg

rates have been under 2%. This necessarily frustrates the Japanese interest rates investor in his quest for a decent yield. A natural avenue would be the constant maturity swap (discussed in Chapter 6). However, it turns out that there is another interesting alternative.

Figure 10.2 compares US and Japanese 5-year swap rates from 1998 to 2007. From 1998 to 2007, the US dollar has tended to have 5-year rates of 4% to 5% (except for a brief period around 2003). Figure 10.3 shows the Japanese versus US swap curves as of 30 November 2006. If you **believed spot USD/JPY would remain unchanged at around 100,** say, why not borrow in yen and invest in dollars? In that case, you would earn the interest rate differential of 2% to 3%. Does this sound like a free lunch?

From the perspective of pricing, it is worth pointing out that since yen rates are lower than dollar rates, forward USD/JPY must be lower than spot USD/JPY. (Recall that Section 3.1

discussed how the fair value of a forward can be determined.) Specifically, in our example above, if spot USD/JPY is 100, yen interest rates are 2% and dollar rates are 5%, then 5-year forward USD/JPY has to be priced at

$$100 \times \left(\frac{1 + 0.02}{1 + 0.05} \right)^5 = 86.5.$$

The forward FX rate is determined from no-arbitrage principles. Specifically, suppose you borrowed ¥100 and bought dollars (to invest) today. The cost of borrowing the yen for 5 years is $100 \times (1 + 0.02)^5$. The value of the dollar investment is $1 \times (1 + 0.05)^5$. You could do a forward contract to sell \$1 in 5 years' time at a strike of X. The yen value of the dollar investment is then $X \times (1 + 0.05)^5$. For no arbitrage, we require the investment and borrowing to give the same result, i.e.

$$100 \times (1 + 0.02)^5 = X \times (1 + 0.05)^5.$$

This gives us the forward USD/JPY value of $X = 86.5$ above.

But if you look at the graph of USD/JPY in the period 1996 to 2007 (Figure 10.4), spot USD/JPY has remained roughly within the 100 to 135 range, regardless of forward USD/JPY suggesting a decrease over time (see Figure 10.5). This is partly due to the Japanese government trying to prevent yen appreciation to avoid hurting exporters, and their willingness to intervene by selling yen. There are other explanations relating to the weak state of the Japanese economy. However, the point is that **forward FX rates need not be realised** in practice, and investors who use the carry trade above are betting that forwards will not be realised. Specifically, they think USD/JPY will remain roughly at current levels.

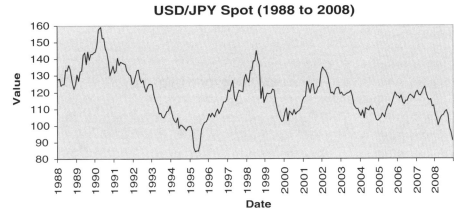

Figure 10.4   Value of spot USD/JPY from 1988 to 2008. Spot USD/JPY has tended to stay within the 100 to 135 range for most of the period since 1996.
Source: Bloomberg

There has been similar interest in AUD/JPY since the Australian dollar has typically yielded rather high interest rates (about 6% to 7%). And from 2006, the surge in commodity prices has strengthened the currencies of commodity-producing countries like Australia.

A note is worthwhile, however. When yen appreciates significantly (e.g. in the mid and late 1990s and from September 2008), there is a scramble to unwind the carry trades, i.e. sell US dollars (or Australian dollars) and buy back yen. This leads to sharp falls in USD/JPY and AUD/JPY. Specifically, in mid-2008, the state of the global economy has led to a flight

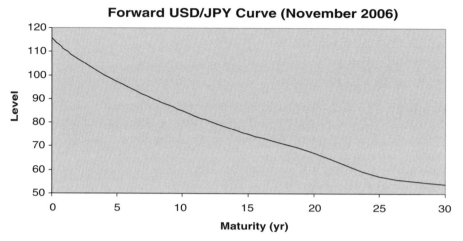

Figure 10.5 Forward USD/JPY curve at November 2006. Since US interest rates across all maturities are much higher than Japanese interest rates, no-arbitrage arguments led to a sharply decreasing forward USD/JPY curve over maturity. Notice how the 30-year USD/JPY forward is less than half of spot USD/JPY.
Source: Bloomberg

to safety and the unwinding of the carry trade has contributed to USD/JPY dropping towards 90 in the space of months. The Australian dollar suffered more drastically. Since mid-2008, sharp falls in commodity prices have led to a steep plunge in AUD/USD (from 0.95 to 0.65 in a matter of months), which has been further exacerbated by the unwinding of the carry trade in AUD/JPY. Figures 10.6 and 10.7 show how AUD/USD and AUD/JPY fared respectively in the credit crisis of 2008.

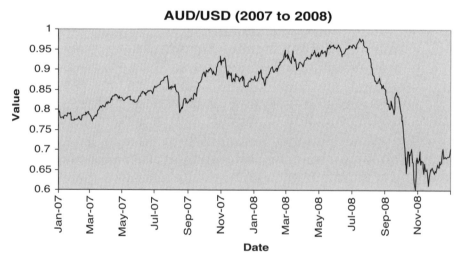

Figure 10.6 Value of spot AUD/USD from 2007 to 2008. AUD/USD plummeted significantly from 0.95 in July 2008 to 0.65 by November 2008.
Source: Bloomberg

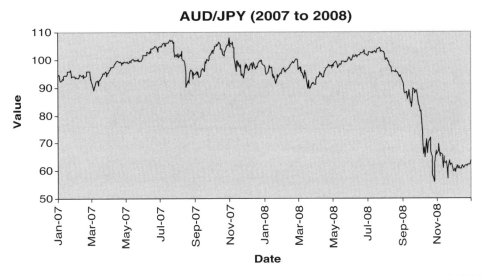

Figure 10.7   Value of spot AUD/JPY from 2007 to 2008. AUD/JPY plummeted from 100 in July 2008 to 60 by November 2008, in sympathy with the plunge in AUD/USD over the same period (see Figure 10.6 above).
Source: Bloomberg

Therefore, the carry trade is far from risk-free.

Key Points

- Yen rates have been near zero (or at least under 2%) versus 4% to 5% for dollar rates.
- The carry trade involves borrowing yen at low interest rates and investing in dollars at higher interest rates.
- The interest rate differential means that forward USD/JPY decreases with maturity, but investors felt that spot USD/JPY would not fall too much from current levels.
- The Australian dollar has high rates, so the AUD/JPY carry trade also existed.
- When yen appreciates, carry trades get unwound, exacerbating its rise.

10.2   LONG-DATED FOREIGN EXCHANGE

This section introduces some key ideas regarding forward foreign exchange for long maturities and long-dated FX options. This is to set the stage for the introduction of PRDCs in the next section.

The investment motivation for long-dated foreign exchange is due largely to interest rate differentials, as discussed above. Take USD/JPY for example. It can be seen in Figure 10.8 that from 2000 to 2007, 30-year yen rates have tended to stay around 2.5% whereas

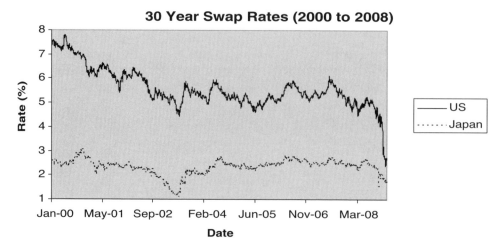

Figure 10.8 US and Japanese 30-year swap rates from 2000 to 2008. From 2000 to 2007, US swap rates have tended to hover around 5% whereas Japanese swap rates have hovered around 2.5% or below, leading to a differential of around 2.5% or more. US swap rates plummeted significantly in 2008, so this differential has narrowed since.
Source: Bloomberg

dollar rates have hovered around 5%. Given a USD/JPY spot of 100, the 30-year USD/JPY forward is

$$100 \times \left(\frac{1 + 0.025}{1 + 0.05} \right)^{30} = 48.5.$$

But most Japanese investors do not believe that USD/JPY will reach 48.5 even 30 years from now and are quite happy to bet against it. (This is especially so if their principal is protected, and the next section explains how this can be done.) This led to the development of a rather lucrative market in long-dated foreign exchange.

Specifically, I would like to address the issue of options in long-dated FX. Let us consider a USD/JPY call option. If X_T is spot at expiry T and strike K, the payoff is

$$\max(X_T - K, 0).$$

Typically to price such an option it is only important to consider the volatility of forward USD/JPY. (This comprises both interest rate volatilities and spot FX volatility.) After all, a forward FX rate depends on both the spot FX rate and the prevailing rates of interest in both currencies. Interest rate volatility tends to be much smaller than spot FX volatility (say 0.5% compared to 10%), so it is usually not necessary to treat it separately where the maturity is short. However, the effect of interest rate volatility grows in proportion to time, whereas the growth of FX spot volatility is only proportional to the square root of time. Thus, for long-dated FX options, a proper treatment of interest rate volatility matters. In particular, the market for long-dated FX options requires a development of long-dated interest rate options for purposes of hedging.

The contribution of interest rate volatility to long-dated FX forward volatility also means that the implied volatility of long-dated FX options has tended to be higher than for short-dated FX options (see Figure 10.9), which means that long-dated FX options are more costly.

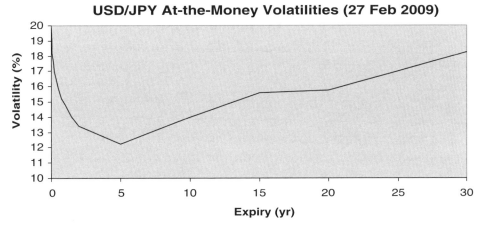

USD/JPY At-the-Money Volatilities (27 Feb 2009)

Figure 10.9   At-the-money volatilities for USD/JPY as of 27 February 2009. (The elevated volatilities at the short end reflect the uncertain economic circumstances following the credit crunch of 2008. But notice how the ATM volatilities rise gradually beyond the 5-year expiry date as interest rate volatilities contribute to total forward volatility.)
Source: Bloomberg

Key Points

- 30-year yen rates were around 2.5% versus 5% for dollar rates, so the 30-year USD/JPY forward is about half the USD/JPY spot. Investors were happy to bet against this.
- Long-dated FX options require proper treatment of interest rate volatilities. They tend to have higher volatilities due to the contribution from interest rate volatilities.

10.3   NORMAL PRDCs

For a normal 30-year bond, on every coupon date (say 6 months) you will get a $3\% \times 0.5 = 1.5\%$ coupon, due to low Japanese rates. (The 0.5 comes in because our coupon is accrued over half a year. For ease of exposition, let us assume in the rest of this chapter that coupons are annual, so that no accrual multiplier is necessary.) Such a low coupon is not very attractive. What if you decide to forgo those 3% coupons in favour of coupons linked to the prevailing FX rate?

Specifically, suppose on every coupon date t, you get

$$L \max (X_t - K, 0),$$

where X_t is FX rate at time t, K is strike and L is a multiplier. (If spot today is 115, then, typically, $L = 0.01$, $K = 95$ for highly-leveraged deals or $L = 0.0016$, $K = 80$ for lower-leveraged deals.)

That is a PRDC in its simplest form (a note comprising a strip of FX options of expiry up to 30 years).

If we look at the graph of forwards (Figure 10.10), for the non-highly-leveraged deals, we see that we are in-the-money for the next 10 years. If USD/JPY remains at 115, we shall get $0.0016 \times (115 - 80) = 0.056$, i.e. a 5.6% annual coupon rather than the paltry 3%. If it drops

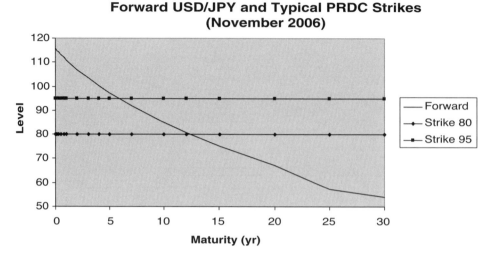

Figure 10.10   Typical forward USD/JPY curve and PRDC strikes around November 2006. For deals with strike 80, the coupons are in-the-money for 12 years; for those with strike 95, the coupons are in-the-money for 5 years.

below 80, we shall get nothing, but the typical Japanese investor is convinced that it will take a long time for USD/JPY to drop below 80 (if ever). Notice that the highly-leveraged deal has a higher strike and a higher multiplier, which means that if USD/JPY stays at 115, you get $0.01 \times (115 - 95) = 0.2$, i.e. a juicy 20% coupon. If it drops below 95 (which is quite possible), you get nothing.

Even if you look at how USD/JPY has dropped from 115 to a low of 90 in late 2008, it does not look like a complete disaster for an investor in a less-leveraged PRDC. As it stands, the coupon is $0.0016 \times (90 - 80) = 1.6\%$. Compare this with the very low 30-year yen yield of 1.72% on 31 December 2009 (or the somewhat better 2.40% on 1 September 2009).

Some Other Features

Some bells and whistles have been added to the basic product to tailor it to customer desires. A good example is the fixed coupon in the first period. Usually, this is something big like 6% or even 8%, which is paid for by having slightly less favourable payoff terms subsequently. Another example is to floor the FX-linked payoff (e.g. at 1%) or to cap the FX-linked payoff (e.g. at 8%). Such details do not overly affect the structure, except insofar as how much of the payoff is FX-linked and how much is protected.

Embedded Early Termination

The above terms (e.g. $L = 0.0016$, $K = 80$) **typically were only made possible by adding embedded early termination features in the PRDC note**. Such features involve protected selling of optionality as discussed in Section 2.3, which is a means of obtaining higher yields. In the absence of such early termination features, the terms would probably look much worse (e.g. $L = 0.0016$, $K = 90$). In practice, most PRDCs involve selling optionality since investors generally seek higher yields (and so I thought it better to just describe the deal earlier in typical terms).

In this case, there are three possibilities **at each coupon date**: allowing the user to call the structure, having the structure cancelled (with the notional repaid) if FX rates stay above a trigger level, or having the structure cancelled if the total coupons received exceed a certain tarn level. Such features need not apply immediately but, say, after the second year. (Chapter 8 has described callability, triggers and tarns in some detail.)

The only comment on callables is that the issuer will call if USD/JPY stays high, ensuring that those sweet juicy coupons cannot be obtained forever. On the other hand, if USD/JPY plummets and stays low, the investor might be stuck with a 0 coupon for the life of the deal.

For triggers, it is worth saying that since forward USD/JPY is decreasing with maturity, the typical trigger levels also step down. So, for example, you have an initial trigger level of 107 starting at the end of year 1, stepping down by 1 each year (see Figure 10.11). Assuming that USD/JPY remains constant at 115.8, it is very likely to trigger out after a few years. (See Chaper 8 on the digital risk of triggers.)

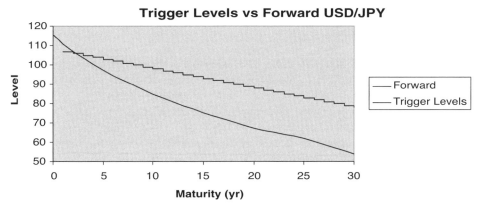

Figure 10.11 Typical forward USD/JPY curve and trigger levels for PRDCs. Trigger levels step down since the forward decreases with maturity.

Tarns are such that if you have been paid total cumulative coupons that reach the tarn level (say 20%), the deal cancels. The danger again is that if USD/JPY drops, you are stuck with 0 coupon for the life of the deal.

It is worth pointing out from a pricing perspective that early termination introduces significant modelling challenges. Whereas a plain PRDC could be trivially priced as a strip of call options via the Black–Scholes equation, the need to capture transition probabilities – and hence model the evolution of FX jointly with stochastic rates to decide if early termination occurs – has required a substantial effort involving many quants and parallelised computing on a cluster of machines (and lots of inaccuracies and rather imperfect hedging nonetheless).

One-Sided Market

It is also worth pointing out that the PRDC market is very one-sided. Basically, clients want to buy optionality on USD/JPY at a low strike (say 80). And they have sold optionality via early termination to dealers at a high strike (say 135 effective strike for callables). By the very nature of this market – for purposes of hedging – dealers need to buy volatility at a low strike

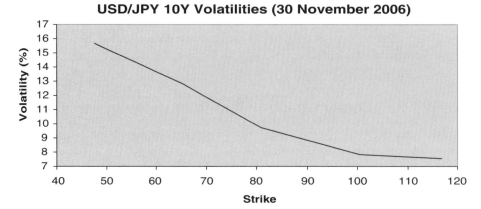

Figure 10.12 USD/JPY 10-year volatility skew as of 30 November 2006. Notice how the volatility increases sharply as strike decreases. This is due to investor demand for options with low strikes and the supply of volatility at high strikes, caused by hedging of PRDCs by dealers.
Source: Bloomberg

and have volatility to sell at a high strike. This leads to a pronounced FX skew in USD/JPY, where volatilities for low strikes are much higher than volatilities for high strikes. Figure 10.12 illustrates how USD/JPY volatilities increase sharply as strike decreases.

It is also sobering to note that the development of the PRDC market pre-dated and spurred the development of a market in long-dated USD/JPY options (for hedging). The systemic risks should be obvious if we note how dealers are all short USD/JPY volatilities at a low strike and long USD/JPY volatilities at a high strike. Furthermore, if yen appreciates significantly, hedging considerations require dealers to buy huge quantities of yen, further exacerbating the problem.

The credit crisis of 2008 led to volatilities for USD/JPY (as well as most other asset classes) skyrocketing. Furthermore, USD/JPY has dropped to around 90 by the beginning of 2009. At such levels of USD/JPY, early termination is extremely unlikely. Investors are still likely to receive coupons (albeit reduced) on less-leveraged PRDCs. For dealers in PRDCs, the problem is much worse, however. The significantly elevated volatilities have led to substantial increases in the cost of hedging, leading to huge losses on the PRDCs sold. The hedging further has the effect of pushing down USD/JPY to much lower levels (e.g. around 90 at the beginning of 2009).

Key Points

- A basic PRDC is a strip of FX options paid instead of coupons of a 30-year bond.
- The options tend to have the same strike, so with a downward-sloping forward, the early maturities are in-the-money.
- The note often has a high initial fixed coupon.
- Early termination via callability, triggers and tarns is common, to enhance yield.
- Trigger levels tend to be step-down as the forward curve is downward sloping.
- The market is one-sided with dealers short volatility at low strikes and long volatility at high strikes.

> • Rapid appreciation of yen in 2008 led to significant increases in volatilities, greatly increasing hedging cost for dealers. Coupons also fell for investors.

10.4 THE REDEMPTION STRIKE

The redemption strike is an embellishment to the PRDC that compromises investor protection. Basically, given a redemption strike R, the investor will receive $\frac{1}{R}$ in the foreign currency (say dollars) at expiry T, instead of receiving his principal in yen. This works out to be $\frac{X_T}{R}$ in yen if spot FX is X_T at expiry. Notice that $\frac{X_T}{R}$ could be less than 1, and thus **the investor loses principal protection**.

In practice, redemption strikes exist on deals with early termination features (callability, triggers or tarns). If early termination occurs, the investor gets back the principal (regardless of redemption strike). However, **if early termination does not occur, the redemption strike applies at maturity**, and the investor could lose significantly if spot drops below the redemption strike at expiry.

Typically, $R = 70$ for a USD/JPY deal, and $R = 50$ for an AUD/JPY deal. Most yen investors do not believe that USD/JPY (or AUD/JPY at least prior to 2008) in 30 years' time can be so low. Notice that the 30-year forward FX rate in 2007 for USD/JPY was about 50 and for AUD/JPY was about 35. Figure 10.13 shows how the typical redemption strike compares with forward USD/JPY rates. A redemption strike therefore makes the deal less costly, and this is compensated to the investor in the form of a higher initial coupon or coupon multiplier. That, coupled with the (perhaps misplaced) confidence that early termination will occur, induced a great deal of investor interest in PRDCs with redemption strikes. If the investor is happy to sacrifice principal protection to gain higher yield, then this is fine. But **such an investor should be aware of the potential losses that can be incurred, as sometimes things do not follow expectations.**

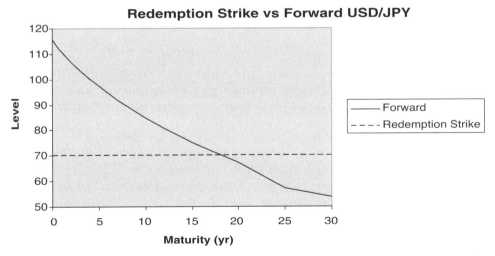

Figure 10.13 Typical forward USD/JPY curve and redemption strike level. The redemption strike of 70 is much higher than the 30-year USD/JPY forward of 53.9, although it is much lower than the USD/JPY spot of 116.

With the sharp decline of AUD/JPY since mid-2008, the PRDCs may well not terminate before maturity. Investors in PRDCs without redemption strikes are at least assured of principal protection, but those in PRDCs with redemption strikes are more vulnerable to FX rate fluctuations in the long years ahead. Notice how AUD/JPY stood at about 63 in late 2008 versus a typical redemption strike of 50. It is not hard to imagine AUD/JPY going below 50 over the next 20 years.

It would probably be useful at this point to compare the features between a PRDC note and the normal carry trade. This is done in Table 10.1.

Table 10.1   Comparing a PRDC note with the traditional carry trade.

Feature	Carry trade	PRDC note
Domestic Principal Amount Assured at Maturity	No. Foreign principal repaid, so domestic value depends on FX rate at maturity.	Yes if deal has no redemption strike; otherwise, foreign principal repaid.
Liquid	Yes.	No liquid market for disposal.
Sensitive to Volatility	No.	Note is more expensive if volatility is high.
Might Terminate when in Investor's Favour	No.	Yes for the many notes which come with early termination features.

From a bank's perspective, the presence of the redemption strike leads to a huge forward risk at expiry (which translates to a huge digital risk on termination). For a normal PRDC, the total FX dependence drops over time as more coupons are paid off. For a PRDC with redemption strike, the redemption strike accounts for much more FX risk than the coupons if early termination is unlikely. When termination occurs, this risk disappears entirely (together with possible gains/losses from the redemption strike). Since termination typically depends on spot FX being above some level, there is a certain jump in payoff as spot moves due to the potential to extinguish the effect of this redemption strike. This is not conceptually dissimilar to how triggers can induce a digital risk.

Key Points

- PRDCs with redemption strikes pay back a foreign currency amount at maturity rather than the yen principal. This is based on an FX rate worse than the forward, hence making the deal cheaper.
- Typically, if the deal terminates early, the yen principal is payable instead.
- Investors in such PRDCs are not assured of principal protection, this was a concern especially for AUD/JPY deals after AUD/JPY plummeted in 2008.
- The redemption strike leads to a huge forward exposure at expiry and hence induces digital risk on termination for the dealer.

10.5   CHOOSER PRDCs

Investors are typically hungry for yield (and a low-yield environment does not really help). Also, declining margins on existing products drive banks to be innovative. If PRDCs become less lucrative, is there a product that could produce higher yields and justify a huge margin? The answer seems to be the "chooser".

First, the chooser is a misnomer: it is the issuer that chooses and not the client. The coupons of a chooser PRDC are based on the minimum of USD/JPY and AUD/JPY payoffs.

Specifically, on every coupon date t, you get

$$L \max \left(\min \left(X_t^{USD/JPY} - K^{USD/JPY}, X_t^{AUD/JPY} - K^{AUD/JPY} \right), 0 \right),$$

where $X_t^{USD/JPY}$, $X_t^{AUD/JPY}$ are the USD/JPY and AUD/JPY spots at time t, $K^{USD/JPY}$, $K^{AUD/JPY}$ are the USD/JPY and AUD/JPY strikes, and L is a multiplier. (If USD/JPY and AUD/JPY spots are currently 115 and 90, then typically $L = 0.01, K^{USD/JPY} = 95$, and $K^{AUD/JPY} = 70$.)

Tarns (and less so trigger features) have been applied to choosers, but callable choosers are a rare breed. The dimensionality of the product makes it non-conducive to PDE pricing and hence makes dealers less willing to apply a callable feature to it.

We also note that as many of these products were really aimed at producing maximum yields, they also came with redemption strikes. If the product does not terminate early (via callability, trigger or tarn features), the yen notional is not repaid at maturity. Instead, the minimum amount by applying the dollar or Australian dollar redemption strikes is paid. Specifically, if $R^{USD/JPY}$, $R^{AUD/JPY}$ are the redemption strikes, then at maturity the amount paid is

$$\min \left(\frac{X_t^{USD/JPY}}{R^{USD/JPY}}, \frac{X_t^{AUD/JPY}}{R^{AUD/JPY}} \right).$$

Typically, $R^{USD/JPY} = 70$, $R^{AUD/JPY} = 50$, which compares poorly with the USD/JPY and AUD/JPY 30-year forwards of about 50 and 35 respectively.

The chooser PRDC is effectively a bet that yen will not appreciate against either the US dollar or the Australian dollar. Noting the policy of the Japanese authorities to avoid yen appreciation against the dollar and the surge in commodities in 2007, this seemed to be a good idea, for a while. This was especially so since some of the deals came with very lucrative initial coupons. For instance, an initial 1-year fixed coupon of 25% was not unheard of when the chooser PRDC (with redemption strike) was first introduced in late 2006.

Recent events since mid-2008 (specifically the huge decline in AUD/USD and hence AUD/JPY) have made the chooser a rather unpleasant bet. With AUD/JPY at 65 and not showing an inclination to recover, many chooser PRDCs (with an AUD/JPY strike of 70) will not pay any more coupon (whatever happens to USD/JPY). On top of getting no coupon for the next 30 years, if AUD/JPY drops below the redemption strike, those deals involving redemption strikes will not even protect the yen principal fully. This is one cautionary tale about the risks of betting on market trends. However, it is only fair to point out that investors in choosers with no redemption strike who have enjoyed a juicy first coupon (of 18%, say) and one or two other big coupons (before AUD/JPY collapsed) might not fare much worse than those who invested in a 30-year bond at less than 3% interest, even if no further coupons are received.

From the perspective of the issuer, the pricing of choosers is very much a question of the choice of correlation between AUD/JPY and USD/JPY. Specifically, the higher the correlation between AUD/JPY and USD/JPY, the higher the cost of the chooser to the issuer, since a rise in one is not likely to be followed by a fall in the other, and the issuer is paying the minimum of the two FX rates. In foreign exchange, volatility of AUD/USD naturally provides implied correlations between AUD/JPY and USD/JPY, and AUD/USD options can even serve as a hedge for such implied correlations. However, whereas the development of PRDCs has spawned long-dated USD/JPY and AUD/JPY options, 30-year AUD/USD options are much rarer. So, a certain amount of arbitrariness is involved in deciding the correlation between AUD/JPY and USD/JPY, and hence the price of a chooser PRDC.

We conclude with a brief comparison of the features of a chooser PRDC versus a normal one in Table 10.2.

Table 10.2   Comparison of the features of a chooser PRDC against a normal PRDC.

Feature	Normal PRDC	Chooser PRDC
Potential Coupon	High if FX (e.g. USD/JPY) remains high (say, around spot).	Much higher than for normal PRDC provided both USD/JPY and AUD/JPY remain high.
Probability of Receiving Coupon	High provided yen does not appreciate too much, so that the FX rate remains closer to spot (than the much lower forward).	Much lower than for normal PRDC, since both USD/JPY and AUD/JPY must remain high.
Principal Repaid at Maturity	Domestic principal assured unless there is redemption strike.	If redemption strike feature exists, possibility for much less principal repayment, since this is based on minimum of USD/JPY and AUD/JPY redemption strikes.
Sensitive to Correlation	No.	Yes, since a low correlation increases the probability of one of the FX pairs falling.

Key Points

- Chooser PRDCs pay the minimum of USD/JPY and AUD/JPY coupons.
- They often come with tarn features and redemption strikes (again the minimum of USD/JPY and AUD/JPY principal amounts).
- The bet is that neither USD/JPY nor AUD/JPY will fall, and this worked out badly in 2008 when AUD/JPY dropped significantly so that coupons and principal are at serious risk.
- Pricing of choosers is heavily dependent on the correlation between USD/JPY and AUD/JPY.

11
Baskets and Hybrids

Modern finance is heavily centred on portfolio theory. The idea is about getting rid of stock-specific risk, for which the investor is not compensated. Whether you subscribe to portfolio theory, it does seem that **many of us would not want all our returns to be tied to the fortunes of one company, so having a diversified portfolio does make sense**. Contrary to the proverbial warning against having all one's "eggs in one basket", the derivatives solution involves a basket of assets.

In this chapter, we concern ourselves with basket products and hybrids. We shall start by discussing how baskets benefit from lower volatility and hence lower option price than their constituent underlyings. Hybrid baskets will be briefly mentioned and we shall then look into other ways of financial engineering with hybrids, e.g. can we have the better of a stock or bond return? Or could we get more yield by having an equity-linked note conditional on EUR/USD staying in some range? Can it perhaps make sense to multiply two payoffs (e.g. rates and equities)? There are endless possibilities, but I hope the above will give the reader an adequate sampling of what is available.

11.1 BASKETS AND THE BENIGN EFFECT OF AVERAGING

A basket is a collection of assets, which may be weighted equally or otherwise. Recall in Section 3.6 how an Asian option has lower volatility than a European option because the returns on each observation date are less than perfectly correlated. (Indeed, correlation is assumed to be 0 based on efficient market theory.) For a basket, less than perfect correlation between the constituent assets leads to a lower volatility as well.

Consider the STOXX 50 index, which comprises the stocks of some of the leading 50 European companies. An investor may be interested in such a basket directly rather than in individual stocks for lots of possible reasons. Perhaps the investor believes in portfolio theory and that idiosyncratic risks of individual stocks will not be rewarded but only systemic market risk will be rewarded. Or perhaps the investor either does not know the individual companies well enough or wants to avoid overexposure to any one name or sector (e.g. the investor thinks the market as a whole will go up, but is not sure whether each of manufacturing, transport and retail will do well). As it turns out, an investor in a tracker fund (i.e. a portfolio of stocks designed to track an index) often does not do much worse than an investor in discretionary funds, where stock selection by the fund manager is permissible.

In any event, European call and put options on indices exist, e.g. options on the STOXX 50 index are traded in Eurex, those on the S&P 500 index are traded in the CME Group, and those on the FtSe 100 are traded in Liffe. While stock indices can be treated (and priced) as single name stocks, they are really baskets. The question is how they relate to the constituent stocks.

The first observation is that whether idiosyncratic risk is rewarded only affects drift (i.e. expected return), which does not matter in option pricing. But baskets have a lower volatility than their constituents. Recall again our example in Section 3.6, which I repeat.

Suppose X and Y are normal variables with 0 mean, standard deviation σ, and correlation ρ. Let $Z = \frac{1}{2}(X + Y)$. Then

$$\text{var}(Z) = \frac{1}{4}(\text{var}(X) + \text{var}(Y) + 2\,\text{cov}(X, Y))$$

$$= \frac{1}{2}\sigma^2(1 + \rho)$$

Notice that any value of ρ less than 1 would cause the variance of Z to be less than that of either X or Y. (This argument on correlations does not require normal variables but the illustration is made more convenient thereby.)

A typical basket is represented as

$$B_t = \sum_{i=1}^{n} w_i S_t^i,$$

where S_t^i is the value of underlying stock i at time t, and w_i is the weight of stock i in the basket ($w_i = \frac{1}{n}$ for an equally weighted basket).

So, **as long as the correlations between the stocks S_t^i are less than 1, the basket has a lower volatility**. Since lower volatility implies lower price of the option, this makes an option on a basket a popular choice. Strictly speaking, correlations are not static. They can and do change with time, affecting the volatility of the basket option. In particular, **correlations of risky assets tend to rise towards 1 in times of crisis**, as there is a flight to safety. Diversification can therefore protect you from a company going bust due to a bad business plan, but not too well against a worldwide financial crisis.

It is worth mentioning that a basket of equities typically has a downward-sloping skew, i.e. options of lower strikes have higher volatilities. This is because of the supply–demand imbalance since most investors are long equity and want downside protection against a crash, and hence buy puts with low strikes. The skew can be more pronounced than for the constituent stocks, since those stocks can be subject to more upside jumps (e.g. success of research in a pharmaceutical company, or launch of a very popular product), and traders obviously need to protect themselves from that. Figures 11.1 and 11.2 show the volatility skew for the S&P 500 and Walmart (a large capitalised US stock).

Finally, of course we could put together arbitrary stocks in a basket we prefer, and not be restricted to, for example, the likes of the STOXX 50 index. If you are a fan of green technology, you could have a basket of stocks of companies involved in this endeavour. Or you could have a basket of commodities such as oil, natural gas, zinc and copper, if you think we are in for a commodities boom (a popular idea in 2007). Or you could have a basket that comprises the STOXX 50, Nikkei 225 and S&P 500 indices if you want exposure to the international markets. (Note that this example involves quantoes since the STOXX 50 index is denominated in euros, the Nikkei 225 index is in yen and the S&P 500 index is in dollars, and most likely payment is in one currency. Chapter 5 has addressed issues in quantoes.)

Or if you were a Brazilian company exposed to both dollar and euro exchange rates and want to hedge (a possible fall in the Brazilian real) more cheaply via a basket, you could have

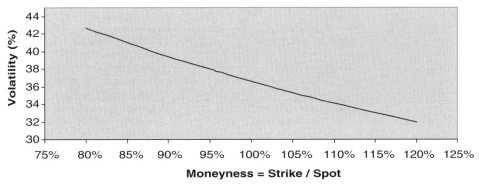

Figure 11.1 S&P 500 volatility skew for expiry 6 months (13 March 2009). Notice the downward-sloping skew, where volatility is higher for lower strikes. Investors tend to own stocks and so seek puts with low strikes to protect them from a market crash. This leads to more demand for low strike volatilities. *Source:* Bloomberg

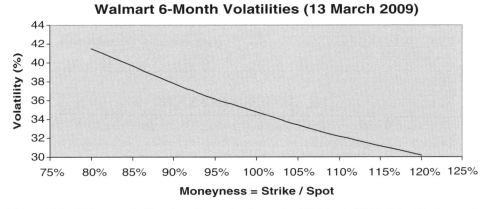

Figure 11.2 Walmart volatility skew for expiry 6 months (13 March 2009). We still observe the downward-sloping skew for this stock. *Source:* Bloomberg

a basket based on their weighted returns

$$B_t = w_1 \left(\frac{USDBRL_t}{USDBRL_0} - 1 \right) + w_2 \left(\frac{EURBRL_t}{EURBRL_0} - 1 \right)$$

and an option that pays

$$\max \left(B_T - K, 0 \right)$$

for some strike K at expiry T.

The possibilities are quite endless.

Before we move on to the next section, Table 11.1 reminds the reader of the key features of an option on a basket versus an option on a single asset.

Table 11.1   Key features of an option on a basket versus an option on a single asset.

Feature	Asset option	Basket option
Volatility	Depends on the asset.	Lower than the average volatility of its constituent assets.
Potential Upside	Can be very high.	Tends to be lower than that of its constituents, since we are looking at an average.
Downside	Option can expire worthless if asset price declines.	A dramatic decline in the value of a basket is less likely than for its constituent assets. So, a lower chance of the option expiring worthless.

Key Points

- Correlations of less than 1 lead to lower volatility for a basket than the average of its constituents, hence a lower price for an option on a basket.
- Idiosyncratic risk (whether rewarded) only affects drift, so does not affect pricing.
- Correlations are not static and tend to rise towards 1 in times of crisis.
- A basket tends to have a more pronounced downside skew than its constituents.
- Stock indices are baskets, but you can construct arbitrary baskets.

11.2   HYBRID BASKETS

We can construct baskets from individual assets. But we can also construct baskets across asset classes. Suppose you were an investor bullish in commodities as well as in equities, as many investors were in 2007. Then you might want a basket that is a weighted average of some stock indices and some commodities.

For example, the following basket can be constructed

$$B_t = w_1 \left(\frac{SP500_t}{SP500_0} - 1 \right) + w_2 \left(\frac{STOXX_t}{STOXX_0} - 1 \right) + w_3 \left(\frac{Oil_t}{Oil_0} - 1 \right) + w_4 \left(\frac{Wheat_t}{Wheat_0} - 1 \right)$$

and your payoff might be

$$\max \left(B_T - K, 0 \right)$$

at the end of the period T.

There is no conceptual difficulty of combining different asset classes in the same basket. Any limits are based more on the expertise of the bank or the capabilities of its systems (to handle cross-asset products) and investor demand. For example, there is less likelihood of an investor betting on a basket comprising FX returns and equity returns together, because the typical retail equity investor does not have a strong directional view on FX, whereas the typical FX investor may be more interested in hedging cashflow exposures. Of course, the more exotic the product, the more the bank would like to add as a profit margin.

But apart from baskets, hybrid products involving more than one asset class can also offer a lot of financial engineering possibilities. For example, an investor may want the better return among two classes of assets, which leads us to the next section.

Key Point

• Baskets involving different asset classes exist.

11.3   "BEST OF" PRODUCTS AND HYBRIDS

A "best of" option basically pays out based on the best of several underlyings. This need not be a hybrid. The following is an example of a "best of" payoff based on two stocks

$$\max\left(\frac{S_T^1}{S_0^1} - 1, \frac{S_T^2}{S_0^2} - 1, 0\right),$$

where S_t^1, S_t^2 are the values of stocks 1 and 2 (e.g. Walmart and Caterpillar) at time t, and $T = 1y$ is expiry.

This pays the higher of the two stock returns if they are positive. It should not be difficult to imagine that such products tend to be expensive. After all, who would not want the higher return if given a choice?

Recall Section 10.5 on chooser PRDCs, where the payoff is really the "worst of" two returns. In that case, the product is cheaper (to the client) when correlations are low (or negative), since **it is more likely that one of the underlyings will fall** (**if the underlyings are likely to move in opposite directions**). Based on a similar logic, a "best of" product is more expensive if the correlations are low, since here we are interested in the best return and welcome underlyings moving in opposite directions. It follows therefore – given that "best of" products are expensive **– they are typically worth betting on only if the investor thinks correlations are lower than priced in the market**. Figures 11.3 and 11.4 show hypothetical paths and the performance of "best of" products when correlations between the underlyings are positive and negative respectively.

Traditional portfolio managers use an equity index (e.g. S&P 500) as benchmark, and seek to outperform it. Beta is the measure of market exposure and the higher the beta is, the more

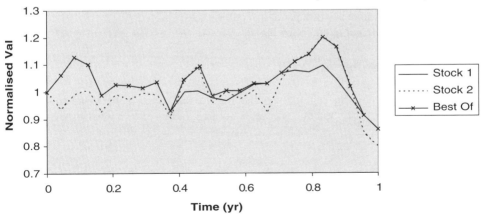

Figure 11.3   Hypothetical paths of two stocks and a "best of" product for high correlation (0.6). The high correlation means the "best of" is not too much better than the worse performing stock.

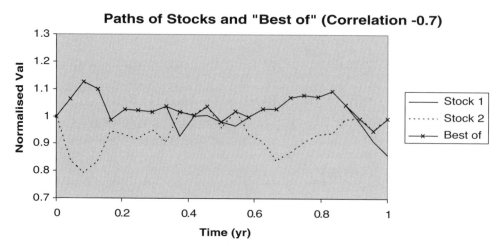

Figure 11.4 Hypothetical paths of two stocks and a "best of" product for high negative correlation (-0.7). The "best of" is clearly more easily distinguished from the worse performing stock.

the expected returns are. If the broader stock market declines, a portfolio manager will seek to justify his returns *vis-à-vis* this benchmark. But alternative asset (hedge fund) managers tend to seek absolute returns, irrespective of the market. They want a certain alpha, which is a return, regardless of the benchmark, so they need something that does not follow a falling market. In this sense, it might be worth having "best of" products in different asset classes because an investor may genuinely want an absolute return, irrespective of a benchmark that may decline. Let us examine a few cases below.

Suppose an investor would like the minimum of the return on British Petroleum (BP) stock over a year or 2%, i.e. she wants the payoff

$$\max\left(0.5 \times \left(\frac{S_T}{S_0} - 1\right), 0.02\right),$$

where S_t is the price of BP stock at time t, $T = 1y$ is the expiry date, and 0.5 is the multiplier applicable so that the note is worth par at inception.

This is really equivalent to the following

$$0.02 + \frac{1}{2S_0} \max\left(S_T - 1.04S_0, 0\right),$$

which is a 2% coupon, plus a call option with strike $1.04S_0$, expiry $T = 1y$ and notional $\frac{1}{2S_0}$. So, as mentioned earlier, a "best of" product is not free. In this case, it involves the purchase of a call option.

Equity with CMS Floor

But perhaps our investor might prefer not to use a fixed rate as her minimum coupon. Suppose we have a steeply upward-sloping yield curve, with generally low interest rates, that are likely to rise as the economy grows. (Such a scenario existed in the Eurozone countries around 2004, as seen in Figure 11.5.)

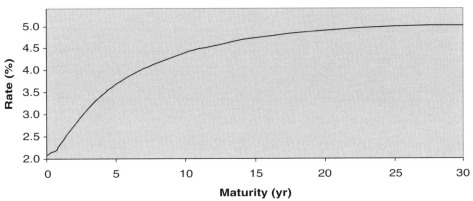

Figure 11.5   Euro swap curve as of 2 January 2004. The yield curve is steeply upward sloping but overall rates are not high.
Source: Bloomberg

A CMS is a nice instrument to deal with this scenario. Furthermore, higher interest rates tend to depress equity markets. Consider a note that pays

$$0.5 \times \max\left(\frac{S_T}{S_0} - 1, R_T^{10y}\right),$$

where R_T^{10y} is the 10-year swap rate.

Our investor would benefit from rising stock prices, but if rising rates adversely affected the stock markets, she would at least get half the 10-year swap rate at the end of the period of 1 year. This instrument is almost tailored to her investment considerations.

Equity with Inflation Floor

Alternatively, suppose an investor would like to have exposure to the markets, subject to a minimum return that protects him from inflation. Consider the following payoff

$$\max\left(0.6 \times \left(\frac{S_T}{S_0} - 1\right), \frac{I_T}{I_0} - 1\right),$$

where S_t is the value of the FtSe 100 index at time t, T is the payment date, and I_t is the value of the Retail Price Index (a measure of inflation) at time t. Figure 11.6 shows the UK Retail Price Index from 1995 to 2008.

Again, our investor would probably compensate for this extra protection by having a lower multiplier on the stock return (0.6 here as opposed to 0.8, say, if the coupon was just floored at 0).

"Best of" Equities and Commodities

Consider another possibility where an investor thinks that various stock markets are likely to go up, but alternatively commodity prices could go up instead. A basket means that the

Figure 11.6 UK Retail Price Index from 1995 to 2008. It has grown steadily but at a low rate until 2008.
Source: Bloomberg

investor would get an "averaged out" return, which may not be great. Perhaps our investor further thinks correlations used in pricing are too high, because, for example, rising commodity prices should have a negative impact on the economy and hence stock prices. **The bet is not fully transparent, since correlation is a model input, but the investor can decide if the quoted deal is agreeable in price**.

In any case, a payoff that involves the "best of " equities and commodities is as follows:

$$0.5 \times \max \left(\frac{SP500_T}{SP500_0} - 1, \frac{STOXX_T}{STOXX_0} - 1, \frac{Oil_T}{Oil_0} - 1, \frac{Copper_T}{Copper_0} - 1, 0 \right),$$

where T is the payment date and the assets above are self-explanatorily labelled.

Such baskets generated some interest in late 2006 and early 2007 when equity markets were still rising, notwithstanding huge increases in commodity prices. Rather curiously, since mid-2008, both equity and commodity prices are falling, most likely since a weakening economy and credit crisis is dragging down company earnings as well as demand for raw material. Figures 11.7 to 11.10 show the prices of the four assets from 2006 to 2008. Again, **this highlights the dangers of unstable correlations, with them going to 1 at the wrong time**.

Table 11.2 recaps the features of "best of " payoffs, including those involving multiple asset classes.

It goes without saying that multi-period versions of the above product exist and the investor could get more yield if early termination features (e.g. callability) are added to the note. Alternatively, early mandatory termination via the tarn feature may be worth while if the economic environment is expected to lead to lower coupons after a period of time.

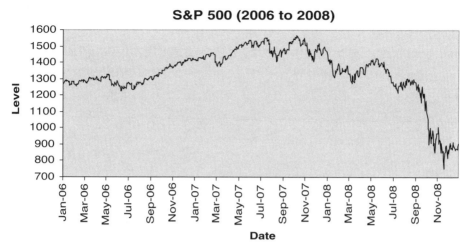

Figure 11.7 Level of S&P 500 index from 2006 to 2008. The S&P grew until October 2007 when it started declining, with particularly sharp falls in late 2008.
Source: Bloomberg

Key Points

- A "best of" product pays the best return of several assets, and is expensive.
- A "best of" is more expensive if correlations are low or negative, so that the underlyings can move in different directions.
- "Best of" products across different assets can help to beat a benchmark, e.g. best of equity and CMS (rising rates mean lower stock returns), best of equity and inflation.
- "Best of" equities and commodities products were popular in 2007 but since 2008 both markets have plummeted.

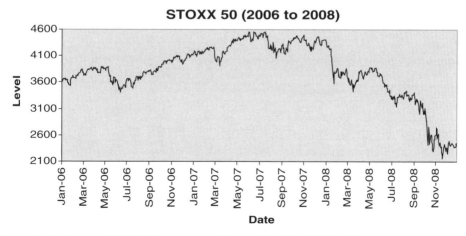

Figure 11.8 Level of STOXX 50 index from 2006 to 2008. The STOXX 50 grew until July 2007 and then started a period of significant decline.
Source: Bloomberg

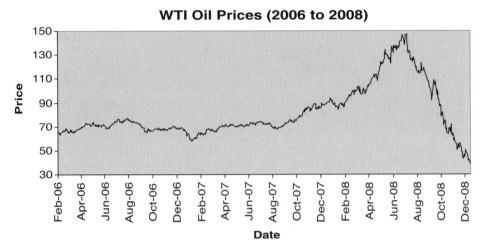

Figure 11.9   WTI oil prices from 2006 to 2008. Oil prices grew explosively from 69 on 30 August 2007 to a high of 146.93 on 14 July 2008, before suffering an equally dramatic implosion to end at 38.74 by 23 December 2008. The explosive growth coincided with the start of the decline of the equity markets from October 2007 (see Figures 11.7 and 11.8).
Source: Bloomberg

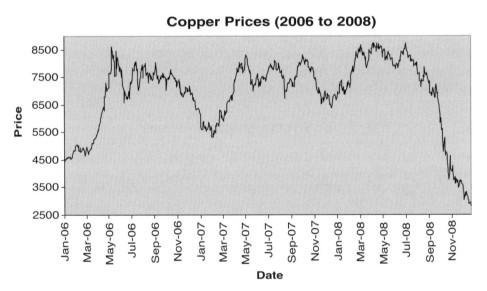

Figure 11.10   Rolling copper futures prices from 2006 to 2008. Copper prices were volatile throughout 2006 but remained around their highs in mid-2007 to mid-2008, before a precipitous decline starting in September 2008.
Source: Bloomberg

Table 11.2   Features of "best of" payoff.

Feature	Normal	"Best of"
Price	Depends on payoff.	Higher than normal payoff.
Potential Upside	Depends on payoff.	Higher than normal payoff. If both assets are negatively correlated, the "best of" can perform much better than the weaker asset.
Remarks		Particularly useful to bet on alternative scenarios (e.g. higher rates versus higher stock prices), provided cost is not too high.

11.4   HYBRIDS AND CONDITIONAL COUPONS

Recall that a general theme of this book is that investors desire yield and they often do so by protected selling of optionality. (This does not contradict their desire for downside protection, which involves buying optionality, often so that the principal is guaranteed.) Our discussions in Chapters 4 (on barriers) and 7 (on range accruals) show just how optionality can be sold by having coupons that are conditional on some other events (e.g. the stock price staying above some barrier during the life of the option).

Indeed, there is no reason why the condition has to be linked to the same underlying as the deal, or even to the same asset class. Section 7.3 on multiple reference accruals ends with an example of an equity payoff conditional on interest rates and FX behaviour.

Equity Payoff Range Accrual Conditional on Rates and FX

To develop the example, consider the payoff

$$1.8 \times \max\left(S_T - K, 0\right) \times \frac{n}{N},$$

where S_T is the value of the STOXX 50 index at expiry T, K is some strike, N is the number of business days from 0 to T, and n is the number of business days where EUR/USD remains between 1.2 and 1.35 and 6-month Euribor stays under 3.5%.

Notice that we added the multiplier 1.8, which is possible only because of our sale of optionality. In particular, suppose that our yield curve is upward sloping, so that Euribor is expected to go above 3.5% after some time. And suppose that the forward curve for EUR/USD projects EUR/USD at 1.4 after 1 year (due to dollar rates being higher than euro rates). Then **by betting against the forward, the investor is getting a lot for his optionality sold (assuming he gets it right)**. As Figures 11.11 and 11.12 show, EUR/USD was trading between 1.2 and 1.35 for most of the period from 2005 to mid 2007, while 6-month Euribor was under 3.5% until September 2006. However, thereafter the dollar weakened and Euribor also rose significantly, putting the rest of the coupons in jeopardy.

Subsequently, in late 2008, EUR/USD fell back to the 1.2–1.3 range and rates dropped sharply, but the equity markets also tumbled. So, **the more conditions attached to a bet, the more possibility of something going wrong**. There is no real free lunch after all.

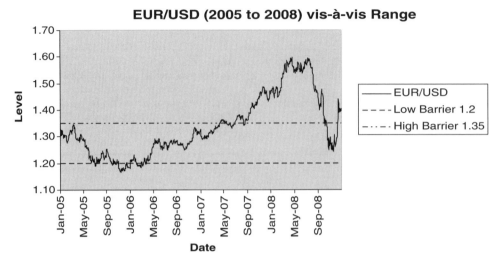

Figure 11.11   Value of EUR/USD from 2005 to 2008 *vis-à-vis* hypothetical range barriers based on 2005 levels. EUR/USD remained between the two barriers for much of the time from January 2005 to May 2007.
Source: Bloomberg

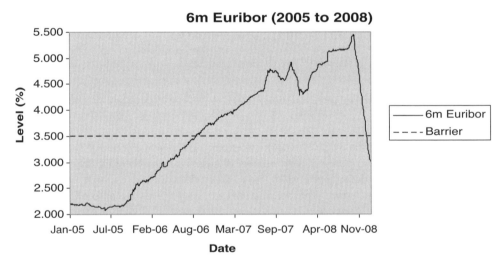

Figure 11.12   Six-month Euribor from 2005 to 2008 *vis-à-vis* hypothetical range barriers based on 2005 levels. Euribor slowly crept up and went past the 3.5% barrier by September 2006. It was not until late 2008 that Euribor fell back below 3.5%.
Source: Bloomberg

CMS Coupon Conditional of FX

To stay on the topic of conditional coupons, consider the following payoff:

$$1.5 \times R_T \times \frac{n}{N},$$

where R_T is the value of the 10-year swap rate at expiry T, N is the total number of weeks from 0 to T, and n is the number of weeks where EUR/USD remains above 1.5 (based on observations on Friday at 12 noon say).

This is an example in which the investor gets a higher multiplier (1.5 as opposed to 0.8 say) on the CMS coupon, by making it conditional on EUR/USD staying above some level. Again, the pitfalls are similar to those in our example above.

It is worth summarising the features of normal and conditional coupons, and we do this in Table 11.3.

Table 11.3 Features of normal and conditional coupons.

Feature	Normal	Conditional
Potential Upside	Depends on payoff.	Tends to be higher than normal coupon, since the condition attached is like selling optionality.
Chances of Not Getting Coupon	Depends on terms of payoff.	Higher than normal coupon, since condition has to be satisfied.

Key Points

- Hybrids can be used for conditional coupons or range accruals to increase yields.
- The more conditions attached to the coupons, the less safe are the coupons.

11.5 MULTIPLYING ASSETS

Why would people multiply two assets together? What sort of twisted payoff would one expect? Is this some kind of "chimera" that is given birth to by financial engineering? Well, as a simple example, if I were a yen investor and wanted to buy Walmart stock, my cost in yen would be

$$S_t X_t,$$

where S_t is the value of Walmart stock on my date of purchase t, and X_t is the value of USD/JPY at time t. I could even have a composite option with a yen strike K and a payoff at expiry T of

$$\max(S_T X_T - K, 0).$$

(Note that this is not a quanto, as there is conversion at the appropriate exchange rate when settling against the strike. Compare Section 5.3 on non-deliverable products.) This might seem specific to FX, and its use in converting assets from one currency to another, but below I shall give another example on how multiplication could be relevant.

Equity Invested at Fixed Annuity Rate

Consider a pension fund that has liabilities over the next 40 years. Payments to retirees are likely to start 20 years from now, so that a more stable cashflow profile would be necessary within 10 years. But if the pension fund invests only in fixed income instruments, it has little chance of earning the required returns to meet its liabilities.

Our pension fund wishes to invest in equities for 10 years, say the S&P 500 index, with principal protection. Furthermore, it wishes to invest in an annuity thereafter to guarantee future cashflows for the retirees. And it wishes to protect itself in case fixed rates fall 10 years from now but wants to benefit from any upside in rates. What should it do?

Let us ignore the principal-protected part. That is like a zero-coupon bond and could be invested in a forward annuity or option on it. The more interesting part is the part that becomes relevant in the event that the stock investment proves successful and yields a positive return. The following payoff profile should keep the investor happy (assuming the cost is bearable):

$$\max\left(S_T - K, 0\right) \max\left(L - R_T, 0\right) \sum_{i=1}^{N} \tau_i Z_{T,t_i},$$

where $T = 10y$ is the expiry date, S_T is the value of S&P 500 at the expiry date, K is the equity strike, R_T is the 30-year swap rate that starts 10 years forward, L is the strike on the swap rate, $t_1, t_2, \ldots, t_N = 40y$ are annual payment dates of the annuity, τ_i are the relevant accrual periods, and $Z_{t,T}$ is the value of a zero-coupon bond with maturity T as seen at time t.

Basically, if there is any return from stock market performance, the payoff protects the pension fund from falling rates, so that it can fix the rate of investment for the amount at a level at least equal to L over the next 30 years.

Admittedly, this made up example is rather complex, and possibly not of interest to most investors. This is rightly the case as **its complexity makes it only suitable for investors with a very strong understanding of the financial markets and their own liability needs, which can be difficult in markets that are fast changing**. But it should serve to highlight that even multiplying assets can make sense. So, this "chimera" hopefully has a purpose in its existence.

Key Points

- It makes sense to multiply an FX with an asset, and you can even have a composite option on a foreign asset with domestic strike after FX conversion.
- Another example is the case of multiplying a stock market return with a swaption, in order to invest future stock market gains at a minimum rate (e.g. for a pension fund), but such complex structures should be properly understood before venturing forward.

12

Some Exotic Equity Products

This chapter gives a flavour of some extremely exotic equity products. The basic premise is to allow for upside participation in stock market returns, while limiting downside risk (e.g. protecting one's principal, or at least some part of it). The anticipated decline (at least for a few years) in equity markets after the bursting of the dotcom bubble of March 2000 certainly inspired the development of many such structures.

Let us begin by explaining that investing in equities historically has not been free of risk. We shall then explore the cliquet, where coupons are based on returns over each period, so that if markets decline in the initial aftermath of the deal, the investor need not be left with an out-of-the-money option. We then explore some much weirder structures, namely the Himalaya, Altiplano, Atlas and Everest. **The exact bet the investor is making in these structures can be obscure**, and certainly I doubt if most investors fully understand the bet. But if we think of these options as **"cheap" (potentially with principal protection), where you sacrifice paltry bond coupons (in a low-yield world) for some bet that could potentially pay out a lot**, then perhaps it might make sense from a risk–reward perspective. These structures may not represent the latest fad (prior to the crash of 2008) but illustrate many of the themes involved in structured equity products.

It is worth mentioning that such exotic features are not restricted to equities. Indeed, they were also applied to commodities (or even baskets comprising both equities and commodities) during the commodities boom of 2007, although interest may be waning following the dramatic decline in commodity prices in 2008.

I really cannot advise on whether to invest in them, but I think it would be interesting to at least know about them.

12.1 A HISTORICAL PERSPECTIVE

The typical investor has a portfolio comprising stocks and bonds. Traditionally, bonds are seen as providing a safe stream of cashflows, while equities are the primary method of achieving a long-term inflation-busting return. Whereas it is said that in the long term the stock market always produces a positive return, how long term does it have to be?

Figure 12.1 shows the level of the S&P 500 since 1990. It has had a meteoric rise from 360 on 2 January 1980 to 903 on 31 December 2008, having fallen from its peak of 1,565 on 9 October 2007. Nevertheless, it appears that long-term investors are still doing nicely.

If, however, we look at the Nikkei 225 in Japan (see Figure 12.2), having reached its peak of 38,916 on 29 December 1989, it has over the last 19 years dropped by 77% to stand at 8,860 as of 30 December 2008. Can the average investor wait more than 19 years?

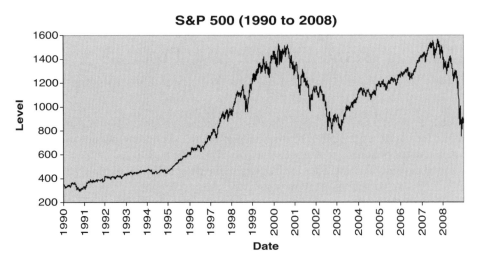

Figure 12.1   The S&P 500 rose spectacularly from 360 on 2 January 1990 to 1,527 on 24 March 2000. It suffered a period of decline to reach 800 on 11 March 2003, but then recovered to a high of 1,565 on 9 October 2007. Thereafter, it went into a tailspin, with particularly steep drops in late 2008.
Source: Bloomberg

But let us return to the USA. Figure 12.3 shows a graph of the S&P 500 from 1966 to 1979. Starting at 92 on 3 January 1966 and ending at 108 on 31 December 1979 is not exactly spectacular – a 17% risky return over 14 years and in an environment that was getting inflationary (towards the late 1970s). Some blame the high inflation for this economic malaise but the point remains that stocks failed to perform in this period.

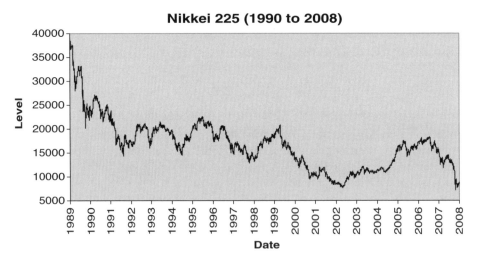

Figure 12.2   The Nikkei 225 reached its peak of 38,916 on 29 December 1989. Thereafter, it has been in a slow decline from which it never recovered. Nineteen years later on 30 December 2008, the Nikkei 225 was just at 8,860.
Source: Bloomberg

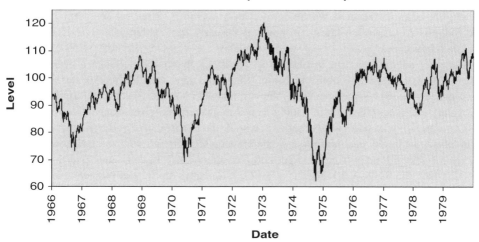

Figure 12.3   Level of S&P 500 index from 1966 to 1979. The S&P 500 mainly moved sideways in the period. It started at 92 on 3 January 1966 and ended at 108 on 31 December 1979, spanning a range of 62 to 120.
Source: Bloomberg

It is said that the developed world (excluding Japan) is in a different era (of high growth and low inflation). But the sharp fall in the S&P 500 of 42% from its peak of 1,565 on 9 October 2007 to 903 on 31 December 2008, and that of other world indices (e.g. STOXX 50 and FTSE 100) by around 40%, not to mention the unprecedented financial crisis enveloping the developed world, should give us cause to reconsider.

While not advocating that we forsake equities, it is only natural to ask if there is a possibility of upside participation while limiting downside risk. In the simplest case, we could have a principal-protected note, where the coupons are used instead to buy call options. And, of course, the possibilities extend from there.

Key Points

- Traditionally, bonds are seen as safe, whereas stocks are seen as a means to seek a high yield.
- The S&P 500 had a meteoric rise from 360 in 1980 to 903 in 2008 despite a sharp fall from its peak of 1,565 in 2007.
- The Nikkei 225 fell from its peak of 38,916 in December 1989 to 8,860 in December 2008.
- The S&P 500 rose from 92 in 1966 to only 108 in 1979.
- In 2008, developed market indices fell sharply (about 40%) from their peaks.

12.2 THE CLIQUET

A cliquet is an instrument whose coupon in a period is based on the return over that period only. Let us see how the environment in the early years of this decade generated interest in this product.

Consider the environment in mid-2002. The stock markets have taken a battering from the burst of the dotcom bubble in March 2000 and have been further devastated by the terrorist attacks of 11 September 2001. The central banks have, however, carried out significant monetary easing and the economy looks as if it might recover, given time.

Our investor, who has a 4-year horizon, would like to participate in the stock market but is concerned that it may decline further in the immediate aftermath. Figure 12.4 shows the level of the STOXX 50 index from June 2002 to December 2007. Let's assume that this is 1 July 2002, where the STOXX 50 index is at 3,131. If she buys a principal-protected note with an embedded call option, her payoff at maturity (1 July 2006) would be her principal plus

$$\frac{1}{3,131} \times \max\left(S_T - K, 0\right),$$

where S_T is value of the STOXX 50 index at expiry T, and $\frac{1}{3,131}$ is a scale factor based on the current spot value of STOXX 50.

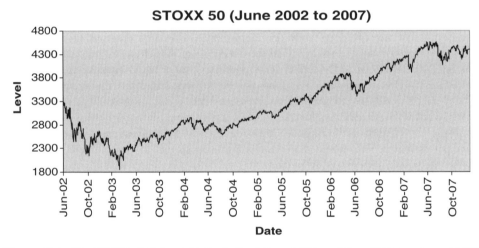

Figure 12.4 The STOXX 50 index initially declined from 3,383 on 3 June 2002 to a low of 1,850 on 12 March 2003, before making a strong recovery over the subsequent years to end at 4,400 on 31 December 2007.
Source: Bloomberg

The strike K applicable (based on current spot of 3,131) might be 3,700. If STOXX 50 declines first and then rises (as in hindsight it did), this option may not even be in-the-money at expiry. So our investor only gets her principal back at maturity (with no coupons). Can we do better than that?

Consider a principal-protected note where the forgone interest is invested in a set of options that pay

$$\max \left(\frac{S_{t_i}}{S_{t_{i-1}}} - K, 0 \right),$$

where t_1, t_2, t_3, t_4 are the annual coupon dates with t_0 being the valuation date, S_t is the value of the STOXX 50 index at time t, and $K = 1.05$ is the strike. This is our cliquet in essence.

If, over each period, the STOXX 50 index rises by more than the strike, a coupon is paid. This is independent of previous periods, so that if the markets first decline and then rise, the investor does not receive coupons initially but subsequently benefits from the rise.

Let's look at the actual performance of the STOXX 50 index and the coupons on this deal. This is captured in Table 12.1.

Table 12.1   Coupons of a cliquet on STOXX 50. Due to the initial decline of the STOXX 50, the coupon at the end of period 1 is 0. However, coupons in subsequent periods are not affected by this initial decline.

Period i	Date t_i	STOXX 50	Coupon (%)
0	1 July 2002	3,127	N/A
1	1 July 2003	2,367	0
2	1 July 2004	2,807	13.6
3	1 July 2005	3,209	9.3
4	3 July 2006	3,663	9.1

Basically, the huge fall between July 2002 and July 2003 led to a first coupon of 0, but the investor benefited from the huge rises thereafter, even though it was not until July 2005 that the STOXX 50 surpassed its value at inception.

A brief note is due on the absence of compounding in a cliquet. For ease of illustration, let us assume that you have a stock that grows at 10% annually, and selling it after 1 year gives a return of 10%. But selling it after 2 years gives a return of $1.1^2 - 1 = 21\%$; selling it after 3 years gives a return of $1.1^3 - 1 = 33.1\%$; and selling it after 4 years gives a return of $1.1^4 - 1 = 46.41\%$. However, **a cliquet pays on the basis of a simple, uncompounded return**, i.e. 10% each year (taking strike as 1). Admittedly, you can invest the returns at the end of each period, but if you were hoping that the magic of compounding would help you to grow your wealth more quickly, you would be disappointed.

As with other products, it is possible to embellish a cliquet to suit investor needs. For example, local caps and floors could be placed, so that the payoff takes the form

$$\min \left(\max \left(\frac{S_{t_i}}{S_{t_{i-1}}} - K, F \right), C \right),$$

where $C = 8\%$ is a possible cap level, and $F = 2\%$ is a possible floor level.

Of course, a floor has to be paid for by the investor, and a cap allows the bank to give the investor more yield. So, perhaps a cap can pay for a floor, hence limiting the risk and reward of the investor.

It is also possible to have global caps and floors. For example, a global floor of 4% means that the investor will get 4% (less any coupons paid during the life of the note) at maturity. And a global cap of 30% means that no further coupons will be paid once the investor has received 30%. This is not the same as the tarn feature, since the deal will not terminate, and the investor still has to wait for maturity to get back her principal. And, of course, early termination (via callability, triggers or tarns) is possible to allow for higher yields.

It should be noted that the cliquet is very much a forward skew product. After all, the bet is on the return over the interval from time t_{i-1} to t_i and not the absolute level. In the equity markets, skew tends to flatten for longer expiries because investors tend to want to buy protection against a huge crash, and banks are anxious for more compensation to make selling such protection worthwhile for short expiries. (Over longer time periods, such an effect is less dominant.) Nevertheless, the development of the cliquet has led to more scrutiny of the pricing of forward skew, as banks realise that they are taking more skew risk at future dates, and price it accordingly.

At this stage, it is worth recapping the features of a cliquet versus a normal European call option. This is done in Table 12.2.

Table 12.2   Features of a cliquet versus a normal European call option.

Feature	European call	Cliquet
Potential Upside	Can be high.	Can be high.
Compounding Effect of Rise in Asset Price over Time	Yes. Payment is only at expiry. As the asset price rises, a subsequent 1% rise means more in absolute terms.	No. Coupons are periodic and return in each period is applied to a fixed notional.
Effect of Sharp Fall in Asset Price Early in Life of Deal	Significantly negative since strike is likely to be set relative to asset price at inception. If asset price falls sharply early on, it is less likely to end above strike at expiry.	Effect limited to return over current period. Returns in subsequent periods are unaffected, since they are relative to asset price at start of that period.
Price	Moderate.	More expensive due to complexity, and higher pricing of forward skew.
Liquidity	High.	Less liquid than European call.

Key Points

- If markets fall sharply before rising, a normal call option is likely to be out-of-the-money at expiry.
- A cliquet pays out based on the returns over each period versus the period starting value, hence subsequent coupons are not handicapped by initial market declines.
- A cliquet does not provide for compounding of returns.
- We can add local or global caps or floors to a cliquet.
- Pricing of a cliquet depends on forward skew.

12.3   THE HIMALAYA

Let me start by telling you what this esoteric beast looks like, and I shall then tell you why some people might like it.

Suppose we have 10 coupon dates and 10 stocks. At the end of the first coupon date, we look at the **returns from deal inception date** (i.e. $R = \frac{S_{t_1}}{S_{t_0}} - 1$) of each of the stocks, pick the best one (say stock C), record it and remove the stock from our basket. At the end of the next coupon date, we look at the **returns from deal inception date** (i.e. $R = \frac{S_{t_2}}{S_{t_0}} - 1$) of the remaining 9 stocks, pick the best (say stock E), record it and remove it from the basket. We continue in this way for the next 8 periods. At the end of the last period, we look at the return of the last stock in the basket (say stock H), and record it. Now, our payoff is

$$
A \max \left(\frac{1}{10} \sum_{i=1}^{10} R_i - K, 0 \right),
$$

where R_i is the return recorded in period i, $K = 10\%$ is the strike, and A is an appropriate multiplier.

This is the Himalaya. It is one of a bunch of "mountain range" products, so named because these products typically depend on the maximum or minimum of a set of stocks, very much akin to the peaks of mountains and troughs of valleys. Although a basket of stocks is involved, there is no averaging. Instead, it is very much about performance of individual stocks.

At first glance, it does not sound too bad. You pick the best return in each period and use this return to determine your payoff. But if a salesperson tries to sell such a note to you in this manner, he is trying to pull a fast one. After all, **you might be recording the best return in each period, but what remains in your basket are the weaker performing stocks in each period**. And over time, your basket comprises only those stocks that have performed badly since the inception of the deal. Since these returns are not floored at 0, **you are basically betting that no stock in your basket performs too poorly since valuation date**.

Let us illustrate with an example involving 5 stocks and 5 coupon periods. For simplicity, let us assume that they have correlation 0, the same volatility of 30%, and spot of 1 today. In Figure 12.5, we can see a potential path of these 5 stocks, and Table 12.3 shows the average return for the Himalaya. Just see how much smaller it is (at −1.2%) compared with the basket average (of 32%)!

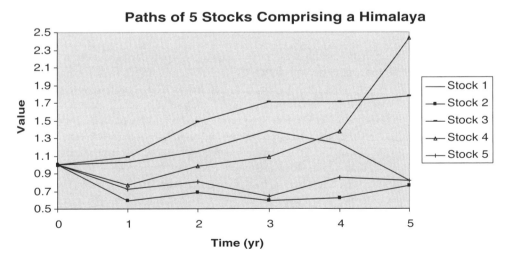

Figure 12.5 Hypothetical paths of 5 stocks comprising a Himalaya. This is used to illustrate the average calculated for the Himalaya in Table 12.3.

Table 12.3 Hypothetical period returns on a Himalaya. The returns are shaded out when the stock is removed from the basket. Because we throw out the stock with the best return at the end of each period, towards the end, we are only left with poor performing stocks. This leads to horrible returns recorded in the last two periods, and a Himalaya average return of −1.2%, somewhat surprising in light of a simple basket average return of 32%.

Time	Stock 1	Stock 2	Stock 3	Stock 4	Stock 5	Period best return	Selected stock
			Returns				
1	3.3%	−40.3%	8.9%	−23.3%	−27.3%	8.9%	3
2	14.9%	−31.4%	48.5%	−1.2%	−19.1%	14.9%	1
3	38.4%	−40.9%	70.6%	8.9%	−35.7%	8.9%	4
4	23.2%	−37.5%	71.4%	37.8%	−14.7%	−14.7%	5
5	−18.3%	−24.1%	77.0%	143.5%	−18.1%	−24.1%	2
		Basket average	32%		Himalaya average	−1.2%	

As a matter of curiosity, let us consider a different product. You still have 10 coupon dates and 10 stocks. At the end of the first coupon date, you look at the returns of all the stocks and pick the worst one R_1^*, record it and remove the stock from the basket. At the end of the next coupon date, you look at the returns of the remaining 9 stocks, pick the worst R_2^*, record it and remove it from the basket. Continue until the end of the last period, where you are left with the last stock and you record the return. The payoff is then defined in the same way as above, i.e.

$$A \max \left(\frac{1}{10} \sum_{i=1}^{10} R_i^* - K, 0 \right).$$

Does not sound too appealing? But surprisingly, **this "worst of" product sometimes costs more than the Himalaya described above**.

To be fair, it may be that there are more stocks than coupon dates (e.g. 12 stocks and 10 coupon dates), so you will not have to live with all the worst performing stocks. But it would be rare for the number of stocks to vastly exceed the number of coupon dates (e.g. 20 stocks and 10 coupon dates).

After all, one of the main reasons why the Himalaya grew popular is because it is cheap. Here there might be the theme of how forwards may not be realised. If, for example, you believe a sector to be very high growth, e.g. commodities in 2007, perhaps you are happy to bet that no asset among those chosen will do badly. (Admittedly, this proved wrong since commodity prices plunged in 2008.) However, the cost of hedging is based on the forward for a stock, which is only affected by the cost of borrowing and dividends of the stock. Any potential growth prospects do not matter. You could therefore get this product cheaply because it is cheap to hedge. In that way, betting against forwards might make this a worthwhile investment.

Let's look at it another way. Suppose you had an investment horizon of 5 years. You wanted only principal protection and were happy to use the sacrificed interest to buy an embedded option. In the low-yield period from 2002 to 2005, with 5-year euro interest rates at 3 to 3.5%, you might not be able to get much optionality. So, a "cheap" bet like the Himalaya, or a deep out-of-the-money call, might be all you could afford. And perhaps you are less than confident of stocks rising sufficiently to make a deep out-of-the-money call worthwhile. The bottom line is that **the Himalaya is probably not a bet most investors can claim to properly understand, but there may not be too many cheap alternatives if you hunger**

for high yields where nominal rates are really low. Still, it should only be the province of sophisticated investors.

Key Points

- A Himalaya comprises a basket of assets. At the end of each period, the best return is recorded and the asset is thrown out of the basket. This continues until the product matures (when typically only one or a few assets are left).
- This product is not worth much since you are left with the worst performing assets over time. It might even be cheaper than a product where you record the worst return and throw the asset out.
- The Himalaya might still be worthwhile since it is a really cheap bet, although most investors are unlikely to understand it.

12.4   THE ALTIPLANO

Like the Himalaya, the Altiplano has quite an obscure manner of payoff. Let's recall the stock market declines following 11 September 2001, and assume that an investor, who is somewhat bullish on the market, still believes that a further deterioration is possible. Let us assume further that the same investor strongly believes that none of a set of 10 stocks will fall too much.

Then perhaps the investor would consider the following payoff at expiry $T = 5y$:

$$
C \qquad \text{if none of } \frac{S_T^1}{S_T^1}, \frac{S_T^2}{S_T^2}, \ldots, \frac{S_T^n}{S_T^n} \text{ is ever less than } H \text{ prior to and including the expiry date,}
$$

$$
\max\left(\frac{1}{n} \sum_{i=1}^{n} \left(\frac{S_T^i}{S_T^i} - 1 \right) - K, 0 \right) \qquad \text{otherwise}
$$

where $C = 50\%$ is a large coupon, S_t^i is the value of stock i at time t, $H = 60\%$ is the barrier level, and $K = 25\%$ is the strike if not all the stocks remained above the barrier.

This is the Altiplano – an instrument that pays a large coupon if no asset in the basket falls below a barrier prior to and including expiry; otherwise, the payoff is based on the average return of the basket.

(There is a variation of the Altiplano where the barrier condition for the large coupon C only applies on the expiry date. The large coupon is obviously more likely to be payable in this variation. As such, it is likely that this coupon will have to be reduced, e.g. to 35%, in order to make the deal viable from the issuer's perspective.)

The investor's primary bet is that none of the stocks in the basket (of 10 stocks say) will ever (at least prior to expiry) fall below 60% of the value at the deal inception date, t_0. If any stock falls below 60% of its value at t_0, he can still get a payoff in the event that the basket itself performs well *vis-à-vis* the strike. This is highly possible as you could have a raging bull market with 9 of the 10 stocks showing significant growth, and one among them going bankrupt due to reasons specific to the company. It is worth saying that this structure can be incorporated into a principal-protected note, ensuring that the investor's principal is safe in any event.

Company-specific reasons for poor performance can never be ignored. Enron was an example of a company that imploded suddenly. But **it is worth highlighting how much some mountain range products tend to be affected by one poor performer amongst many**.

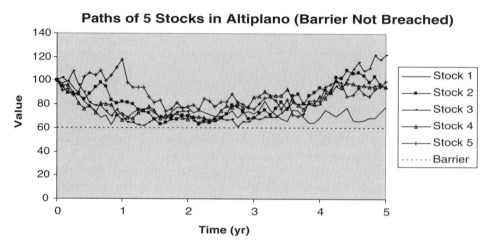

Figure 12.6   Hypothetical paths of 5 stocks comprising an Altiplano. The barrier of 60 has not been breached, so the investor is entitled to the huge coupon at expiry.

If such products are also long-dated, it is questionable if the investor is taking too much company-specific risk. If anything, this seems to be the opposite of diversification.

Let us consider an example as to the possible payoff. Figures 12.6 and 12.7 show hypothetical paths of 5 stocks comprising an Altiplano. For simplicity, we assume 0 correlation between the 5 stocks, the same volatility of 20% and a spot of 100 today. Notice how the two graphs look rather similar. In Figure 12.6, the 60% barrier was not breached, so the investor is entitled to a 50% coupon at maturity (in 5 years). In Figure 12.7, however, Stock 3 clearly breached the barrier, so the investor is now entitled to a payoff of

$$\max\left(\frac{1}{5}\sum_{i=1}^{5}\left(\frac{S_T^i}{S_T^0}-1\right)-25\%,0\right)=\max(-5.28\%-25\%,0)=0.$$

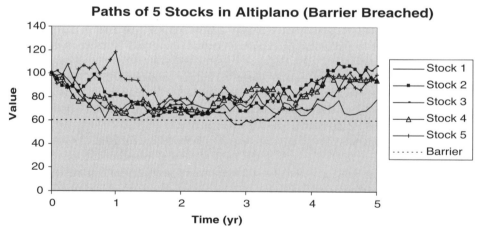

Figure 12.7   Another set of hypothetical paths of 5 stocks comprising an Altiplano. (These are the same as in Figure 12.6 except for Stock 3.) The barrier of 60 has been breached by Stock 3, so this becomes a basket option.

Quite a difference! Recall our discussion in Chapter 3 on digital risk. This looks very much like it.

Of course, it is possible to make this structure less dependent on individual companies by allowing at most two of the stocks (for example) in a larger basket (e.g. of 15 stocks) to breach the lower barrier without extinguishing the coupon. But the higher the number of exceptions, the more expensive will be the structure.

A key rationale for interest in such a structure is, firstly, that it is likely to be cheap. A bet on the minimum of a set of many stocks (say 10) being above some level is a bet on a low probability event, at least from a pricing perspective, since pricing does not account for potential upward growth in the stock prices but only the cost of hedging. Let us assume that our reference basket is a bunch of liquid technology stocks (prior to the burst of the dotcom bubble). An investor (before March 2000) may feel that no stock in the bunch is likely to decline significantly (wrong in hindsight), but that is not priced in. **The liquidity of the stocks in the basket is important, since hedging by the banks of such contracts would otherwise significantly affect the price of the stocks.** This was often the case in practice, much to the chagrin of the companies affected.

> **Key Points**
>
> - An Altiplano pays a huge coupon if no stock in the basket falls below some level during the life of the deal; otherwise, it becomes an option on the basket.
> - There is a lot of company-specific risk in this product. Excluding one or two stocks from the high coupon condition may help to some extent.
> - Liquidity of stocks in this product is important as hedging can distort markets.

12.5 THE ATLAS

In earlier sections, we discussed how a single stock can cause a lot of harm to the payoff of a mountain range product. Suppose that the economic environment is not certain. Perhaps we are in late 2008, where stock markets have taken a big tumble amid the credit crisis. An investor is overall bullish on stocks, thinking they are oversold, but is afraid that individual companies may not withstand the crisis. In particular, the investor does not really want one of her stocks to cause her grief. For example, if, in a basket of 10 stocks, one goes bankrupt (and hence has a return of -100% assuming no recovery), while the others each have a return of 10%, the average return is -1.1%. What should she do?

One solution is a basket that excludes the worst k (e.g. $k = 2$) performers. However, that by itself would be costly, so usually you offset the cost by excluding the best m (e.g. $m = 3$) performers as well. In a basket of 25 stocks, you would then have excluded the worst 2 and best 3 returns and obtained an average over the remainder. This product, which pays on the basis of the return of a basket excluding the best and worst performers, is called the Atlas. At expiry, the payoff is

$$\max\left(\frac{1}{n^*}\sum_{i=1}^{n^*}\left(\frac{S_T^i}{S_0^i}-1\right)-K,0\right),$$

where $S_t^1, S_t^2, \ldots, S_t^{n^*}$ are the values at time t of the n^* stocks not excluded from the basket, T is period end date, and K is strike.

In a sense, this is a very different product from either the Himalaya or the Altiplano. It is a true basket product in every sense of the word, and the correlation effect and lower volatility discussed in Chapter 11 are all relevant. In fact, this is even a more benign product than the normal basket option discussed in Chapter 11, since by throwing out extreme values, volatility is even less. From that perspective, the investor should expect a reduced risk of poor performance but also a more limited upside in this product.

As an illustration, we have in Figure 12.8 a plot of the possible paths of 5 stocks and their overall average (having excluded the best and worst performer). You can observe how much less volatile is the result of throwing away extrema.

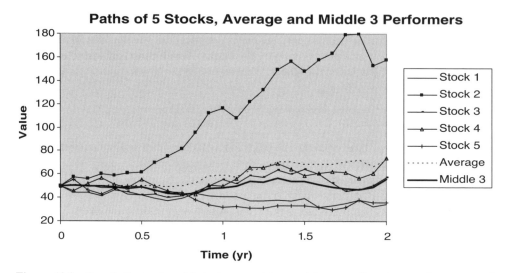

Figure 12.8 Hypothetical paths of 5 stocks comprising an Atlas, as well as the overall average and the middle 3 performers. The overall average, and especially the overall average of the middle 3, varies much less than the individual stocks.

Key Points

- An Atlas throws away the best and worst performers and pays on the basis of the average of the remainder.
- An Atlas is less volatile than a typical basket and has a very different payoff profile from the Himalaya or the Altiplano.

12.6   THE EVEREST

The Everest is actually quite simple compared to the other mountain range products. Contrary to the name of the world's tallest mountain, the Everest is a payoff based on the minimum of a set of stocks, so it is more akin to the valleys of high mountains than to the peaks. Perhaps the higher one climbs, the bigger the potential fall.

The payoff is basically based on the minimum return of a basket of stocks over a period. The payoff is

$$L \times \min_{1 \le i \le n} \left(\frac{S_T^i}{S_0^i} \right),$$

where S_t^i is the value of stock i at time t, T is the period end date, and L is a leverage factor.

The Everest typically involves many stocks (e.g. all 30 stocks in the DAX 30 index) and can be based on the return over a very long period (e.g. 10 years). It is likely to be cheap, being the minimum return of a huge basket of stocks. (Of course, company-specific risk can be mitigated if the payoff is, instead, based on the second lowest return, for example.)

It goes without saying that since the payoff is cheap to hedge, it would be compensated for by a large multiplier L, which is determined from the value of interest sacrificed after the bank has added a profit margin.

Key Points

- An Everest pays the minimum of a large basket over a long horizon.
- It is likely to be cheap, if we ignore expected growth (or decline) in the stocks, as is the case for the pricing of derivatives.

12.7 PRINCIPAL PROTECTION OR LACK THEREOF

This chapter cannot do justice to the myriad of structured equity products available. There are all sorts of such products, including those that give the investor the better of relative versus absolute outperformance, e.g. the coupon could be

$$\max \left(\frac{StockA_T}{StockA_0} - \frac{STOXX_T}{STOXX_0}, \frac{StockA_T}{StockA_0} - 1 \right),$$

or those that pay a coupon linked to absolute deviation of final spot from initial spot. The latter resemble bets on volatility, which form the subject of Chapter 13. Nevertheless, it is worth concluding by examining the crucial feature of principal protection.

There are lots of structured equity products where the principal is not protected at maturity. There is no reason in principle why we cannot add principal-protection features, but some equity investors may have higher risk appetites and seek correspondingly higher yields. After all, many equity investors would have bought a stock outright if they had not invested in a structured note.

Thus, perhaps, the investor receives principal repayment linked to the performance of the stock market (e.g. $\frac{S_T}{S_0} \times 0.9$, where S_T is the value of a stock index at maturity T). In 2006 to 2007, it was common for structured equity notes to consist of a lower barrier. If this lower barrier was breached at any time prior to maturity by an index or even perhaps by one stock in the basket, then less than the full principal was repayable. In some cases, the principal repayable is a certain percentage of par, e.g. 60%. In other cases, it may even be dependent on the performance of some stocks in the basket, e.g. the value of the poorest performing stock as a proportion of its value at the inception of the deal.

Investors should be aware of the risks involved in such investments. In the simpler cases (such as the example above that pays 0.9 times the performance of the stock market), this is no more risky than a simple stock investment. But where more complex conditions are applied as regards principal repayment – for example, principal repayment of

$$\min\left(\frac{S_T}{S_0}, 1\right) \text{ or } \min\left(\frac{S_T^1}{S_0^1}, \frac{S_T^2}{S_0^2}, \ldots, \frac{S_T^n}{S_0^2}\right),$$

– the investor can be in real danger of receiving a very low principal repayment at maturity while not retaining much upside. It is one thing where an investor takes a calculated bet (even one she does not fully understand) with sacrificed coupons, knowing that potential losses are limited, but it is altogether a different matter when the investor has a lot more at stake.

Many investors lost heavily in 2008 on the lower barrier structures, as described above. These barriers were typically at 60% to 75% of the value of spot at deal inception (around 2006 to 2007), and the equity markets in 2008 had fallen by over 40% from their peaks. Consequently, these investors were left with notes that would repay less than the full principal upon maturity.

Key Points

- Structured products in equities sometimes do not offer principal protection.
- It is important to realise that some have higher risks than a stock.

13

Volatility and Correlation Products

This chapter provides an introduction to products that depend directly on volatility and correlation. These products are of less interest to a typical investment professional, and more usually the preserve of hedge funds (who want to take outright bets on volatility and correlation) or banks (for their hedging needs). However, with the reduction of suitable investments for yield seekers in the economic environment post-2008, and continuing market volatility, they may be worth knowing about. If for no other reason, there should at least be some curiosity value.

We start by looking at variance swaps and their sisters, volatility swaps, and the significant risks involved in such deals will be explained. We then move on to options on variance swaps, which may be preferable for investors, provided that they find the rather high cost palatable. Correlation swaps are then examined.

13.1   VARIANCE AND VOLATILITY SWAPS

Let us start with some motivation behind volatility trading, before describing the variance swap itself.

Volatility is of concern to investors. Typically, an investor prefers a safe investment whose price does not fluctuate too much. From a bank's perspective, the Black–Scholes framework as discussed in Chapter 3, shows how the **cost of delta hedging an option** (and hence its price) depends only on the cost of funding, and the **volatility of the underlying**. (Any expected growth or decline in the underlying is irrelevant.) The higher the volatility, the more frequently hedging has to take place. The higher the price of the underlying, the higher its delta, and delta hedging requires you to maintain an amount of the underlying equal to its delta. Figure 13.1

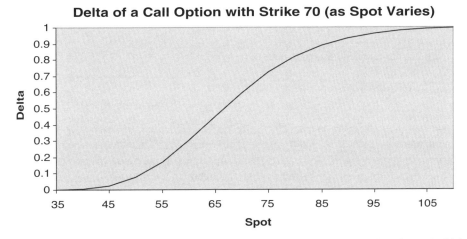

Figure 13.1   Delta of a call option with strike 70 as spot varies. The higher the value of spot, the higher the delta of the call option. This means that delta hedging involves buying high and selling low, since you need to hold an amount of stock equal to its delta.

shows the delta of a call option as a function of spot. **This means that you are buying high and selling low.** So a bank may naturally be interested in managing its exposure to volatility.

An investor also may be interested in speculating on volatility directly. After all, there are quiet periods when volatility is low and other periods when volatility is high. A typical investor usually has a stronger view on the direction of the market than whether it would be volatile. However, if there is a crash, as in 2008, you may not be sure of market direction (since you don't know when the market has bottomed out), but you are guaranteed high volatility. It should be stressed, however, that selling volatility is not for the faint of heart, and should really be left to sophisticated investors (e.g. hedge funds). **A variance swap is after all a contingent liability instrument, and selling variance can lead to potentially unlimited losses (much akin to shorting a stock).**

Still, let us come to the variance swap, which allows us to trade volatility directly. We can define the log-return of an asset from time t_{i-1} to t_i as

$$R_i = \log\left(\frac{S_{t_i}}{S_{t_{i-1}}}\right),$$

where S_t is the value of the asset at time t. (Usually, the intervals for measuring returns are daily, but they can also be weekly or even monthly.)

The realised variance over the period from $t_0 = 0$ to $t_N = T$ is then

$$V = \frac{1}{N}\sum_{i=1}^{N} R_i^2 - \overline{R}^2,$$

where $\overline{R} = \frac{1}{N}\sum_{i=1}^{N} R_i$ is the mean. Note that some variance swaps are defined without mean adjustment, i.e. $V = \frac{1}{N}\sum_{i=1}^{N} R_i^2$.

A variance swap is an instrument that allows you to either pay or receive realised variance versus some pre-agreed strike. A variance swap with a strike K has a payoff at maturity T (in years) of

$$\frac{252}{T}(V - K)$$

if you are buying realised variance, and

$$\frac{252}{T}(K - V)$$

if you are selling realised variance. (The $\frac{252}{T}$ factor is included because typically the trades are based on annualised variance, and there are approximately 252 business days per year.)

Variance increases significantly when there are jumps in the value of the underlying (be it a stock or a foreign exchange rate). With the financial turmoil resulting from the credit crunch, 2008 has been an extremely volatile year for almost all asset classes, while 2007 has been rather mild in comparison. From the diagrams of the S&P 500 (Figure 13.2) and its daily log-returns (Figure 13.3), it should be no surprise that the realised variance for 2008 at $40.9\%^2 = 0.167$ is significantly higher than the $16.1\%^2 = 0.0259$ for 2007.

Figures 13.4 and 13.5 show the values of EUR/USD from 2007 to 2008, and its daily log-returns. We see how volatility has dramatically increased between 2007 and 2008 as investors

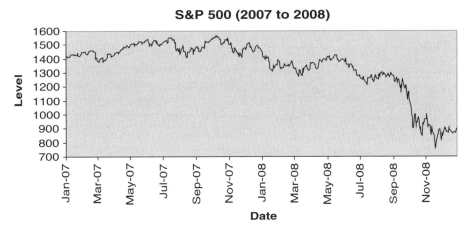

Figure 13.2 Level of S&P 500 index from 2007 to 2008. The S&P 500 plummeted sharply in late 2008, leading to a huge rise in realised volatility.
Source: Bloomberg

take flight to the safety of the dollar. In particular, the annualised realised variance for 2007 is $6.2\%^2 = 0.0038$, whereas that for 2008 is $13.7\%^2 = 0.0188$.

It is clear that buying variance would have been a very profitable strategy for 2008, whereas selling variance would have been disastrous. Buying variance can also be particularly interesting for single-name stocks, where huge one-day swings are possible.

It should be noted that the volatility of the underlying outside the measurement period is not captured by a variance swap. If you have daily observations, these are typically based on end-of-day prices (or quotes at some specified time). **Huge intraday swings will not**

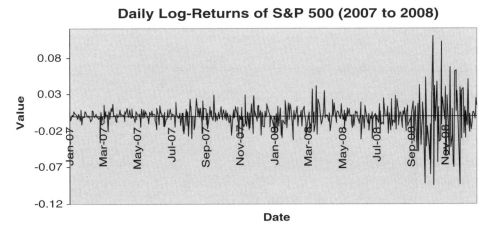

Figure 13.3 Daily log-returns of S&P 500 from 2007 to 2008. The absolute values of log-returns increased significantly from September 2008 due to the huge declines in the S&P 500 index from that period. This is captured as higher realised volatility.
Source: Bloomberg

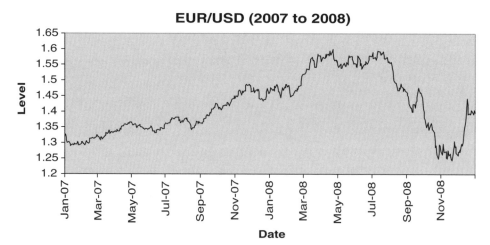

Figure 13.4 Value of EUR/USD from 2007 to 2008. EUR/USD fell sharply since August 2008 as investors rushed to the relative safety of the dollar, following a worsening of the credit crunch. This led to a sharp increase in realised volatility.
Source: Bloomberg

lead to increased realised variance on the variance swap. In 2008, there were often large intraday swings but where the end of day prices hardly changed (see Figure 13.6). In a similar vein, realised variance typically will be higher if observations are daily rather than weekly or monthly.

Huge intraday swings, however, cause problems for institutions trying to hedge a variance swap entered into with a client, since over a one-day period (where observations are daily) the hedger is exposed directionally to movements in the price of the underlying asset.

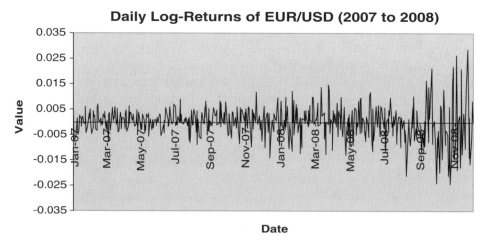

Figure 13.5 Daily log-returns of EUR/USD from 2007 to 2008. The fall in EUR/USD since August 2008 is reflected in the higher absolute values of log-returns in late 2008, i.e. higher realised volatility.
Source: Bloomberg

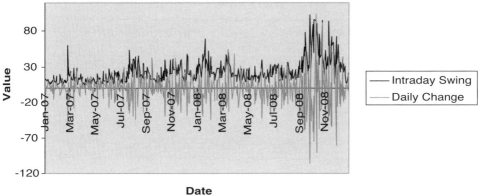

Figure 13.6   Daily changes versus intraday swings of S&P 500 from 2007 to 2008. It appears that the intraday log-returns often do not correspond directionally with the daily log-returns.
Source: Bloomberg

Some variance swaps (especially those on single-name stocks) have a clause limiting the payoff to 2.5 times (or some other multiplier) volatility strike (or $2.5^2 = 6.25$ times variance strike). Prior to 2008, it was seen as extremely unlikely for realised variance to be more than 6.25 times strike. As such, the value of the protection from this cap was usually not priced in. But if you did a variance swap on the S&P 500 in the beginning of 2008, it might be at a strike of $17\%^2$, which means that the cap would be set at $(2.5 \times 17\%)^2 = 42.5\%^2$. The realised variance for 2008 at $40.9\%^2$ is getting close to reaching this cap. The increase in realised volatility in 2008 for single-name stocks has been much greater than for the stock indices (since many huge institutions experienced financial turmoil), so that the cap of 2.5 times volatility strike would certainly have been surpassed.

The presence of this cap no doubt limited the loss incurred by a seller of variance; but, arguably, if a buyer of variance did this as a hedge, it made the hedge less than fully effective. A cap on the payoff is like an option on a variance swap, which we consider in the next section.

Actually, some cap on the payoff is needed, especially for single-name stocks. After all, a company can go bankrupt and the stock price can drop to 0. This would lead to infinite realised variance (and astronomical payoffs), since we are considering log-returns that approach $-\infty$ as the stock price falls to zero!

Pricing of Variance Swaps

If we assume that the underlying follows a continuous distribution, then variance swaps (with frequent fixings) can be statically replicated via basic call and put options across a spectrum of strikes with expiry equal to the maturity of the swap. (Static replication was covered in some detail in Chapter 6.) This means that **it is more natural to trade in terms of variance swaps than volatility swaps**, even if it is more natural to think in terms of volatility than of variance. Static replication means that no model assumptions are required and, as such, more confidence can be had in the pricing of the instrument. However, as discussed above, jumps are rather important in their impact on realised variance, so it is not clear how much faith should be placed in the above static replication technique. Selling variance is a dangerous thing and banks are likely to want to charge a significant margin to take this risk.

The strike for variance swaps is typically set at a premium to historical realised volatility. This partly reflects how implied volatility (used in static replication of variance swaps) is usually higher than historical realised volatility. Prior to the collapse of Lehman Brothers in September 2008, many hedge funds found it profitable to sell realised variance in a variance swap, taking advantage of the strike being at a premium to historical realised volatility. But the sharp spikes in volatility of all asset classes consequent to Lehman's collapse has led to many such hedge funds being badly burnt. This may reduce the number of participants in this market going forward.

As a refresher, Table 13.1 compares the characteristics of a variance swap *vis-à-vis* an at-the-money European option.

Table 13.1   Features of a variance swap *vis-à-vis* an at-the-money European option.

Feature	At-the-money European option	Variance swap
Sensitivity to Volatility	High while forward remains close to strike. However, if spot moves significantly away from strike, volatility becomes less important.	Always high.
Pricing Method	Standard.	Replication is an approximation, but does not account for jump risk.
Liquidity	High.	Much less than for a European option.

The Volatility Swap

Nevertheless, volatility swaps do exist, and a volatility swap with strike K^* has a payoff at maturity T of

$$\frac{252}{T}\left(\sqrt{V} - K^*\right)$$

if you are buying volatility.

As mentioned above, it is more natural to trade in variance. Because of the square root, there is negative convexity (with respect to realised variance), and the payoff of a volatility swap grows less than linearly with respect to realised variance, as Figure 13.7 demonstrates. Thus, the strike K^* for a volatility swap should be less than $\sqrt{K}$, where K is the strike of the variance swap.

Furthermore, volatility swaps cannot be replicated even assuming that the underlying has a continuous distribution. As such, a model is required to price it (or at least estimate the value of the negative convexity).

Key Points

- Volatility is important since higher volatility means that cost of hedging is higher.
- In times of a crash (e.g. 2008), volatility skyrockets.
- A variance swap is a contingent liability instrument.

- Variance increases significantly when there are jumps.
- Volatility skyrocketed in 2008, so that the typical cap at 2.5 times volatility strike (not priced in prior to 2008) often turned out to be effective. Many hedge funds suffered horrible losses in 2008 from selling realised variance.
- Variance swaps can be replicated (in the absence of jumps) while volatility swaps cannot. Volatility swaps require a negative convexity adjustment.

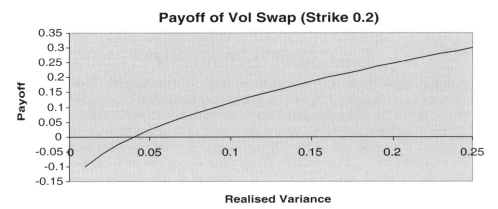

Figure 13.7   Payoff of a volatility swap with strike 0.2 as realised variance varies. The payoff of a volatility swap grows less than linearly as a function of realised variance. Hence, a negative convexity adjustment is necessary with respect to the variance swap strike.

13.2 OPTIONS ON VARIANCE SWAPS

As mentioned earlier, some variance swaps cap the payoff at 6.25 times the variance strike K (i.e. 2.5 times the volatility strike), notwithstanding actual realised variance. This means that the seller of variance has also bought a call option on a variance swap with strike $6.25K$.

Clearly, the payoff for a call option on a variance swap with strike K is

$$\frac{252}{T} \max(V - K, 0)$$

while that of a put option is

$$\frac{252}{T} \max(K - V, 0)$$

where V is realised variance, and T is expiry.

Options on variance swaps certainly can be used for speculation, and if an investor wishes to bet that variance will fall, it is much safer to buy a put option on a variance swap. Notwithstanding their simple descriptions, these instruments are difficult to price, and the seller of such options is undertaking huge risks. After all, volatility and hence variance are low under normal market conditions, but spike upwards sharply when markets crash. For example, as a result of the economic devastation from the credit crunch of 2008, realised volatility on the S&P 500 index jumped from 16.1% in 2007 to 40.9% in 2008, and for EUR/USD from 6.2% in 2007 to 13.7% in 2008. It appears that sellers of call options on variance swaps are selling insurance against the risk of a crash. So, it is not expected that such options will be cheap, especially going forward, since some institutions and even more hedge funds found themselves to have sold variance too cheaply in 2008.

Key Points

- Options on variance swaps exist, but are not cheap.
- Volatility spikes in times of crisis, so options on variance swaps are like insurance against a crash.

13.3 CORRELATION SWAPS

Like volatility, but for fewer products, correlation is of interest to hedgers. When you buy an option on a basket (as covered in Chapter 11), you are certainly not hoping that the assets comprising the basket will move in different directions. For a product involving multiple underlyings, correlation can have a significant impact on the price. Correlation affects the total volatility of a basket option. For a structured note with barriers based on the levels of interest rates and foreign exchange, correlation affects the probabilities of both rates and FX breaching the barriers. For an exotic equity product that considers the relative performance of several stocks (as covered in Chapter 12), correlation affects the likelihood of a stock that has performed better than another thus far, nevertheless yielding a lesser return over the period.

So, from a bank's perspective, correlation assumptions form a heavy part of the pricing of products with multiple underlyings. However, typically the complexity of such products means that only rather simple assumptions are made as to the correlations of the underlyings *vis-à-vis* each other. Moreover, outside the realm of pure foreign exchange (where for example volatilities of AUD/USD, USD/JPY and AUD/JPY can be used to hedge their correlations), there is generally no effective way to hedge correlation risk. So a product that allows a user to lock in her correlations can be of interest to the banks.

Consider our definition of returns as in Section 13.1. Define by A_t the value of another asset at time t, and similarly define the log-returns by

$$r_i = \log\left(\frac{A_{t_i}}{A_{t_{i-1}}}\right).$$

Then the realised correlation between the log-returns of the two assets is

$$\rho = \frac{\text{cov}(R, r)}{\sqrt{Vv}},$$

where

$$\text{cov}(R, r) = \frac{1}{N}\sum_{i=1}^{N} R_i r_i - \bar{R}\bar{r}$$

is the covariance between the log-returns of the assets,

$$V = \frac{1}{N}\sum_{i=1}^{N} R_i^2 - \bar{R}^2$$

is the realised variance of the first asset, and

$$v = \frac{1}{N} \sum_{i=1}^{N} r_i^2 - \bar{r}^2$$

is the realised variance of the second asset.

A correlation swap is an instrument that allows you to pay or receive realised correlation versus a pre-agreed strike. A correlation swap with strike K has a payoff at maturity T of

$$\rho - K$$

for the party that is buying correlation.

The cost of hedging PRDCs (described in Chapter 10) involves both rates and FX and their correlation *vis-à-vis* each other. Given widespread involvement in the PRDC market among dealers, there has recently been demand for a correlation swap based on USD/JPY and, say, the 10-year dollar swap rate with maturity 1 year, to lock in the correlation between interest rates and FX.

An investor can also seek to use a correlation swap to achieve returns based on certain market views. It is well known that in a crisis, correlations tend towards 1, since all assets tumble together. If an investor feels that this is not fully reflected in the strike of a correlation swap, then he can buy correlation. It should be remarked that correlations can only range between -1 and 1, so there is a natural limit to the risk of an investor in a correlation swap. However, **correlation swaps are contingent liability instruments and may not be suitable for most retail investors**.

Correlation swaps are relatively new, and there is no accepted methodology to price them. So they can be quite expensive, as banks try to price conservatively.

Similar to variance swaps, correlation swaps are disproportionately affected by jumps. So, if on one day two assets move strongly in opposite directions, then the realised correlation will fall significantly. Figure 13.8 shows the graphs of the Nikkei 225 and S&P 500 (whose

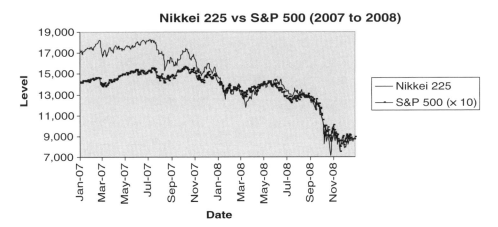

Figure 13.8 Levels of S&P 500 index versus Nikkei 225 index from 2007 to 2008. The S&P 500 and Nikkei 225 seem to fall together since the end of 2007. However, the realised correlation of daily log-returns is only 23.8%, whereas that for S&P 500 vs next day Nikkei 225 is 52.7%. In contrast, the correlation of weekly log-returns is 83.2%, which fits better with the picture.
Source: Bloomberg

values have been multiplied by 10 to enable the plot to be on the same scale). It is clear that they both plummeted significantly in 2008. However, the realised correlation of log-returns for 2007 is 9.7% and that for 2008 is only 23.8%! This is partly because Japan and the USA cover different time zones, and whereas longer term the markets seem to move together, events that affect the USA after the close of the Japanese markets will only be reflected in Japanese stock prices the next day. Curiously, since the Japanese market is more likely to take its cue from the performance of the US market the day before, taking observations of log-returns of S&P 500 versus next day Nikkei 225 yields a much higher 52.7%! Furthermore, if we take weekly observations (say each Friday), the correlation for 2008 would be a whopping 83.2%! **So that is a warning to be careful as to how exactly you define the terms of the correlation swap, since it can make a big difference**!

Key Points

- Correlation is important for hedging multi-underlying products.
- PRDC hedging can be assisted by correlation swaps on a swap rate versus USD/JPY.
- Correlations tend to go to 1 for risky assets in times of a crisis.
- Correlation measures are disproportionately affected by jumps.
- Weekly correlations tend to be much higher than daily correlations of returns across different stock indices.

14

Fund Derivatives

Many retail investors do not buy stocks directly but instead invest in either mutual funds or investment trusts. These investors might feel that they have neither the time nor the expertise to properly select suitable companies themselves, or they might not have enough capital to construct a diversified portfolio comprising a reasonable mix of stocks. As such, the professional fund management business grew as equity investments gained popularity with the public, not least aided by stories of impressive returns under some stellar fund managers.

Derivatives have been used by stock investors to engineer personally preferred payoff profiles. For example, a call option gives the investor the right but not obligation to buy a stock at a certain strike at expiry, so that her loss is limited if the stock price collapses. Can we have similar structures regarding mutual funds?

It turns out that to a limited extent, financial engineering on mutual funds is possible. In this rather brief chapter, we shall begin by explaining how the inability to sell short a fund severely restricts the range of products available. We shall then describe Constant Proportion Portfolio Insurance, which is a popular strategy for synthesising an option as pertains to mutual funds, but can carry significant risks to the investor. Finally, we shall explore some considerations pertaining to the funds that are chosen as the underlying of a derivative.

14.1 FUND DERIVATIVES PRODUCTS

Let us begin by defining mutual funds and investment trusts, and describing how they differ from ordinary assets. This difference explains why fund derivatives on offer tend to be of a more limited variety than derivatives on ordinary assets.

Mutual funds tend to be open-ended trusts, where new investors can subscribe for units at a price set by the fund manager, and the fund manager will use the monies to invest in new stocks. Investment trusts, on the other hand, are closed-ended companies, where the fund manager merely decides how to invest existing monies in the fund, and the proceeds can be traded like shares of a normal company.

It is not possible to borrow shares of mutual funds for purposes of short selling (i.e. selling units you do not own), since such shares do not exist. This means that **unlike a stock (or other asset), you can only sell units in mutual funds if you own them.**

Recall that in Sections 3.3 and 3.4 we discussed how financial institutions that sell derivatives are not concerned with whether the underlying moves up or down as they offset the risk by delta-hedging, i.e. by constantly maintaining an amount of stock equal to the delta of the derivative. Figures 14.1 and 14.2 show the Black–Scholes delta profiles of a European call and put option respectively.

Notice that delta is negative for a put, so that short selling is essential if a seller of a put is to hedge his exposure. **The inability to sell short units in a mutual fund means that typically put options on mutual funds will not be offered.** More generally, financial institutions will be reluctant to offer products that allow an investor to benefit from a decline in the price of a

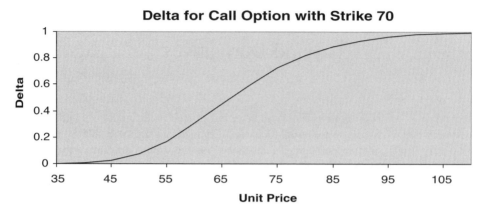

Figure 14.1   Delta of a call option as the unit price varies. The delta of a call is always non-negative (between 0 and 1).

unit of a mutual fund for this reason, so that typically the only derivatives available on mutual funds are those that reward an investor if the value of the fund rises.

Regarding the range of available products, we can have call options on baskets of funds (for even more diversification) since the payoff benefits if each fund in the basket rises in value. Options on the better of two funds can be problematic because it invariably requires selling short one of the funds, as part of hedging. For that reason, mountain range products (as covered in Chapter 12) are non-starters. The cliquet call, which is not a mountain range product, is fine however, since over each period, it benefits from the rise in value of the fund.

Furthermore, as we have discussed in Chapter 8, early termination can be used to enhance the yield of a structured note. There is no reason why callability, trigger or tarn features cannot be applied to limit the amount payable on a structured note involving funds. However, puttability can lead to scenarios where short selling is necessary, and hence is not generally suitable.

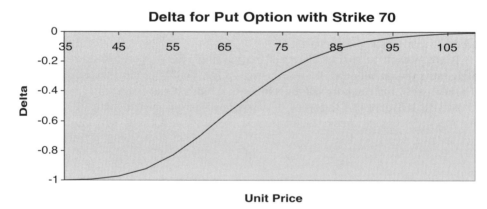

Figure 14.2   Delta of a put option as the unit price varies. The delta of a put is usually negative (between −1 and 0). This means that you have to sell short the underlying (i.e. borrow the underlying to sell it).

The difficulty in making available products that allow an investor to benefit from a falling value of a mutual fund, is due to an inability to sell short units of the fund. However, **if a financial institution has lots of clients that are buying products that benefit from a rise in value of the fund, it would have acquired lots of units of the fund for hedging purposes**. It follows that if it wanted to, **our financial institution could sell products that benefit from a decline in the value of the fund, provided that the aggregate hedging portfolio does not require selling short the fund**.

Table 14.1 presents the key differences between an option on a fund versus a normal stock option.

Table 14.1   Key differences between option on a fund versus a normal stock option.

Feature	Option on fund	Stock option
Payoff Types	Tend to be limited to bets on funds rising in value.	Payoffs linked to fall in value also possible.
Bets on Relative Performance Available	Usually not available.	Yes.
Liquidity	Not liquid.	High.

Key Points

- Mutual funds tend to be open-ended, with investors subscribing for new units. Investment trusts, on the other hand, manage existing monies.
- You cannot borrow shares of mutual funds for short selling. This restricts the range of products available since short selling is required to hedge some types of products (e.g. the put option).
- We can have call options on baskets of funds, cliquets on funds, but not "best of " products or mountain range products on funds.
- Early termination via callability, trigger or tarn features does not pose problems.

14.2   CONSTANT PROPORTION PORTFOLIO INSURANCE

Not all financial institutions offer fund derivatives, partly because of hedging difficulties (e.g. many funds tend to trade less frequently and in smaller volumes than large capitalised stocks and especially stock indices) and partly because the range of products available is more limited. Another reason for the reluctance to offer fund derivatives is that it is uncertain which volatility to use in pricing the derivative. For example, if a fund manager decides to temporarily sell his stocks and switch to bonds (in anticipation of a market crash), the fund's volatility would suddenly plummet.

But some institutions have instead offered clients synthetic derivative products, i.e. where the institution invests clients' monies in a certain style, in order to mimic certain payoff profiles.

Consider the simple call option. In Section 3.3 and 3.4, we discussed how the financial institution can dynamically replicate the payoff at expiry of a call option by trading in the underlying. This basically involves holding a certain amount of asset (equal to the delta of the option) at each point in time. If you look at the delta profile of a call option in the previous section (see Figure 14.1), you will see that the delta increases as the stock price increases. This means that the above strategy requires you to buy more asset as the asset price increases, and sell some amount of the asset as the asset price decreases. This buy high–sell low strategy determines how a financial institution prices an option. (Note that this strategy depends on model assumptions for the asset, since the option's delta is computed from the model.)

A synthetic call option is one where the financial institution implements the above strategy on behalf of the investor, rather than promising the actual payoff of a call option. There is a very big difference between this synthetic option and an ordinary call option. **In this synthetic option, the investor is taking the risk of the strategy not producing the same payoff as an option; in the case of an ordinary call option, the financial institution takes the risk that the hedge does not work.**

Constructing the Portfolio Insurance in Practice

Constant Proportion Portfolio Insurance (CPPI) is about ensuring that the value of the portfolio does not fall below a certain amount (termed the floor). (This is very similar to partial principal protection covered in Section 2.1 and referred to throughout the book.) Suppose you wish to ensure that the portfolio value at maturity $T = 5y$ is at least 90% of your principal. Let V_t be the value of your portfolio at time t and let $Z_{t,T}$ be the value of a zero-coupon bond with maturity T as seen at time t. Consider the following investment strategy:

If $V_t > 0.9 \times Z_{t,T}$, you maintain $\alpha \left(V_t - 0.9Z_{t,T} \right)$ units of the mutual fund;

$V_t \leq 0.9 \times Z_{t,T}$, you hold the entire portfolio in zero-coupon bonds,

where α is a constant, hence the name "Constant Proportion" in CPPI.

This is supposed to synthesise a call option on the fund, together with an assurance that you will get at least the floor (i.e. 90% of your principal) at maturity.

Who Bears the Different Types of Risk?

If asset prices follow a diffusion process, the above strategy will ensure that your portfolio will never fall in value to below the floor (i.e. $V_T > 0.9$ always). However, reality is not so kind. When a sudden market shock occurs, asset prices collapse, and the issuer will not be able to rebalance the portfolio quickly enough to avoid it falling below the floor. Furthermore, in times of a crash, liquidity dries up, and rebalancing is horribly expensive.

Issuers of notes with CPPI strategies invariably guarantee the floor; thus, the issuer bears the risk of price shocks causing the portfolio value to drop below the floor. This guarantee is the main risk to the issuer, since the investor otherwise fully bears the risk of the strategy not performing as expected.

If the portfolio value falls below the floor, the investor will no longer be invested in the underlying and, as such, will only be entitled to the floor (e.g. 90% of the principal) at maturity of the note (notwithstanding any potential future rises in the price of the underlying).

In this sense, **the worst case scenario for the investor is when the fund's value plunges shortly after investment in the note, and breaches the floor. The investor is then only entitled to a zero-coupon bond at maturity.** The payoff behaves like a barrier option which can be extinguished during its life by a fall in the value of the underlying.

The 1987 Stock Market Crash

As Figure 14.3 clearly shows, the S&P 500 index dropped by a whopping 20.5% on 19 October 1987 compared to the previous Friday. Clearly, any form of portfolio rebalancing was impossible, since it was very much a one-way market. In particular, hedging of put options required huge quantities of stocks to be sold as the markets dropped. This definitely exacerbated the fall in the S&P, and it is doubtful if it did the hedgers any good ultimately. The 1987 stock market crash also gave portfolio insurance a horrible reputation. Issuers of CPPI would have suffered huge losses by having to make good their guarantee on the floor, while being unable to cut their exposure to the falling market.

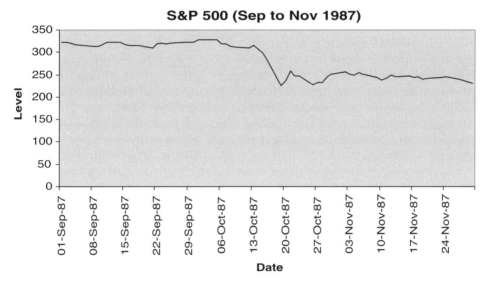

Figure 14.3 S&P 500 index from September to November 1987. The sharp 20.5% fall was on 19 October. Under such market conditions, any model-mandated delta-hedging is impossible.
Source: Bloomberg

A point made earlier in this section cannot be overstressed: **A CPPI is different from a call insofar as the investor now bears the risk of the payoff being worse than the model would suggest. However, as the issuer guarantees that the portfolio value will remain above some floor**, that at least should give some solace to an investor.

Key Points

- A strategy of holding a delta amount of a stock replicates the payoff of a call option, but this is subject to reality corresponding to model assumptions.
- Constant Proportion Portfolio Insurance (CPPI) is where the issuer executes a strategy of holding a constant multiplier of portfolio value in excess of a minimum (termed the floor), so as to mimic an option payoff.
- The investor bears the risk of a CPPI strategy not performing in accordance with model assumptions. However, the issuer guarantees that the portfolio value will remain above

a floor. When this occurs, the investor is entitled to only the floor at maturity, since he is no longer invested.
- The S&P 500 dropped 20.5% on 19 October 1987. Clearly, any strategy relying on dynamic hedging would fare horribly in an event like this.

14.3   THE IDEAL UNDERLYING FUND

The ideal fund for use as an underlying in a fund derivative or a CPPI strategy is one that is reasonably liquid, where volumes are high and bid–offer spreads are small. After all, **hedging considerations will require frequent rebalancing of the portfolio**. It would not be good if hedging activity can drive up the price of units in a thinly traded mutual fund. In practice, liquidity and cost considerations will mean that hedging is much less frequent than for derivatives in other assets (e.g. stocks or FX). Perhaps this occurs weekly or even monthly.

Since investment trusts are traded like other stocks, they might be easier candidates for hedging. It might also be possible to short these trusts, and hence create derivatives that benefit an investor if the fund's value declines. However, their liquidity must be taken into account in deciding if they are suitable candidates for use as the underlyings of derivatives.

Currently, funds of funds are also available. These are funds that invest in other mutual funds and investment trusts, rather than stocks and bonds directly. They allow an investor exposure to different popular funds, while not being completely tied to the performance of any one fund. From the perspective of its use as an underlying in a derivative, a fund of mutual funds requires very little different consideration from a normal mutual fund. Perhaps, one would expect volatility to be lower due to the diversification effect, but that is all.

Hedge funds are also seen as an interesting avenue for investors to explore, as they tend to focus on alpha (i.e. absolute returns not correlated to the broader stock market). However, **hedge funds make poor candidates as underlyings for derivatives**. As they are not always open to all investors and can be restricted to only a small subset, liquidity can be an issue. Furthermore, they tend to have restrictive investment conditions, e.g. tying in capital for certain periods, and perhaps even restrictions on withdrawal, which might be activated when the fund's value plummets. This means that rebalancing your exposure to a hedge fund is likely to be very inconvenient. Whether funds of hedge funds are suitable for use as underlyings of derivatives depends on the liquidity considerations and withdrawal restrictions.

Key Points

- To be suitable for use as an underlying of a fund derivative or CPPI strategy, a fund should be liquid with high volumes and small bid–offer spreads.
- Investment trusts might be easier candidates since they are traded like stocks.
- Funds of funds can also be used as underlyings for fund derivatives.
- Hedge funds are generally not suitable for use in fund derivatives, since they tend to be illiquid and might have restrictions on withdrawals.

15

The Products Post-2008

In the preceding chapters I have given the reader an overview of a wide range of structured products in interest rates, equities and foreign exchange. Such products thrived during the golden days of derivatives, which ended sometime in late 2007. Since then, the credit crisis has devastated the financial markets and the wider economy, and probably altered the investment landscape permanently.

In this final chapter, it is perhaps worth speculating on which of the above structured products might survive the credit tsunami, with the increased regulations to follow and the risk aversion of both financial institutions and investors. We can also, perhaps, consider what lessons might be learned and incorporated in some of these structured products for the future. Certainly, the credit aspects of these trades also deserve more consideration and so we shall explore them briefly.

This chapter is, by its nature, speculative. I profess no special insight into the future and can only hope my thoughts will not be proved too far wrong as events unfold in the years ahead.

15.1 THE PRODUCTS LIKELY TO SURVIVE THE CREDIT CRUNCH

Hopefully, by now, you will have seen that derivatives span a very diverse range, and that not all derivatives are dangerous. Considering that derivatives have been with us in some form or other for decades, if not centuries, it is very unlikely that they will die out any time soon. With investors and financial institutions nursing heavy losses, especially in the credit arena from products they never understood, I believe the trend in the foreseeable future is towards simpler and more liquid products. Corporates will be less willing to choose cheap hedges that do not fully protect them; investors will be less keen to make a headlong rush for yield, heedless of risk; and financial institutions will be more reluctant to compete aggressively for deals on esoteric products that they do not fully comprehend.

Consequently, the less exotic and more entrenched of the derivatives discussed in the book are likely to survive the storm. However, it is quite possible that some of the more esoteric instruments dreamed of in the days of excesses for financial engineering may never again see the light of day. Let us now consider the various instruments in turn.

Forwards

As discussed in Chapter 3, a forward contract is an agreement to buy or sell an asset at a certain future date at a predetermined price. Clearly, there will always be parties who are interested in locking in the price for an asset (e.g. a producer locking in the cost of raw materials), so forwards are here to stay.

One stumbling block is the potential for interference by regulators. In particular, in late 2008, a temporary ban on short selling of various financial stocks was imposed to relieve pressure on the battered financial community. But if a client enters into a short position in a forward contract with an institution, the institution needs to sell short the underlying to hedge. (Actually, any derivative that pays out more if an asset declines in price needs to be hedged by selling short the underlying asset.) Therefore, any ban on short selling automatically affects the ability to make available short positions in forward contracts. It is, however, unlikely that permanent bans on short selling will be imposed, as regulators are aware of its importance in the functioning of the market.

With increased concern regarding counterparty risk, there may be a switch to greater usage of futures where possible, since these are exchange traded and the exchange (backed by a collection of clearing member financial institutions) is the central counterparty to all contracts. Nevertheless, the daily settlement of futures contracts in exchanges can be of concern to some hedgers, as perhaps they prefer to only have liabilities that match their own cashflow profiles, e.g. at the date they have the asset to sell.

Vanilla Options

As mentioned in Chapter 3, a call option gives the holder the right to buy the underlying at the strike at expiry. A put option gives the holder the right to sell the underlying at the strike. Such instruments allow the holder to benefit from the performance of an underlying (up or down), with limited risk if her view proves wrong.

Calls and puts are the essence of financial engineering, as they allow for an asymmetric payout. Considering that many investors seek to protect their principal (via investment in some sort of zero-coupon bond), a somewhat more leveraged (but protected) use of the remaining value of their investment must be made to earn any meaningful return. Hence, these products will always be in demand.

Being among the most basic of derivatives (and not of too many varieties), short- to medium-term (i.e. < 2 years maturity) calls and puts on bonds, stock indices, major stocks and major FX pairs against the dollar are liquidly traded in exchanges, so there is not too much to worry about counterparty risk. If current concerns about counterparty risk persist over time, it might just mean that there will be a shift to exchange trading of more of such products. For example, at least prior to the credit crunch, the FX market has been heavily dominated by over-the-counter (rather than exchange-traded) transactions. Or, another possibility is for trades that were initially done between two institutions to be thereafter transferred onto a futures exchange, which now becomes the central counterparty to both sides of the trade. This idea is discussed further in Section 15.3.

The average-rate Asian option is also here to stay. As Chapter 3 describes, the payoff is based on the average value of the underlying over the period. To the extent that extreme events are less likely to affect the average than the value on the expiry date itself, Asian options are less volatile than European options and may be preferable in some cases. They are particularly popular in commodities.

Barriers

As discussed in Chapter 4, barriers are essentially a way of buying options on the cheap. For example, knockout barriers are just calls or puts that extinguish if the underlying breaches some level. Due to heightened volatility and huge market moves in 2008 following the credit crisis, lots of barriers have knocked out, leaving their holders without the options they thought they had.

To that extent, lessons should be learned that barriers are cheap for a reason, i.e. they can be extinguished and that possibility should not be forgotten. If you were looking for a hedge, a barrier is less likely to be suitable. After all, suppose you want to protect yourself from a decline in EUR/USD to below 1.25. You can buy a put with strike 1.25. Suppose, instead, you had a put with an additional up barrier of 1.4. If EUR/USD hit 1.401, and then fell back below 1.25, your put protection is gone. For this reason, at least in the near future, I expect less use of barriers in hedging by corporates.

If you were a speculator, however, such a contract may not be too bad, in that if EUR/USD hit 1.4, you might no longer expect it to fall below 1.25. So, the issue is not the product, but what you really want from it, and what you can afford to go wrong. Thus, barriers, at least in FX, are likely to continue to be in some demand.

Quantoes

With the prevailing teachings on a diversified portfolio, there is definitely interest in investment in foreign assets. To the extent that an investor may be interested in exposure to foreign assets but not the foreign exchange risk, quantoes will remain useful. After all, Chapter 5 describes how a quanto is just settlement of a foreign asset in the domestic currency without the prevailing FX conversion.

The Plain Vanilla Swap

As discussed in Chapter 6, this basic instrument has two legs, one paying a pre-agreed fixed rate and another paying a floating rate, based on some index (e.g. Libor). Considering that there will always be institutions that need to manage their cashflows (e.g. lock in a fixed rate of borrowing or return), swaps will always be relevant.

The credit crisis of 2008 has seen Libor rates surpassing government yields by a substantial amount (e.g. over 3% for 3-month dollar Libor in September 2008) for a short period. After all, Libor is the average of rates at which major banks borrow from each other. And in the immediate aftermath of the default of Lehman Brothers, the fear of further bank failures was extremely high and banks too were hoarding cash to stave off their own liquidity crises.

Clearly, counterparties that make payments tied to Libor were adversely affected by the sky-high Libor rates *vis-à-vis* government paper (whatever their own credit ratings). So, one can only speculate that, perhaps, government bill/bond yields (plus an appropriate spread) might be used as a benchmark for some new contracts as opposed to Libor.

Alternatively, consider the Overnight Interest Swap (OIS), which reflects overnight borrowing. Where two counterparties (typically financial institutions) have a collateral agreement with daily mark-to-market and settlement, positions are naturally funded overnight. As of early 2009, the credit crunch has led to liquidity being at a premium so that 3-month borrowing costs much more than overnight borrowing. If a corporate is perhaps interested in doing a swap, but prefers not to be caught up in future liquidity crises, then it may use the OIS rate plus a spread (rather than Libor) as a benchmark for floating rate payments.

In any event, the swap will exist in some form or other.

Constant Maturity Swaps

These are basically instruments where a floating long-term rate (e.g. 10-year swap rate) is paid periodically (e.g. every 3 months). As discussed in Chapter 6, they are typically synthesised by a portfolio of swaptions.

I very much suspect that the Constant Maturity Swap (CMS) is here to stay. After all, historically the yield curve has tended to be upward sloping. This is especially so when interest rates are low. Japan has had more than a decade of zero interest rates (at the short end), with the long end between 2% to just under 3%. So, why receive a short-term rate if you can receive a long-term rate?

Traditionally, receiving a long-term rate requires taking the fixed leg of a swap, but if the level of rates overall increases you will be hurt. The CMS, however, allows you to receive a long-term floating rate, so that you can not only benefit from long-term rates being higher than short-term rates, but can also participate in overall increases (or decreases) in future interest rates.

This would sound especially attractive in the current environment (post-2008) where short-term rates have been kept low (near zero for developed economies) to stimulate growth in an unprecedented economic crisis. Many developed economies are looking a bit like Japan in 2000 some years after its stock market and real estate crash. Figures 15.1 and 15.2 show the US and UK swap curves, respectively, as of 17 February 2009. Also, as many people found it unattractive in 2000 to lock in to 30-year government bond yields of under 3% in Japan, do you really find it attractive to lock in to current 30-year US government yields of under 3.5% (as at the beginning of 2009)?

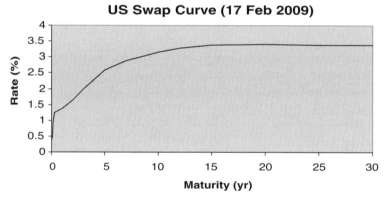

Figure 15.1   US swap curve as of 17 February 2009. The yield curve is very upward sloping, with the very short end under 1% and the long end just over 3%. Overall rates are very low.
Source: Bloomberg

We could end up with the Japanese scenario of low interest rates and an upward-sloping curve over a long horizon. Alternatively, since various governments are considering spending their way out of the recession, we could end up with runaway inflation and rates would rise steeply. Typically, as seen in the early 1980s, short-term rates rise sharply and the curve gets inverted. Such a scenario would badly hurt holders of long-term bonds. If you had a 30-year bond with a 5% annual coupon, how would you feel if 30-year rates went up to 12%? On the other hand, in a CMS you will benefit if 30-year rates skyrocket to 12%. (Of course, if the curve gets inverted, the receiver of 3-month Libor might get an 18% coupon, but if the curve remains steeply upward sloping, a 3% 30-year rate is better than a 0.5% 3-month rate.)

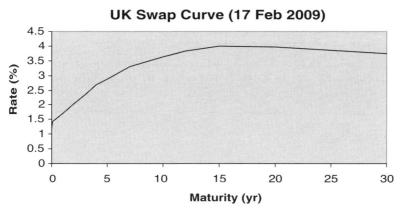

Figure 15.2   UK swap curve as of 17 February 2009. UK rates are at a historic low, at least in the short end. The curve is also steeply upward sloping.
Source: Bloomberg

As discussed, CMS products are likely to remain in demand and, similarly, spreads on CMS are likely to be in demand. After all, if the yield curve is to remain upward sloping, is it not a good idea to bet on the 10-year vs 2-year spread? Remember investors seek yield, and you need to be creative to get yield, especially in a market where 30-year bonds yield 3% to 4%.

It should be noted that volatilities have increased significantly since the credit crisis in 2008, and since CMS products have to be synthesised with swaptions, they are somewhat more costly. As such, demand for these products has to be seen in the light of their increased costs versus the desirable payoff profiles.

Another caveat is that with the huge spread between Libor and government yields, there may be concerns about the effect of credit and liquidity on the current CMS rate. After all, swap rates are computed from Libor rates. Alternatively, Constant Maturity Treasuries could be utilised. This is basically where the yield on a long-term government bond (e.g. 10-year bond) is used as the reference rather than the swap rate.

Range Accruals

As discussed in Chapter 7, the payout of a range accrual is based on the number of days that a variable stays within some range. This is a very useful concept since your payout is less random if it does not depend totally on whether the S&P 500 index is above 900 on a certain expiry date. Investors (and financial institutions) typically prefer less volatility, all things being equal.

Perhaps people will try not to introduce too many complexities, e.g. where the payoff is based on different underlyings to those used to determine if the range condition is satisfied. This is not a given, but it can be said that in the more risk-averse environment post-2008, there will be greater emphasis on trading or investing only in products that one understands.

Early Termination

Early termination (Chapter 8) is basically about protected selling of optionality (i.e. where the investor possesses the underlying or some other options). In that sense, it is a fundamental concept to structured products. If you want higher yields, selling optionality is one of the ways to get it. Callability, triggers and tarns have proved rather popular methods of early termination, and they will probably be utilised in the years ahead.

Most investors are after all seeking a higher yield. If notes are structured to give the investor a big initial coupon, she may be happy for the note to terminate early, as she is then free to reinvest again under prevailing market conditions.

Pathwise Accumulation

This class of instruments might be our first dodo-to-be in the list. In plain, they are too complex for their own good. The skyline, as described in Chapter 9, involves coupons that are linked to previous coupons. The coupons increase over time, provided that some condition is met (e.g. Euribor stays under 4%) but otherwise fall to 0, and this is the new reference coupon. That means that one bad coupon can significantly affect future coupons in the deal.

An investor may well have strong views about the path of interest rates, and may be willing to take a bet like this if it is sufficiently cheap. However, with significant losses to both financial institutions and investors in the credit arena in 2008, certainly there is less appetite by financial institutions and investors to take risks that they do not properly understand. So, perhaps such products will not sit well with the new theme of simplicity.

Power Reverse Dual Currencies (PRDCs)

The carry trade stimulated by significantly lower yen rates than dollar rates has spawned this rather interesting product (Chapter 10). It is basically a bet that USD/JPY (or AUD/JPY) will remain at about spot, rather than yen appreciating to levels corresponding to forward FX rates. Some of the economic rationales (at least insofar as USD/JPY is concerned) remain, e.g. Japan does not want a strong yen *vis-à-vis* the dollar and prefers to facilitate export-driven economic growth.

Nevertheless, recent yen strengthening (USD/JPY has dropped to 90 by the end of 2008 against 115 in 2006, AUD/JPY has dropped to 60 by end of 2008 against 90 in 2006) has hurt investors badly (via lower or zero coupons for the foreseeable future). Furthermore, if such investors had redemption strikes in the deals, they might only get reduced principals back at expiry (depending on the FX rate at that time), especially since early termination is unlikely if yen remains strong. Banks are hurting even more, insofar as PRDCs involve selling options on dollar calls and implied volatilities have skyrocketed, and the cost of hedging has led to horrendous losses in a one-way market.

The outlook for PRDCs is bleak, as the drop in long-term dollar interest rates to about 3% means that the interest rate differential (versus yen) is much lower, making it difficult to establish a profitable business in new PRDC issuance. Basically, when USD/JPY was 115 and the 30-year USD/JPY forward was 50 (in 2006), a strike of 70 to 100 would be feasible. With USD/JPY at 90 and 30-year USD/JPY forwards at 53 in early 2009 (see Figure 15.3), the strikes would have to be within 65 to 75 (and possibly with much lower leverage).

AUD/JPY PRDCs are also dead, as they were a bet on the strength of the Australian dollar which was popular when commodity prices were skyrocketing in 2006 to 2007. With sharp declines in the prices of commodities in 2008, and AUD/USD dropping from 0.95 to about 0.65, this bet seems rather rash in hindsight.

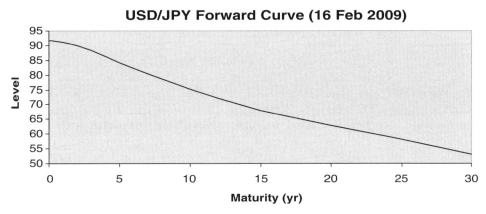

Figure 15.3 USD/JPY forward curve as of 16 February 2009. Notice how spot USD/JPY is 92 while 30-year forward USD/JPY is 53. While the forward curve is still downward sloping, it is less steep than in 2007 and much of 2008.
Source: Bloomberg

Nevertheless, it is not inconceivable that other FX bets against forwards *à la* PRDCs might emerge. Most developed economies have slashed rates to almost zero by the end of 2008. Developing economies, however, may have high interest rates (over 10%). Suppose you expect the Brazilian real not to depreciate in line with its forward, can you not have a USD/BRL PRDC? I admit that this is a very different instrument, insofar as USD/BRL is not expected to display the same stability as USD/JPY, and there are no policy considerations on keeping the Brazilian real strong or the US dollar weak. But if you wish to do a carry trade (i.e. borrow dollars and invest in the Brazilian real), why not go for PRDCs which are likely to involve more protection of your principal. In this case, the huge interest rate differential will justify a shorter expiry (e.g. 5 years). The problem now is to find a willing issuer. And please refrain from the redemption strike unless you are really greedy.

Baskets and Hybrids

Baskets, too, will likely retain their appeal. After all, a basket offers diversification. Correlations tend to increase in times of crisis. (It would be nice if investors finally learned that diversification is not a silver bullet, and they should still monitor their risks.) It is nevertheless still safer to have one's returns tied to a collection of stocks than to the vagaries of the fortunes of one company. And, for that matter, it may not be bad to have a basket of bonds, stocks and commodities, especially if they are consistent with one's views.

The more complex hybrids may fall prey to the desire for simplicity, but as a whole the need for yield enhancement will probably ensure that some of them survive.

Equity Exotics

Equity products will always feature heavily in the offerings of structured products. After all, the typical investor is familiar mainly with stocks and bonds, and stocks are seen as the primary means of achieving an above-inflation return in the long run. But in markets where losses in stock investments are a very real possibility, perhaps instruments that offer upside participation with limited downside risks will be much sought after. The plain vanilla option is a simple example.

Consider the case where you expect a stock market rally, but prior to that there could be further declines. Suppose the FtSe 100 index is now at 4,150. You buy a 2-year European call option on FtSe with strike 4,900. If, after year 1, FtSe drops to 3,700, it would be quite unlikely to exceed 4,900 at the end of year 2.

In that sense, a cliquet (as featured in Chapter 12) is a useful alternative. A cliquet gives you an option on the return over each period. Suppose the FtSe is 4,300 in year 2. The return would be $\frac{3,700}{4,150} - 1 = -10.8\%$ in year 1 and $\frac{4,300}{3,700} - 1 = 16.2\%$ in year 2. In this case, you are likely to still get a coupon in year 2, dependent on the strike of the cliquet. Cliquets are likely to remain popular in these distressed market conditions, although with the high volatilities in equities (and high forward volatilities), they are likely to be expensive for many investors.

On the other hand, some of the more esoteric of the exotic equity products may not survive. Recall the Himalaya: (1) you have a basket of stocks; (2) in each period, you record the best return and throw it out of the basket; (3) you consider the remaining stocks in the next period and do the same; and (4) continue until maturity, where the coupon is based on the averaged returns. It sounds much too convoluted for an investor to understand its worth, and banks can also possibly get the pricing seriously wrong as there is significant correlation dependence, to say the least. Apart from it being cheap some years ago, it is not clear why anyone would want to do it.

Other products, such as the Everest which is very long-dated (typically over 10 years) and involves a huge basket, may also lose popularity, since clients may not want to be exposed to counterparty risk with financial institutions over too long a horizon. Banks, too, may become wary of pricing complex products with too many underlyings over long horizons. (Too many items could be overlooked or simply go wrong.)

Variance Swaps

Many hedge funds entered into variance swaps (Chapter 13) where they were paying realised variance, since historically (i.e. prior to the devastation of 2008) the fair-value strike was typically higher than the expected value of realised variance. However, it is probable that most sellers of realised variance lost a lot of money as volatilities skyrocketed in 2008 (and buyers, of course, profited). Variance swaps have proved useful in transferring volatility risk, and as such would be in demand. However, institutions and hedge funds have realised that they have not always understood these products properly and some may reconsider their involvement. To that extent, there is likely to be a reduction in the market for variance swaps. The market for the more esoteric options on variance swaps is likely to shrink even more dramatically, since many of the players who got badly burned are not likely to return.

Fund Derivatives

As long as the general public does not lose faith in equities, there will be demand for mutual funds and investment trusts. And of course, fund derivatives would be of interest. Some investors may lose interest in fund managers and the strategies they pursue, since many have failed to outperform the falling market despite the fees charged. These investors might instead prefer to invest in exchange-traded funds that track a broad market index (e.g. STOXX 50). To that extent there will be a corresponding drop in the demand for fund derivatives.

Concerns on product complexity will not be an issue, since most fund derivatives are among the simpler of equity derivatives. Whether Constant Proportion Portfolio Insurance (CPPI) remains popular is another question since risk-averse investors might prefer to let a financial institution take the risk of the strategy not performing as per model assumptions. Then again, the rather high levels of volatility in the market, in the wake of the credit crisis of 2008, might induce some investors to take their chances rather than pay over-the-top for option protection.

Key Points

- Derivatives, as a species, are likely to be around for a while, although certain subspecies might not survive.
- There will always be a demand for the simpler products, e.g forwards, options, barriers, quantoes, swaps.
- Various products and features will continue to exist because there is a compelling reason regarding yield enhancement and risk tailoring, e.g. CMS, range accruals, early termination, cliquets, baskets, simple hybrids, variance trades and fund derivatives.
- Complex products that involve fairly sophisticated bets might be less favoured in a world of more discerning investors, e.g. skylines, snowballs, some mountain range products. The survival of other products might depend on the economic environment (e.g. USD/JPY PRDCs are at risk if dollar rates remain low).

15.2   INCORPORATING SOME LESSONS LEARNED

Of course, after every crisis, there will be recriminations and reflections on what should be done differently. In a crisis of the magnitude of the credit crisis of 2008, perhaps there might even be arguments to redesign the entire financial landscape. In this case, derivatives have been severely tarnished. But I should remind the reader that derivatives are very different from each other, and the crisis really involved extremely complex credit products (e.g. ABS CDOs, CDOs squared, sub-prime CDOs) that were poorly understood, but nevertheless heavily oversold. At its heart, it was an issue of easy credit, which could have spawned an albeit lesser crisis in the absence of derivatives.

Simplifying Products

Many lessons could be learned (even as pertains non-credit products), and one of them is about the need to understand the products with which we are dealing. The nice thing is that the term sheets for most structured products in interest rates, equities and foreign exchange, are only a few pages long (say under 15), and an investor is likely to read them. (In contrast, prospectuses for Collateralised Debt Obligations in the credit world tend to run up to a few hundred pages, and hence may not receive the same level of scrutiny.)

An investor does not need to be able to price a product to understand its risks and rewards. People have tended to be too focused on whether they have got a good price, as opposed to the potential losses from unforeseen events. Suppose you bought a reverse knockout option which gives you the right in 1 year to sell GBP/USD for 1.7, but in the event that GBP/USD drops below 1.4 at any point, the option expires worthless. The idea of the knockout was to make the option cheaper. Whether you got a fair price for it is not as important as understanding that if GBP/USD drops to 1.401, you would make $1.7 - $1.401 = 0.299, whereas if it drops to \$1.399, you would get 0! (To be fair, reverse knockouts usually have rebates so that you will not have such an extreme scenario in practice.) If you are comfortable with such a risk, go for it. But it is essential to understand that such a risk is there if you invest in the structure.

I would expect that some products would be simplified in the years ahead, insofar as investors would only invest in products they understand. Consider the PRDC from before. Many such structures had a redemption strike which means that the principal repaid will depend on the FX rate at expiry if the deal does not terminate early. The idea for this was again to get an increased yield, but investors ended up subjected to exchange rate risk on their principal in addition to low or non-existent coupons for the life of the bond. In the light of this, perhaps such features will meet much more investor scrutiny for other products.

Redefining Benchmarks

Libor and Euribor have been the benchmarks for interest rates for well over a decade. During the 1990s and all the way until 2007, interbank lending rates have tended to be a small stable spread on top of government rates. Until 2008, banks have tended to be willing to quote rates for bespoke maturities, whereas government yields are dependent on new issuance of government debt, which is not always liquidly available. Hence, a benchmark based on AA credit rating and taken as some average of banks' lending rates seemed sensible.

However, with the implosion of Lehman Brothers, the interbank markets froze and Libor/ Euribor spreads above government yields skyrocketed (to over 3% for 3-month dollar lending in September 2008, and over 1.5% for 3-month euro lending in December 2008) for a short period. This certainly may affect confidence in Libor or Euribor. Notwithstanding that Libor represents the cost of funding by banks, would a client be happy to pay significantly elevated short-term rates on a floating leg of a swap just because interbank lending has seized up so that Libor is no longer a reliable reference? After all, the fixed rate they were due in the swap (agreed upon at possibly better times) clearly would not reflect a deterioration in the credit situation.

One alternative would be to go for government yields (plus the appropriate spread) as the benchmark rate. In that sense, swap rates would be replaced by government bond yields and Constant Maturity Swap products would effectively be replaced by Constant Maturity Treasury products. I am not predicting an end to Libor or Euribor, but I think some clients would be interested in a different benchmark (e.g. government yields) when the dust from the credit crisis finally settles. Another alternative might be to use rates on Overnight Interest Swaps.

Key Points

- The credit crisis may provide some impetus to simplify products. At least, investors might be less willing to invest in structures that they do not understand.
- Certain benchmarks might have to be revisited. For example, Libor or Euribor has been the benchmark for floating rate resets. However, a crisis in interbank lending starting in September 2008 may make market participants consider if there are alternatives that are less sensitive to changes in liquidity or credit conditions.

15.3   CREDIT CONSIDERATIONS

There are also various modifications that might potentially be made to structured products in the light of credit concerns that have come to the forefront as a result of the multiple bank implosions and bailouts in 2008.

Frequent Coupons and Shorter Maturities

Various structured notes (especially in the equity arena) do not pay periodic coupons but only pay the principal plus a market-linked coupon at maturity (typically up to 5 years in the future). Perhaps a better approach for the investor would be to receive frequent coupons (say quarterly or semi-annually) based on the performance over the appropriate period. Of course, a default by the issuer prior to repayment of the principal will still hurt, but at least some of the loss would be mitigated, especially for very long-dated notes. For example, if 30-year rates were 3%, the current value of a $100 principal zero-coupon bond payable at maturity is only $100 \times \frac{1}{1.03^{30}} = \$41.20$.

On that same note, perhaps investors should reconsider the appropriateness of very long-dated structured notes. In interest rates, 30-year notes are common, and PRDCs are typically 30-year notes, too. There could be economic reasons for such notes (e.g. the shape of the forward curve) but perhaps with the heightened concerns on counterparty credit, shorter maturities (e.g. up to 10 years) might nevertheless be preferable in the majority of cases. Rather curiously, some institutions naturally need long-dated investments because they have long-dated liabilities (e.g. pension funds), so it would not be sensible to discontinue long-dated structured notes. However, some mechanism to ensure that counterparty default does not threaten payments is essential in these circumstances.

Zero-Coupon Government Bonds

Traditionally, governments have been seen to be risk-free in their local currency debts, since they have the option of printing money (however politically unpalatable). The credit crisis of 2008 has led to significant spreads for insuring government debt of even G7 countries (e.g. 0.3% to 0.5% for the USA in November 2008, and over 1% for the UK in December 2008). This suggests that the market fears potential defaults nonetheless. Even so, it is not clear what one can buy that is safer than government debt, so we might have to just hope for the best, and treat government debt as risk-free.

We discussed earlier how principal protection can be achieved by buying a zero-coupon bond for less than its principal (with the remainder left to fund our structured coupons). Of course, if the zero-coupon bond were that of any non-government issuer, there is a non-negligible risk of default. Clearly, Lehman-issued "principal-protected" structured notes failed to repay the principal when Lehman Brothers defaulted, much to the chagrin of investors who misunderstood the idea. Yet, true principal protection is still possible if a zero-coupon government bond is purchased. (Or a compromise might be a zero-coupon bond from a highly-rated corporate that is considered to be recession-proof.) This would admittedly leave less money to invest in the structured coupons, but if you are thinking of investing in a 30-year structured note (as in our pension fund), that may be a price worth paying for the security of the principal repayment.

It may be necessary to have some mechanism for separating the government bonds from the issuer's assets (e.g. via a trust) to ensure that they are ring-fenced for the investor in the event of the issuer's default. Actually, the investor might be able to hold these zero-coupon government bonds and just get the financial institution to sell the structured coupons.

More Exchange-Traded or Exchange-Cleared Products

Of course, counterparty risk can be mitigated by having more exchange-traded products. Basically, the clearing house of a futures exchange serves as a central counterparty (backed by clearing member financial institutions) to any trade undertaken. Daily settlement based on traded prices of the underlying for or against a position holder ensures that, in the worst scenario, the amount owed by any party is kept to a few business days' worth of market swings.

In contrast, if you had a structured note, payments are only made at the appropriate coupon date or may even only occur at maturity. An argument against exchange-traded products is that the over-the-counter market provides more flexibility to tailor the product to the exact maturities and position sizes sought by the investor. However, the counterparty risk argument far outweighs this flexibility (especially for liquid products).

Perhaps in the simple case, a structured note could be designed so that it comprises a zero-coupon government bond and an exchange-traded option, with the bank holding these on trust for the investor. This is too simplistic for the majority of structured products, but it is not inconceivable that more use could be made of exchange-traded products in the design of future structured products.

As of early 2009, the majority of deals (by volume) in interest rates, foreign exchange, equities and credit are traded over-the-counter (OTC) rather than in futures exchanges. With strong pressure from governments for better management of counterparty risks and more transparency, various futures exchanges (e.g. Eurex, the CME Group, NYSE Liffe, Intercontinental Exchange) have recently introduced the service of clearing OTC products.[1] The idea is as follows: As before, contracts are done privately between the two institutions, except that thereafter the deals are transferred onto the clearing house of the futures exchange (for a charge). Basically, the exchange becomes the central counterparty to both sides of the trade, being responsible for making good performance. To protect itself from its potential losses in the event of default, the exchange imposes margin requirements on both parties. These margins are calculated on the basis of the potential 1-day move in the asset, and open positions are settled daily on the basis of mark-to-market values of similar exchange-traded deals.

This approach allows clients to benefit from the flexibility of privately negotiated deals, while having a very robust mechanism to almost completely eliminate counterparty risk and guarantee performance of the transaction. As it stands, the facility is offered on only a very limited number of products. In fact, this idea has been driven mainly in view of the demand by regulators to move a sizeable proportion of the unregulated Credit Default Swap market onto regulated exchanges. In the near future, however – having been given time to germinate – exchange clearing of OTC trades is likely to be used on an industrial scale for a large number of vanilla OTC products, since the benefits of counterparty risk management, particularly for

---

[1] I was aided in my description of exchange clearing of OTC products by a GARP event in April 2009 that I attended on Migrating Counterparty Risk in OTC Derivatives, with Byron Baldwin from Eurex and Samuel Ely from HSBC Securities Services presenting.

mid- and long-dated deals, are compelling. This is especially so with the hindsight of the devastation on financial institutions wrought by the credit crunch of 2008.

Of course, if a client prefers not to have to worry about cashflow issues resulting from daily settlement on a deal based on mark-to-market, she will still be able to continue doing traditional OTC deals. Since such clients will inevitably exist, some deals will always be traded with no involvement of the futures exchanges.

Puttability

A puttable note allows an investor to sell it back to the issuer. Based on our earlier discussion of optionality, this is clearly a valuable feature. Whereas callability makes a note cheaper, puttability makes it more expensive. Since investors typically want higher yields, this seems to work against that theme.

Nevertheless, it is possible to have a deep out-of-the-money put, say at 70% of notional. This may not be attractive for an investor in normal circumstances. However, should the issuer default, losses are likely to be far greater than 30% of notional. As such, this can serve as a last line of defence, so that an issuer can demand repayment of 70% of the notional value of a note when the issuer is teetering on the brink of default.

Break Clause

A break clause is basically something that allows the investor to seek repayment of the value of the structured note in exchange for terminating it. It is possible to make it triggerable by certain events (e.g. ratings downgrade of the issuer or increase in Credit Default Swap spread of the issuer), or always available.

To make this possible, it is necessary to seek third party valuers to determine a fair value, perhaps a collection of financial institutions as specified in the terms of the contract (subject to possible replacement if necessary). Clearly, the issuer would not like this, as it may value the note differently from these other institutions. One possibility is for some penalty to be applied should the investor exercise this clause (e.g. repayment is 5% to 10% less than fair value). This should also serve to protect the investor in the event of imminent default of the issuer, although I suspect the simplicity of the puttability feature might make it more compelling.

Key Points

- Having structured notes pay coupons frequently (e.g. quarterly) rather than just at maturity would help to reduce credit risk, as would offering shorter-dated structures. Some institutions (e.g. pension funds) have need for long-dated assets.
- Zero-coupon government bonds can be used to ensure that the investor gets back her principal at expiry, although that leaves less value for structured coupons.
- Notwithstanding flexibility considerations, making more use of exchange traded products can alleviate credit concerns. Exchange clearing of OTC products is a new concept that deals with counterparty risk while retaining flexibility.
- Adding a puttability clause (even if deeply out-of-the-money) can protect investors from bankruptcy of the issuer.
- Inserting a break clause (perhaps with a penalty) can also save investors if the issuer's credit condition falls sharply, although puttability is a simpler solution.

Some Final Thoughts

If you have come this far, I certainly hope you enjoyed reading this book as much as I enjoyed writing it. I stress again my purpose in writing this book is to explain in simple terms the economic rationale for exotic products in the realm of interest rates, equities and foreign exchange to the average investment professional, and to discuss the risks undertaken by an investor in such products.

By covering a bunch of complex products from CMS to range accruals, and even the more esoteric breed of PRDCs, snowballs and Himalaya, I hope to show that these products have arisen due to economic circumstances that make them worth selling (from the bank's perspective) or worth buying (from the investor's perspective). And I hope to have shown that not all derivatives are dangerous (especially since some offer principal protection), but that some can be dangerous, especially if the investor misunderstands what can go wrong. Indeed, investors are sometimes misold these products or have made inappropriate assumptions as to the risks involved.

It is worth stressing that many of the products described are illiquid, so if you buy them from a bank, it is not too easy to dispose of them when things go wrong. But that makes it all the more essential that you understand what can go wrong, and whether you are prepared to hold the contract until maturity. Furthermore, noting that you might be stuck for some time with such contracts from the institution that sold it to you, you have to ask if you trust that institution's creditworthiness.

I am not saying that the above investments are available to an average individual, since they often require a fairly high principal investment. But they would be available to many funds, which is partly why the book was written. If at the end you conclude that derivatives are not for you, that does not defeat the purpose of this book. In fact, I would be glad that you have come to such a decision having seen what derivatives really are. If, however, you feel that it has whet your appetite for derivatives, I hope you would carefully look at the structures available and make sure you are fully aware of the risks you are undertaking in the contract. This is not a solicitation of business, and neither is it an investment manual. If you wish to invest, I suggest you seek further advice and try to understand more of the options in which you are going to invest.

The end of 2008 has seen a period of unprecedented financial turmoil, which started from the credit crisis, for which complex credit derivatives, namely Collaterised Debt Obligations (CDOs), and more complex variants of such (namely Asset Backed Securities (ABS) CDOs and CDOs Squared) have to take a lot of the blame. But such weird structures are by no means representative of the derivatives market (outside credit) in general. Also, if you think of credit, at best you get your notional back and (high) coupons along the way, while at worst you get nothing. This is quite the opposite of principal-protected derivatives, where at worst you get your principal back (unless the bank defaults but that would also hit its normal bonds), but may lose any coupons. In the case of credit you are selling insurance, while in the case of some structured notes, you are buying insurance. I know there are huge profits to be gained in selling insurance, but can the average person afford the losses when something goes wrong? (I say this even if the pricing was not flawed, as it often was for the above-mentioned credit derivatives.)

This is not a book about credit. I have focused on explaining products that are more part of my expertise, but which I also feel might continue to be of interest in the years ahead. Looking to the future, with record (or near record) low interest rates in most developed economies, how can an investor get a higher yield? With stock markets in serious turmoil, are you the brave soul who wants to go head on against the financial tsunami without principal protection? The Japanese have waited 19 years and have still not recovered the peak of their market (and that is a huge understatement). How long can you wait? And no one knows if we are in a period of impending deflation or if the attempts of governments to spend their way out of the financial crisis will lead to possible runaway inflation. As for hedge funds, some see them as a means of good returns in a time of falling markets. However, risk-free is a poor description of such investments, and the practice of some funds restricting redemptions when market conditions have inflicted heavy losses on them, does not offer encouragement.

Sadly, I cannot predict the future. I am not suggesting that you invest in something or avoid investing in something else. But I do suggest that it is prudent to look at all possible options for your investments. Knowledge really cannot hurt, and on that note, I wish you good fortune in the years ahead.

Glossary

Below is a list of key terms used throughout the book, as well as others that a reader might find useful. Most of the terms used are defined when first encountered, but the glossary could nevertheless help to remind a reader of what they refer to.

Alpha A measure of returns that are independent of the market.

Altiplano A product that pays a large coupon if no stock within a large basket falls below some barrier level. Otherwise, the product pays as though it were an option on the basket.

American Option An option that can be exercised at any date prior to expiry.

Annuity A series of fixed cashflow payments over regular intervals.

Appreciate If an asset appreciates, it increases in value.

Asian (Average-Rate) Option An option based on the average price of the underlying over time rather than the price on the expiry date.

At-the-Money Roughly speaking, an option is at-the-money when strike is close to spot or forward (where the convention differs for different markets).

Atlas A product on a large basket of assets. It excludes some of the best and worst performers and the payoff is based on an average of the remaining assets.

Bank of England Central bank of the United Kingdom.

Bank of Japan Central bank of Japan.

Barrier A barrier instrument is one where there is a discontinuous change in payoff upon crossing some level. A knockout barrier extinguishes (i.e. becomes worthless) if the barrier is breached. A knockin barrier however only becomes activated if the barrier is breached. A double barrier option has two barriers (typically one above and one below the spot at deal inception). Breaching either barrier extinguishes the instrument.

Basis Point (bp) 0.01 of 1%.

Basket A collection of assets of the same type or otherwise (e.g. a basket of stocks and commodities).

Bermudan Option An option that can be exercised on certain fixed dates prior to expiry. Typically, for a note that pays coupons on regular intervals, the exercise dates correspond to coupon dates.

Beta A measure of returns that are correlated to the market. If beta is greater than 1, then the instrument is supposed to be more volatile (and hopefully yield more) than the market benchmark.

Black–Scholes Options pricing developed largely due to the seminal work of Black and Scholes that showed how dynamic hedging can be used to eliminate risk in a derivative *vis-à-vis* the underlying. The Black–Scholes model assumes geometric Brownian motion (i.e. a specific process) and the resultant equation was first solved by Merton to produce the Black–Scholes formula, which is extremely popular in derivatives pricing.

Bund German government bond.

CAC 40 An index based on some of the largest 40 companies (by market capitalisation) in France.

Calibrate To choose model parameters so that the prices from the model match market quotes for liquid instruments.

Callable A note that can be repaid at the discretion of the issuer. By repaying the principal the issuer will no longer be liable for coupons on the note. Typically the issuer will call when it is in his interest and not in the interest of the investor; so callability makes a note cheaper.

Cap To cap a payoff is to limit the maximum amount payable. However, a cap is also used to refer to an instrument that comprises a portfolio of caplets, each of which is a call on interest rates.

Caplet A call option on interest rates.

Cash-Settled Swaption Contrary to intuition, this is not just an option on a swap that is settled in cash. Instead, the payoff is defined differently, solely in terms of the swap rate.

Chooser PRDC A type of PRDC where the coupon payable is the minimum of USD/JPY and AUD/JPY payoffs.

Clearing House An institution that processes the trades transacted on a futures exchange, and guarantees performance of the contracts in its capacity as the central counterparty to all trades.

Clearing Member A member of a futures exchange that deals directly with the clearing house of the exchange (which acts as central counterparty to all trades). All trades on a futures exchange must go through a clearing member.

Cliquet An instrument whose payoff is based on the returns over each period (e.g. the value of the stock at year 3 versus that at year 2).

CME Group A major US futures exchange formed by the merger between the Chicago Board of Trade and Chicago Mercantile Exchange in July 2007.

CMS Spread An instrument that pays on the basis of the difference in value between two CMS rates.

Conditional Coupon A coupon that gets paid under certain conditions (e.g. if Euribor stays under 3.5%).

Constant Maturity Swap (CMS) An instrument that pays on the basis of a long-term floating rate (e.g. 10-year swap rate) but is reset at much shorter intervals (e.g. every 3 months).

Constant Maturity Treasury (CMT) Similar to the CMS but where the reference rate is based on government bond yields.

Constant Proportion Portfolio Insurance (CPPI) A strategy that attempts to mimic the payoff of an option. If the portfolio value is above some minimum, an investment in the asset is made equal to some multiplier times the excess. Otherwise, the entire amount is invested in zero-coupon bonds.

Consumer Price Index An index of inflation based on a representative basket of consumer products.

Contingent Liability This is where a position can lead to losses exceeding one's initial investment, as a result of adverse market movements.

Correlation A measure of linear co-dependence between two random variables.

Correlation Swap A contract that pays the difference between realised correlation and some strike.

Counterparty The other entity with whom you have entered the transaction.

Coupon An amount payable under the terms of an instrument. This amount could be fixed, or dependent on market conditions.

Credit Default Swap (CDS) An instrument which allows a party to receive compensation if a reference name defaults, in exchange for regular (insurance) payments by that party.

DAX 30 An index based on some of the largest 30 companies (by market capitalisation) in Germany.

Delta The sensitivity of an instrument with respect to a unit change in the value of the underlying.

Deposit An instrument that earns interest over a period of time.

Depreciate If an asset depreciates, it decreases in value.

Derivative An instrument whose value depends on that of an underlying (e.g. the value of an option depends on that of a stock).

Digital A digital option pays 1 if the underlying is above some level at expiry (for call), or if the underlying is below some level at expiry (for put).

Discount Curve A representation of the price of zero-coupon bonds payable at each expiry.

Discount Factor The value today of a zero-coupon bond with notional of 1.

Dow Jones Industrial Average An index based on some of the largest 30 industrial companies (by market capitalisation) in the USA.

Dynamic Replication A hedging strategy that ensures that one can match a given payoff under any market conditions, by trading in the underlying and possibly some options. The amount of the underlying (and options) to hold depends on model assumptions.

Equity A stock (also termed share).

Eurex A pan-European futures exchange, comprising the German and Swiss exchanges, among others.

Euribor Stands for Euro Interbank Offered Rate. It is the average of quotes for lending in euros by major banks, sponsored by the European Banking Federation and ACI The Financial Markets Association.

Euronext A pan-European stock exchange, part of the NYSE Euronext group.

European Central Bank (ECB) Central bank of the Eurozone countries (i.e. countries that use the euro as currency).

European Option An option that can only by exercised on expiry date.

Everest A long-expiry option in which payment is based on the minimum of a large basket of stocks.

Exchange A regulated and organised market that facilitates trading of assets by bringing together different market participants.

Exchange Cleared Product An OTC product (i.e. between two private counterparties) that is thereafter transferred onto a futures exchange, which becomes the central counterparty to both sides of the trade, and guarantees performance to both parties.

Exchange Traded Product A product that is traded on a futures exchange, which acts as the central counterparty to both sides of the transaction.

Exercise Exercising an option is using it to acquire or dispose of the asset at the strike.

Expectation An average, computed on the basis of probabilities of different outcomes materialising.

Expiry The date when a European option can be exercised. Also the last date for an American option to be exercised.

Fader A variation of the range accrual, where the accrual multiplier is applied to a call or put style payoff.

Fed Funds Refers to borrowing by qualifying banks direct from the Federal Reserve.

Federal Reserve Central bank of the United States.

Fixed Rate Bond An instrument that pays fixed coupons at regular intervals (e.g. semi-annually), as well as the principal at maturity.

Floating Rate Note (FRN) An instrument that pays floating coupons (based on some benchmark index like Libor) at regular intervals, as well as the principal at maturity.

Floor To floor a payoff is to ensure that a minimum amount is payable. However, a floor is also used to refer to an instrument that comprises a portfolio of floorlets, each of which is a put on interest rates.

Floorlet A put option on interest rates.

Foreign Exchange (FX) The conversion from one currency to another.

Forward An agreement to either buy or sell an asset at a pre-agreed price (strike) at a future date (maturity). Such an instrument is typically traded privately between two counterparties.

Forward Price The fair value of the strike of a forward, so that the forward contract is worth zero today, based on no-arbitrage principles.

Forward Rate The fair value of the interest rate between two future points in time, so that it is consistent with the yield curve.

Forward Rate Agreement (FRA) An agreement to fix the rate of lending or borrowing for the period between two future dates.

FTSE 100 An index based on some of the largest 100 companies (by market capitalisation) in the United Kingdom.

Fund of Funds A fund that invests in other mutual funds, investment trusts or hedge funds.

Futures An exchange-traded instrument that provides for buying or selling an asset at a pre-agreed price (strike) at a future date. Typically, there is daily settlement of profit and loss on the position, based on the closing price of traded futures contracts. The exchange is the central counterparty to all futures contracts.

Gilt UK government bond.

Hedge To protect oneself from adverse market moves by taking positions to offset one's exposure.

Hedge Fund These are lightly regulated (or unregulated) investment entities, with much greater leeway to invest client monies and use leverage. They tend to have restrictions on withdrawals.

Himalaya A product on a large basket. At each coupon date, it records the best return (from deal inception date) of assets still in the basket and throws out the asset. This continues until the last coupon date. The payoff is based on some average of these returns.

Hybrid Products that depend on multiple asset classes (e.g. rates and FX).

Implied Volatility The volatility required in the Black–Scholes formula to match market quotes.

In-the-Money An option that is in-the-money can be exercised at a profit immediately (if exercise is permissible).

Inflation A measure of the rise of prices of goods in general, hence reducing the purchasing power of money.

Intercontinental Exchange A US futures exchange.

Inverse Floater A note that pays coupons on the basis of a reference strike minus Libor, if greater than zero.

Investment Trust A closed-end trust for collective investment, where the fund manager invests monies in the trust. These trusts can normally be traded like any other shares.

Libor Stands for London Interbank Offered Rate. It is the average of quotes for lending by major AA-rated banks, and covers various currencies (US dollar, sterling, Japanese yen, etc.). It is calculated by the British Bankers' Association.

Libor-in-Arrears (LIA) An instrument where the fixing date for the LIBOR rate is the same as the payment date. For a normal floating rate coupon, fixing is done at the beginning of the reference period, while payment is at the end (e.g. 6 months later).

Liffe A pan-European futures exchange, acquired by Euronext in January 2002. It is currently part of the NYSE Euronext group.

Long To go long is to buy.

Margin An amount of collateral set aside to cover potential losses from market movements. This is usually required by exchanges when you enter into a contingent liability position.

Martingale A variable whose expected value at a future point in time is its current value.

Maturity The date when the principal of a bond or note is to be repaid, and also when a forward has to be settled.

Measure Using a different numeraire induces a change in measure. Basically, this just means that the probabilities used in the computation of expectations change. It is something to be aware of in pricing derivatives.

Money Market Account A fictional (risk-free) deposit in a bank, which is continuously compounded.

Monte Carlo (MC) A valuation method that involves random numbers. These are used to generate random paths for the value of a security. Averaging these paths and discounting gives the price.

Mountain Range Products The collective name for some exotic equity products (e.g. Himalaya, Altiplano, Atlas and Everest). These tend to involve a basket of stocks, and some of them pay on the basis of the minimums or maximums.

Mutual Fund An open-ended trust, with a mandate to invest in stocks and bonds. Investors subscribe to units in the fund, and the fund manager invests the new monies.

Nikkei 225 An index based on some of the largest 225 companies (by market capitalisation) in Japan.

No Arbitrage This is the main principle underlying derivatives pricing. Basically, it says that riskless profits should not exist, so that if you can construct a (possibly dynamic) portfolio that matches a payoff, then the portfolio must have the same value as the payoff.

No-Touch A no-touch option pays 1 at expiry if, during the life of the option, the barrier is never breached.

Non-Deliverable A non-deliverable product is one that is settled in a foreign currency (with appropriate FX conversion). This is often because the natural currency is not freely convertible, or otherwise inconvenient to use.

Novation This involves substituting a third party in place of one of the parties to a transaction. The third party assumes all rights and obligations of the party removed from the transaction.

Numeraire This is a unit of measure of value. It must be a domestic asset whose value is always greater than 0. So, a stock can be a numeraire, as can a bank account (assumed to be risk-free growth).

NYSE Euronext A group comprising cash and futures exchanges in the USA and Europe, resulting from the merger between the New York Stock Exchange and Euronext in April 2007.

OAT French government bond.

One-Touch A one-touch option pays 1 at expiry if at any time during the life of the option the underlying breaches a barrier. The barrier is above spot for an upside one-touch and below spot for a downside one-touch.

One-Way Floater A product that pays floating coupons on the basis of interest rates. However, each coupon is contractually guaranteed to be at least the value of the previous coupon. So coupons increase as rates rise, but stay the same as rates fall.

Option An instrument that gives one the right but not obligation to buy (call option) or sell (put option) an asset at a future date (expiry) at a pre-agreed price (strike).

Out-of-the-Money An option that is currently not worth exercising.

Overnight Interest Swap (OIS) A swap where one party pays the overnight rate.

Over-the-Counter (OTC) These are deals done between private parties outside an organised exchange.

Par When a note is worth par, its present value is equal to its principal.

Partial Differential Equation (PDE) An equation that relates partial derivatives. This also leads to a valuation method that involves constructing a lattice of points. Valuation is done either by moving forward or backward in time on the lattice.

Power Reverse Dual Currency (PRDC) A very long-dated instrument whose coupons are linked to FX rates (typically in USD/JPY or AUD/JPY). Typically, the bet is that the yen will not appreciate in quite the manner suggested by forward FX rates. If the note has a redemption strike, the domestic value of the principal repaid at expiry is not assured.

Premium The price of an option.

Present Value (PV) The value today of an instrument or set of future cashflows.

Principal The face value of a bond or structured note. At maturity, typically the principal is repaid in full, unless it is linked to market variables. Also, coupons tend to be quoted with reference to the principal.

Principal Protection A note that has principal protection is one where the principal will be repaid at maturity, notwithstanding movements of market variables. This means that the principal is as safe as that of a bond. However, it should be stressed that the principal repayment is typically still subject to the credit risk of the issuer.

Probability The likelihood of an event occurring; 1 means that an event is certain.

Puttable A note that can be repaid at the discretion of the investor. This is a valuable right, since the investor will put the note when it is in her interest, e.g. when market moves have made existing coupons not worth receiving. So, puttability makes a note expensive.

Quanto An instrument where the payoff is in a non-natural currency of the underlying but where no FX conversion takes place (e.g. Microsoft stock paid in euros).

Range Accrual An instrument that pays based on the number of days in a reference period that an underlying stays above or below some barrier.

Retail Price Index An index of inflation that is based on a representative basket of retail products.

Risk-Neutral Hedging is meant to ensure that a payoff can be replicated. As such, the drift of the underlying is not relavant, only the cost of hedging. This leads to risk-neutrality.

S&P 500 An index based on some of the largest 500 companies (by market capitalisation) in the USA.

Self-Quanto (also Auto-Quanto) An instrument whose payoff is based on an FX rate quoted as ccy1/ccy2, but settled in ccy1 rather than the natural ccy2, with no FX conversion.

Short To go short is to sell. Often short selling refers to selling an asset you do not own (e.g. by borrowing it).

Skyline A product in which payment is based on the previous coupon plus an increment if the market variable (e.g. Libor) stays under some level. Otherwise, the coupon is zero and accumulation starts from zero for the next coupon.

Snowball A product in which payment is based on the previous coupon, plus strike minus some market variable (if greater than 0). Otherwise, coupon is zero and accumulation starts from zero for the next coupon.

Speculate To bet on the movements of market variables in the hope of earning a profit.

Spread The difference between two market variables (e.g. the 10-year swap rate and the 2-year swap rate).

Static Replication Construction of a portfolio today that will match a given payoff at a future point in time under any market conditions. This portfolio and the payoff must therefore be worth the same today. No model assumption is involved.

STOXX 50 An index based on some of the largest 50 companies (by market capitalisation) in Europe.

Strike The exercise price of a forward or an option.

Structured Products Instruments created by financial institutions and specially tailored to a client's market views and investment preferences, allowing the client better control over the risk–reward tradeoff.

Swap An instrument that involves exchanges of cashflows. In a vanilla swap, one party pays a floating rate (based on some index such as Libor) and the other party pays a pre-agreed fixed rate at each coupon date. Usually, no exchange of notional takes place.

Swaption An option that gives one the right to enter into a swap.

Tarn Stands for target redemption note. A condition that leads to early principal repayment (and hence termination of coupons) of a note, if the total coupons paid have exceeded some level. This makes the note cheaper as it limits the total coupons payable.

Terminal Distribution The distribution of a variable as seen at one future point in time.

Totem Benchmark market quotes based on market consensus (i.e. average from various banks) made available for various vanilla and semi-exotic flow products. It is provided by the institution Markit.

Transition Probability The probability of moving from one state at a point in time, to another state at a future point in time.

Trigger (also AutoCall) A condition that provides for early termination (by repayment of principal) of a note if some level has been breached. Typically, this is set in such a way as to benefit the issuer in order to make the note cheaper.

Vanilla Refers to simpler products. For options, these typically include European calls and puts and digitals.

Variance The square of volatility, another measure of how much a variable moves.

Variance Swap A contract that pays the difference between realised variance and some strike.

Vega The sensitivity of an instrument with respect to a unit change in the value of implied volatility.

Volatility (Vol) A measure of how much a variable moves on average. The higher the volatility, the higher the price of an option since it costs more to hedge.

Volatility Smile/Skew A representation of varying volatility for different strikes.

Volatility Swap A contract that pays the difference between realised volatility and some strike.

Volatility Surface A representation of volatilities for different expiries and strikes. In interest rates, you need one more dimension for maturities of the underlying swaps.

Yield Curve A representation of the rates of borrowing for different maturities.

Zero-Coupon Bond A bond that pays no coupons but only the principal at maturity.

Appendices

This collection of appendices contains technical material relevant to the contents of the book. The level of mathematics required to understand it will be much higher than expected for the vast majority of readers of the book. It is partly provided for completeness, and partly because certain categories of readers (e.g. quantitative analysts in investment banks) might find it useful. Nothing in the flow of the book requires understanding the material in these appendices.

CHAPTER 3

This technical appendix shall elaborate on various topics, such as change of measure as well as the derivation of the Black–Scholes equation.

The Radon–Nikodym Derivative

Our martingale pricing equation earlier gives the following relation

$$V_t = B_t E^{Q_B}\left[\frac{V_T}{B_T}\right] = A_t E^{Q_A}\left[\frac{V_T}{A_T}\right].$$

In particular, this relates the two measures Q_A and Q_B via

$$E^{Q_B}\left[\frac{V_T}{B_T}\right] = E^{Q_A}\left[\frac{V_T}{A_T}\frac{A_t}{B_t}\right] = E^{Q_A}\left[\frac{V_T}{B_T}\frac{dQ_B}{dQ_A}\right],$$

where the ratio $\frac{dQ_B}{dQ_A} = \frac{B_T/B_t}{A_T/A_t}$ is the Radon–Nikodym derivative.

So, changing measure from Q_B to Q_A involves multiplication by the Radon–Nikodym derivative.

Girsanov's Theorem

Let W_t be a Brownian motion under measure Q. Suppose we wish to change to measure Q^* with corresponding Brownian W_t^*. Then Girsanov's Theorem gives

$$dW_t = dW_t^* + \lambda(t)dt,$$

where $\lambda(t)$ satisfies the following equation involving the Radon–Nikodym derivative

$$\frac{dQ^*}{dQ} = \exp\left(\int_0^t \lambda(s)dW_s - \frac{1}{2}\int_0^t \lambda^2(s)ds\right).$$

Basically, Girsanov's Theorem states that change of measure only involves a change in drift. The volatility remains unchanged. This is quite useful, since it means that we can calibrate our model volatilities without regard to the measure we are in. Furthermore, we shall see in the appendix to Chapter 5 that this also means that the quanto correction only involves a change to drift and not to volatility.

The Black–Scholes Equation

Suppose that the stock price process S_t at time t follows geometric Brownian motion, specifically

$$dS_t = \mu S_t dt + \sigma S_t dW_t,$$

where μ is the real world drift, σ is volatility, W_t **is a Brownian motion (representing randomness)** and dS_t represents the change in S_t.

Let $V_t = V(S_t, t)$ be the price of any option on S_t (e.g. a call option). Itô's lemma gives

$$
\begin{aligned}
dV_t &= \frac{\partial V_t}{\partial t}dt + \frac{\partial V_t}{\partial S_t}dS_t + \frac{1}{2}\frac{\partial^2 V_t}{\partial S_t^2}(dS_t)^2 \\
&= \frac{\partial V_t}{\partial t}dt + \frac{\partial V_t}{\partial S_t}(\mu S_t dt + \sigma S_t dW_t) + \frac{1}{2}\sigma^2 S_t^2 \frac{\partial^2 V_t}{\partial S_t^2}dt \\
&= \left(\frac{\partial V_t}{\partial t} + \mu S_t \frac{\partial V_t}{\partial S_t} + \frac{1}{2}\sigma^2 S_t^2 \frac{\partial^2 V_t}{\partial S_t^2}\right)dt + \sigma S_t \frac{\partial V_t}{\partial S_t}dW_t
\end{aligned}
$$

since $(dt)^2 = dtdW_t = 0$ and $(dW_t)^2 = dt$.

(It is beyond the scope of this book to explain stochastic calculus but the interested reader is referred to such excellent texts as Oksendal (1998) or Brzezniak and Zastawniak (1998).)

Suppose we construct a portfolio involving short 1 option and long Δ stock. Then the value is

$$\Pi_t = -V_t + \Delta S_t.$$

Furthermore,

$$
\begin{aligned}
d\Pi_t &= -dV_t + \Delta dS_t \\
&= -\left(\frac{\partial V_t}{\partial t} + \mu S_t \frac{\partial V_t}{\partial S_t} + \frac{1}{2}\sigma^2 S_t^2 \frac{\partial^2 V_t}{\partial S_t^2}\right)dt - \sigma S_t \frac{\partial V_t}{\partial S_t}dW_t + \Delta\mu S_t dt + \Delta\sigma S_t dW_t
\end{aligned}
$$

Notice that if $\Delta = \frac{\partial V_t}{\partial S_t}$, the dW_t terms cancel and we are left with

$$d\Pi_t = -\left(\frac{\partial V_t}{\partial t} + \frac{1}{2}\sigma^2 S_t^2 \frac{\partial^2 V_t}{\partial S_t^2}\right)dt_t.$$

But since we have eliminated risk (by removing the dW_t terms), the portfolio must grow at the risk-free rate r, i.e.

$$d\Pi_t = r\Pi_t dt_t = r\left(-V_t + \frac{\partial V_t}{\partial S_t} S_t\right) dt.$$

This leads to the celebrated Black–Scholes partial differential equation

$$\frac{\partial V_t}{\partial t} + rS_t \frac{\partial V_t}{\partial S_t} + \frac{1}{2}\sigma^2 S_t^2 \frac{\partial^2 V_t}{\partial S_t^2} = rV_t.$$

The Feynman–Kac Theorem

The Feynman–Kac Theorem relates the Black–Scholes PDE to the martingale equation. Specifically, it says that for a derivative $V_t = V(S_t, t)$ such that

$$\frac{\partial V_t}{\partial t} + rS_t \frac{\partial V_t}{\partial S_t} + \frac{1}{2}\sigma^2 S_t^2 \frac{\partial^2 V_t}{\partial S_t^2} = rV_t$$

with terms defined above,

$$V_t = E^Q \lfloor e^{-rT}\Phi(S_T, T)\rfloor$$

where $V_T = \Phi(S_T, T)$ gives the payoff at expiry T.

Derivation of Black–Scholes Equation

Consider the martingale equation

$$V_t = B_t E^Q\left[\frac{V_T}{B_T}\right],$$

where $B_t = \exp(rt)$.
  For a call option, $V_T = \max(S_T - K, 0)$.
  Since $dS_t = rS_t dt + \sigma S_t dW_t$,

$$S_t = S_0 \exp\left(rt - \frac{1}{2}\sigma^2 t + \sigma W_t\right)$$

where $W_t \sim N(0, t)$. Then

$$V_0 = \exp(-rT) E^Q[\max(S_T - K, 0)]$$

$$= \exp(-rT)\frac{1}{\sqrt{2\pi}}\int_{z^*}^{\infty}\left(S_0 \exp\left(rT - \frac{\sigma^2 T}{2} + \sigma\sqrt{T}z\right) - K\right)\exp\left(-\frac{z^2}{2}\right)dz$$

where

$$S_0 \exp\left(rT - \frac{1}{2}\sigma^2 t + \sigma\sqrt{T}z^*\right) = K \Rightarrow z^* = -\frac{\log\left(\frac{S_0}{K}\right) + rT}{\sigma\sqrt{T}} + \frac{\sigma\sqrt{T}}{2}$$

Thus,

$$V_0 = S_0 \exp\left(-\frac{\sigma^2 T}{2}\right) \frac{1}{\sqrt{2\pi}} \int_{z^*}^{\infty} \exp\left(\sigma\sqrt{T}z - \frac{z^2}{2}\right) dz$$

$$-K \exp(-rT) \frac{1}{\sqrt{2\pi}} \int_{z^*}^{\infty} \exp\left(-\frac{z^2}{2}\right) dz$$

$$= S_0 \frac{1}{\sqrt{2\pi}} \int_{z^*}^{\infty} \exp\left(-\frac{1}{2}\left(z - \sigma\sqrt{T}\right)^2\right) dz - K \exp(-rT) N\left(-z^*\right)$$

$$= S_0 \frac{1}{\sqrt{2\pi}} \int_{z^*-\sigma\sqrt{T}}^{\infty} \exp\left(-\frac{y^2}{2}\right) dy - K \exp(-rT) N\left(-z^*\right)$$

$$= S_0 N\left(-z^* + \sigma\sqrt{T}\right) - K \exp(-rT) N\left(-z^*\right)$$

$$= S_0 N(d_1) - K \exp(-rT) N(d_2)$$

where

$$d_1 = -z^* + \sigma\sqrt{T} = \frac{\log\left(\frac{S_0}{K}\right) + rT}{\sigma\sqrt{T}} + \frac{\sigma\sqrt{T}}{2}$$

$$d_2 = -z^* = \frac{\log\left(\frac{S_0}{K}\right) + rT}{\sigma\sqrt{T}} - \frac{\sigma\sqrt{T}}{2}$$

The derivation of the formula for a put option follows in a very similar manner.

Pricing Asian Options on a PDE

An Asian option has a payout based on the average of an underlying. This clearly depends on the path of the underlying. Suppose the average is based on continuous observations (daily observations are good enough in practice). Define

$$I(t) = \int_0^t S_u \, du,$$

where S_t is the value of the underlying at time t. Then the average of the underlying up to time t is $\frac{I(t)}{t}$.

The relevant PDE (assuming we do not have stochastic volatility or jumps) is now

$$\frac{\partial V_t}{\partial t} + S_t \frac{\partial V_t}{\partial I_t} + rS_t \frac{\partial V_t}{\partial S_t} + \frac{1}{2}\sigma^2(S_t, t) S_t^2 \frac{\partial^2 V_t}{\partial S_t^2} = rV_t.$$

This is Markovian in two state variables (i.e. both the underlying and the average process), and hence can be efficiently treated via PDE techniques.

If, however, our observations for averaging are much less frequent (e.g. monthly), then a continuous averaging assumption may not be appropriate. We could resort to auxiliary state variables, using a collection of PDEs where the auxiliary state variable represents the average (or accumulated sum), and joining them as we backward induct through time. (This idea will be revisited in the appendix to Chapter 8.)

Notice that pricing an Asian option is clearly more challenging than for a normal European option. However, hedging it is more pleasant, since as time progresses, there is less uncertainty. At time t, we only need to delta hedge the remaining part from time t to expiry T, i.e. $\int_t^T S_u du$ in our continuous average example.

CHAPTER 4

It is worth mentioning a few things to promote the understanding of barriers.

The Reflection Principle

Consider a Brownian motion W_t. Due to symmetry, if $W_t = y$ for some time t, it has equal likelihood of moving down to x or up to $2y - x$ at a future time T (see Figure A.1.)

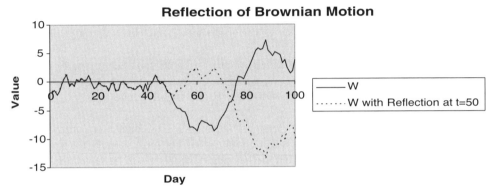

Figure A.1   Diagram showing reflection principle in Brownian motion.

Thus,

$$P\left(\max_{0 \le t \le T} W_t > y \text{ and } W_T \le x\right) = P(W_T > 2y - x).$$

Barrier Replication

Section 4.2 refers to replicating a barrier via a portfolio of options. Let us put this more concretely. Suppose we have a call option of expiry T with strike K and knockout barrier $H < K$. Let us construct a replicating portfolio.

Suppose the option has not knocked out by time T, then it is worth the value of a European call option, so our portfolio must consist of one European call option with strike K and expiry T. (Suppose its value is $C(t, K, T)$ as seen at time t.)

Now, suppose we split our time grid into times $t_0 = 0, t_1, \ldots, t_{n-1}, t_n = T$. At time t_{n-1}, if the underlying $S_{t_{n-1}} = H$, then the barrier option must be worthless. So, we need our portfolio to be worthless too. We construct our portfolio by adding an amount w_{n-1} of a digital put option with strike H and expiry t_{n-1}. (Suppose its value is $P(t, H, t_{n-1})$ as seen at time t.)

We solve for w_{n-1} by setting

$$w_{n-1} + C(t_{n-1}, K, T) = 0.$$

Similarly, at time t_i, we need to add an option with strike H and expiry t_{i+1} and solve for w_i in the equation

$$w_i + \sum_{j=i+1}^{n-1} w_j P\left(t_i, H, t_j\right) + C\left(t_i, K, T\right) = 0.$$

This ultimately gives us the portfolio value

$$\sum_{j=1}^{n-1} w_j P\left(0, H, t_j\right) + C\left(0, K, T\right)$$

as of valuation date.

Notice that in our replication, we require the evaluation of unexpired options. This requires the implied volatility for a realised spot at a future point in time. This means that our **replicating portfolio is not model independent but depends on the forward skew** of the underlying. For example, stochastic volatility produces a more pronounced forward skew than local volatility, which affects the price of barrier options. (More on stochastic and local volatility will be seen in the appendices to Chapters 10 and 12.)

Since our replication is not model independent, we could consider trying to zero out some other sensitivities, e.g. the vega. We could do this by introducing another instrument at each expiry, e.g. a normal put option with strike H and slightly longer expiry (e.g. to next replication point) in this case.

Only if we make such simplifying assumptions as assuming constant volatility (e.g. in the Black–Scholes world), do we get a static replication. For most models, our replication is merely a framework for valuation, but the hedging portfolio has to be rebalanced as spot moves.

Pricing Barriers on PDEs and Monte Carlo

It is worth mentioning that PDEs offer a natural mechanism to price barrier options. After all, PDEs require boundary conditions, and these boundaries are naturally the barrier levels.

On the other hand, pricing barriers on Monte Carlo can be unstable because of the discontinuity of the payoff at the barrier level. Some tricks such as smoothing the payoff by a function like $\tanh(x)$ rather than the using the indicator $1(x)$ may help to achieve better numerical convergence.

CHAPTER 5

Quantoes only affect drift as opposed to volatility. We can show this as follows. Consider a foreign asset process A_t specified by

$$dA_t/A_t = \mu_A(A_t, V_t, t)\,dt + \sigma_A(A_t, V_t, t)\,dW_t^A$$

$$dV_t/V_t = \mu_V(V_t, t)\,dt + \sigma_V(V_t, t)\,dW_t^V$$

where V_t is the variance process of A_t, and $dW_t^A dW_t^V = \rho_{AV}(t)\,dt$.

(This covers the general case of local and stochastic volatility. To consider pure local volatility, take V_t as constant.)

Also, let the domestic money market account B_t be defined by

$$dB_t = r_t B_t dt.$$

Self-Quanto

Let us assume that this is a foreign exchange process, but instead, we have domestic the wrong way round. In this case, suppose that EUR/USD is our currency pair, but we choose a numeraire B_t based on the euro as the domestic currency (instead of dollar). EUR/USD is then an "inverted" process.

In this case, we have a foreign (dollar) money market process B_t^f defined by

$$dB_t^f = r_t B_t^f dt.$$

To get a domestic (euro) asset we need to divide by the EUR/USD rate, getting $\frac{B_t^f}{A_t}$. This leads to the martingale equation

$$\frac{B_t^f}{B_t A_t} = E^Q \left[\frac{B_T^f}{B_T A_T} \right].$$

which gives the drift

$$\mu_A(A_t, V_t, t) = r_t^f - r_t + \sigma_A^2(A_t, V_t, t)$$

for our "inverted" process.

Specifically, take note of the quanto-adjustment term of $\sigma_A^2(A_t, V_t, t)$.

Normal Quanto

Consider further a foreign exchange process X_t specified by

$$dX_t/X_t = \mu_X(X_t, U_t, t) dt + \sigma_X(X_t, U_t, t) dW_t^X$$

$$dU_t/U_t = \mu_U(U_t, t) dt + \sigma_U(U_t, t) dW_t^U$$

where U_t is the variance process of X_t, and all correlations are given by

$$E\left[dW_t^i dW_t^j\right] = \rho_{ij}(t) dt.$$

Then assuming conversion to domestic currency is by multiplication (i.e. $A_t X$ represents the price in domestic currency), we have

$$\frac{A_t X_t}{B_t} = E^Q \left[\frac{A_T X_T}{B_T} \right].$$

Thus,

$$d \left(\frac{A_t X_t}{B_t} \right) \Big/ \frac{A_t X_t}{B_t} = [\mu_A(A_t, V_t, t) + \mu_X(X_t, U_t, t) + \rho_{AX}(t) \sigma_A(A_t, V_t, t) \sigma_X$$

$$\times (X_t, U_t, t) - r_t] dt + \sigma_A(A_t, V_t, t) dW_t^A + \sigma_X(X_t, U_t, t) dW_t^X$$

$$= 0 dt + \dots dW_t$$

by the martingale property.

But we know that

$$\mu_X(X_t, U_t, t) = r_t - r_t^f$$

under the domestic numeraire B_t, so

$$\mu_A(A_t, V_t, t) = r_t^f - \rho_{AX}(t)\,\sigma_A\,(A_t,\,V_t,\,t)\,\sigma_X(X_t,\,U_t,\,t)\,.$$

(NB I have ignored the presence of a dividend yield or third currency rate here. There are no complications from these. My emphasis is on the quanto-adjustment, however.)

Thus, we need an adjustment of $-\rho_{AX}(t)\,\sigma_A(A_t,\,V_t,\,t)\,\sigma_X(X_t,\,U_t,\,t)$ for the drift of our foreign asset A_t.

It can similarly be shown that if conversion to domestic currency is by division, the quanto adjustment is $\rho_{AX}(t)\,\sigma_A(A_t,\,V_t,\,t)\,\sigma_X(X_t,\,U_t,\,t)$.

PDE Considerations

Notice that if volatility is dependent on spot, then pricing a quanto increases the dimensionality by at least 1. So that whereas you can price a single asset derivative under local volatility in a one-factor model, a quantoed version unfortunately requires a two-factor model. For PDEs, increasing the dimensionality is extremely computationally expensive.

Note on Hedging

Hedging is an attempt to neutralise (i.e. set to zero) various Greeks. In particular, delta hedging and vega hedging are pursued.

Consider a quanto asset A_t where conversion is by multiplication. (It is similar for conversion by division.) The drift is

$$\mu_A(A_t, V_t, t) = r_t^f - \rho_{AX}(t)\,\sigma_A(A_t,\,V_t,\,t)\,\sigma_X(X_t,\,U_t,\,t)\,,$$

whereas the drift of a foreign asset would have been $\mu_A(A_t, V_t, t) = r_t^f$ with respect to the foreign measure.

(The volatility remains the same at $\sigma_A(A_t,\,V_t,\,t)$.)

This means that in practice the vega hedge for a quanto contract is no different from before. And the delta hedge is based on the drift with the quanto adjustment.

Intuitively, suppose you sell a quanto call option on British Petroleum (BP) payable in dollars. Then rather than buy a fixed delta amount of stock, you need to buy a delta amount that is divided by the GBP/USD rate. The ideas are better described in de Weert (2008) but a brief description follows.

Suppose the delta of a normal BP stock is Δ. If GBP/USD is currently 1.4, then you need to maintain a pound delta of $\Delta/1.4$ for your quanto. Similarly, if GBP/USD rises to 1.6, you need to maintain a pound delta of $\Delta/1.6$. Notice there is no optionality with regard to GBP/USD itself. But your hedge portfolio P&L will be reflected by how GBP/USD moves *vis-à-vis* BP stock. Hence, the delta has a dependence on correlation.

CHAPTER 6

This appendix covers an assortment of topics regarding interest rate products and their modelling.

Black's Formula for Caplet

A caplet pays

$$\max\left(L_T - K, 0\right) \tau Z_{T,T+\tau}$$

at expiry time T where L_T is Libor rate as seen at time T, K is strike and $Z_{t,T}$ is the value of a zero-coupon bond with maturity T as seen at time t.

But $L_t = \left(\frac{Z_{t,T}}{Z_{t,T+\tau}} - 1\right)\Big/\tau$. So,

$$(L_T - K)\tau = \frac{Z_{T,T}}{Z_{T,T+\tau}} - 1 - K\tau = \frac{Z_{T,T} - (1 - K\tau) Z_{T,T+\tau}}{Z_{T,T+\tau}}.$$

As this is the ratio of two assets, it is a martingale under the $T + \tau$-forward measure with numeraire $Z_{t,T+\tau}$.

Thus, the value of a caplet is

$$C_t = Z_{t,T+\tau} E^{T+\tau}\left[\max\left(L_T - K, 0\right)\right]$$

and we can integrate in the same way as in the appendix to Chapter 3 to get

$$C_0 = Z_{0,T+\tau}(L_0 N\left(d_1\right) - K N(d_2)),$$

where

$$d_1 = \frac{\log\left(\frac{L_0}{K}\right)}{\sigma\sqrt{T}} + \frac{\sigma\sqrt{T}}{2}, \quad d_2 = d_1 - \frac{\sigma\sqrt{T}}{2}.$$

Black's Formula for Swaption

A swaption has payoff

$$\max\left(R_T - K, 0\right) A_T$$

where $A_t = \sum_{i=1}^{n} \tau_i Z_{t,t_i}$ is the annuity, and

$$R_t = \frac{Z_{t,t_0} - Z_{t,t_n}}{\sum_{i=1}^{n} \tau_i Z_{t,t_i}} = \frac{Z_{t,t_0} - Z_{t,t_n}}{A_t}$$

is the swap rate as seen at time t.

So, choosing the annuity A_t as numeraire,

$$R_T - K = \frac{Z_{t,t_0} - Z_{t,t_n}}{A_t} - K = \frac{Z_{t,t_0} - Z_{t,t_n} - K A_t}{A_t}$$

is the ratio of two assets and is thus a martingale. This gives the value of a swaption as

$$S_t = A_t E^A\left[\max\left(R_T - K, 0\right)\right]$$

and we can integrate in the same way as in the appendix to Chapter 3 to get

$$S_0 = A_0(R_0 N(d_1) - K N(d_2)),$$

where

$$d_1 = \frac{\log\left(\frac{R_0}{K}\right)}{\sigma\sqrt{T}} + \frac{\sigma\sqrt{T}}{2}, \quad d_2 = d_1 - \frac{\sigma\sqrt{T}}{2}.$$

Cash-Settled Swaptions and IRR as Numeraire

For a cash-settled swaption, the payoff is

$$\max(R_T - K, 0)\, \Lambda(R_T),$$

where

$$\Lambda(R_t) = \sum_{i=1}^{n} \frac{\tau_i}{(1 + R_t \tau_i)^{t_i/\tau_i}}.$$

Note that the IRR $\Lambda(R_t)$ cannot take the place of a numeraire as it is not a proper asset in its own right (being instead a function of swap rates).

For practical purposes, however, Black's formula is used to get

$$S_0 = \Lambda(R_0)\,(R_0 N(d_1) - K N(d_2)),$$

and for all intents and purposes we can tweak σ to get the price needed to match market quotes.

(Moreover, the approximation is fairly accurate versus the true price of a cash-settled swaption.)

However, the inconsistency leads to problems. For example, put–call parity no longer holds. Actually, put–call parity is hard to define, since in this case, we should end up with a "cash-settled swap", which is an imaginary instrument that is also not easy to value.

More telling is that if we use Black's formula with our cash-settled swaptions to get an implied density, the density will not integrate to 1. (We can obtain the implied density as $\frac{\partial^2 S_0(K,T)}{\partial K^2}/\Lambda(R_0)$, where $S_t(K, T)$ is the price of a cash-settled swaption with strike K and expiry T as seen at time t.) This means that our CMS replication may not produce a unique CMS par rate, but the CMS par rate obtained depends on our choice of CMS caplet strike in our replication. (The computed CMS par rates should be very close however.)

Linear Swap Rate

One means of dealing with the problem of the inconsistency of pricing cash-settled swaptions is via resort to the linear swap rate model, as espoused by Hunt and Kennedy (2004, Chapter 13).

(Note that Hunt and Kennedy proposed the Linear Swap Rate model but **did not necessarily advocate** its use as described below. Nevertheless, the usage below seems to be standard industry practice.)

This posits that

$$\frac{Z_{t,T}}{A_t} = a_T + b_T R_t,$$

where a_T and b_T are coefficients to be determined.

Specifically, we require

(1) $\quad \dfrac{Z_{0,T}}{A_0} = a_T + b_T R_0$

$\Rightarrow a_T = \dfrac{Z_{0,T}}{A_0} - b_T R_0,$

and

(2) $\quad \dfrac{\sum\limits_{i=1}^{n} \tau_i Z_{0,T_i}}{A_0} = 1,$

giving

$$\sum_{i=1}^{n} \tau_i \left(a_{T_i} + b_{T_i} R_0 \right) = 1$$

$$\Rightarrow \sum_{i=1}^{n} \tau_i a_{T_i} = 1 \quad \text{and} \quad \sum_{i=1}^{n} \tau_i b_{T_i} = 0$$

Equipped with this approximation, we can use physically-settled swaptions to replicate (and hence calibrate to cash-settled swaptions), and then use these calibrated physically-settled swaptions to replicate CMS products to produce a unique CMS par rate.

There is certainly consistency, although the appropriateness of this approach is subject to debate. After all, we are using imaginary physically-settled swaptions, calibrated to real cash-settled swaptions to price real CMS products. This is somewhat convoluted logic to say the least.

Time Lag

The problem of time lag in paying the CMS rate is also a thorny one. Basically, CMS replication works well if we get paid the swap rate on its observation date. However, an adjustment has to be made where (as is usually the case) payment is at the end of the period (e.g. after 3 or 6 months).

A simplistic approach is to use a lognormal style adjustment for payment delay. However, this is unlikely to be consistent with the convexity adjustment from replication.

Alternatively, if one had applied the Linear Swap Rate model and used physically settled swaptions to replicate CMS products, then the payment delay could also be naturally handled via the Linear Swap Rate model.

CMS Spread Options

The issue of the inconsistent use of Black's formula on cash-settled swaptions leading to an implied density not integrating to 1 is especially troublesome for CMS spread options.

It is worth mentioning that for CMS spread options, we know the marginals since we could get each CMS rate by replication. And in fact, we have the implied distributions of the CMS rates by taking the second derivatives numerically.

So, typically these CMS marginals are then joined by a copula (e.g. Gaussian copula) with a correlation in order to obtain the price of a CMS spread option. The Gaussian copula works as follows: Suppose we have a draw z from the marginal distribution. Then we can apply the marginal cumulative distribution to get $F(z)$. Next, we apply the Gaussian inverse cumulative distribution to get $\Phi_N^{-1}(F(z))$ as a Gaussian variate. We apply our correlations to this variate and thus get correlated processes.

There are issues regarding the Gaussian copula approach. In particular, there are criticisms that it does not necessarily produce good transition probabilities. However, we are interested only in European style CMS spread options, i.e. payoff is only at expiry. So, only the terminal distribution matters.

In fact, whereas implied volatility uniquely determines the price of a European vanilla option, implied correlation uniquely determines the price of a European CMS spread option. It has to be remarked that European CMS spread options are rather liquid, and strike-dependent correlations are needed to match the market.

So, actually, the whole idea of modelling CMS spread options may be more akin to finding a good method to interpolate from prices of a given set of CMS spread options to price CMS spread options outside this set.

There is not a lot of real interest rate modelling involved here.

Callable CMS Products and Interest Rate Modelling

It has been mentioned that CMS products can be priced via replication. Even CMS spread products can be priced merely by choosing the appropriate implied correlation. However, when callability is added, there is a need to produce a proper model for the term structure of interest rates. This is necessary to determine the transition probabilities and to decide on when to exercise the call.

This is not a book on modelling, so I shall not propose to cover much material here. But to give a brief flavour, there are three main types of interest rate models: short rate models, Libor Market (BGM) models, and Markov-Functional models.

Whatever the interest rate model, the requirement is to match the current discount curve, and calibration involves choosing volatilities and correlations to match the price of liquid market options (mainly swaptions but sometimes also caplets).

Short Rate Models

This is the oldest class of models, and possibly the class with the most widespread usage amongst banks.

The basic assumption is that the evolution of the entire yield curve can be described by an instantaneous short rate r_t, which satisfies

$$Z_{t,T} = E_t^Q \left[\exp\left(-\int_t^T r_s ds \right) \right],$$

where $Z_{t,T}$ is the value of a zero-coupon bond that matures at time T as seen at time t and expectations are taken under the risk-neutral measure Q.

The HJM model (from Heath, Jarrow and Morton, 1992) specified via continuous forward rates is defined via

$$Z_{t,T} = \exp\left(-\int_t^T f_{t,s}ds\right),$$

where $f_{t,T}$ is the instantaneous forward rate applicable to time T as seen at time t.

It turns out that the HJM framework is equivalent to the short rate framework, so I shall henceforth refer to them interchangeably.

A popular short rate model is the Hull–White (Gaussian) model, i.e.

$$dr_t = (\theta(t) - ar_t)dt + \sigma(t)dW_t,$$

where $\theta(t)$ is a time-dependent mean reversion level, a is the mean reversion speed, and $\sigma(t)$ is the instantaneous short rate volatility. (Note that the drift of the short rate model comes automatically by matching the current discount curve. Mean reversion actually does not affect drift in the risk-neutral world but instead leads to volatility dampening.) The popularity of this model is due to the availability of analytic formulae for the forward discount bond, as well as for caplet and swaption pricing.

Another popular short rate model is the Cheyette model (Cheyette, 1992). This is nice because it is Markovian in a small number of state variables. (It is desirable for a model to be Markovian in a small number of state variables, partly because PDE methods are only effective if the model is Markovian in up to three state variables. Also, a model which is Markovian in fewer state variables requires less computation time in Monte Carlo.) A one factor Cheyette model is specified via the equations

$$dx_t = (-\kappa x_t + y_t)dt + \eta(x_t, y_t, t)dW_t$$

$$dy_t = \left(\eta^2(x_t, y_t, t) - 2\kappa y_t\right)dt,$$

where κ is the mean reversion speed and $\eta(x_t, y_t, t)$ is the local volatility.

The forward discount bond price is given by

$$Z_{t,T}(x_t, y_t) = \frac{Z_{0,T}}{Z_{0,t}}\exp\left(-G(t, T)x_t - \frac{1}{2}G^2(t, T)y_t\right),$$

where $G(t, T) = \frac{1-e^{-\kappa(T-t)}}{\kappa}$.

This is Markovian in two state variables. A 2-factor Cheyette model is Markovian in five state variables.

A further short rate model of interest is the quadratic Gaussian model. This posits that the short rate is a quadratic function of a Gaussian variable.

Specially,

$$r_t = a(t) + b(t)Z_t + c(t)Z_t^2,$$

where $Z_t = \int_0^t \sigma(s)dW_s$, with $a(t)$, $b(t)$, $c(t)$ and $\sigma(t)$ being deterministic functions of time t, and W_t is a Wiener process.

A 2-factor quadratic Gaussian model can produce a smile and not just a skew (and indeed can be interpreted as incorporating stochastic volatility). This is desirable. However, the equations required to solve for the drift to match the discount curve, and for calibration to caplets and swaptions are rather involved. More details can be found in Tezier (2005) or Assefa (2007).

Libor Market Models

The idea came from Brace, Gaterek and Musiela (1997). Basically, consecutive spanning Libor rates L_t^i (i.e. those that together cover the entire time period of interest) are modelled directly via the processes

$$dL_t^i = \mu \left(\left\{ L_t^j \right\}_{j=1}^n, t \right) dt + \sigma \left(L_t^i, t \right) dW_t^i,$$

where $\sigma \left(L_t^i, t \right)$ are volatilities, $\mu \left(\left\{ L_t^j \right\}_{j=1}^n, t \right)$ are drifts and W_t^i are Brownian motions.

If only modelling one Libor rate, a lognormal BGM model reduces to Black's model under the appropriate measure (i.e. where the numeraire is the discount bond with maturity corresponding to the accrual end date of this Libor rate). However, in general, since **we require the same measure for all the Libor rates**, the drift corrections required are often unpleasant and involve other Libor rates (as indicated above).

This means that even a one-factor BGM model involving n forward Libor rates is Markovian only in n state variables. Thus, PDE methods are typically inappropriate. (Attempts to "freeze the drift" based on time 0 approximations have often led to huge inaccuracies.) Monte Carlo methods, which are the only possibility, are time-consuming and can pose problems in application to callability since determination of the early exercise boundary in Monte Carlo is not always straightforward.

However, BGM models give most control over the evolution of forward rates and their correlations and this makes them preferable for highly path-dependent products, e.g. accumulators like snowballs where future coupons depend on previous ones. (Such products are covered in Chapter 9.)

Markov-Functional Models

The approach was suggested by Hunt, Kennedy & Pelsser (2004). The framework just requires that discount bonds be representable by a small number of Markovian factors. It is possible to choose to model Libor rates directly, so that calibration to market is straightforward while keeping the dimensionality of the problem low. This class of models is the least explored in the banking industry thus far.

It is worth mentioning that for simple interest rate products, a 1-factor model is required (representing roughly a parallel shift of the curve as a mode of stochasticity). And for CMS spread products, at least 2 factors are required (representing a parallel shift and a steepening of the two stochastic modes).

Furthermore, subsequent developments have included adding stochastic volatility to short rate models or BGM models. This is partly due to a desire to capture a smile as opposed to just a skew, and the prevailing view that stochastic volatility can sometimes produce more appropriate forward volatility dynamics than local volatility models.

CHAPTER 7

A few technical details on pricing range accruals are relevant here.

Portfolio of Digitals

Consider the range accrual that pays

$$\frac{n}{N},$$

where n is the number of business days in the 6-month period where EUR/GBP is above 0.81.

As discussed earlier, this is a portfolio of (albeit payment delayed) digitals each with notional $\frac{1}{N}$ and strike 0.81 and with expiries on each business day. But there are 132 digitals here, so the pricing effort is undesirable. (For digitals, it is tolerable. But perhaps we still prefer not to do 132 pricings for such a simple instrument.)

A common approach is to price the digital with the longest expiry and the digital with the shortest expiry. We can then interpolate over expiry to get the price of the other digitals, since we expect prices to vary smoothly, based on time to expiry.

Decorrelation

Consider our payoff

$$\frac{n}{N} \times L_T,$$

where L_T is the Libor rate at fixing date T (start of period), and n is the number of business days in the period (from T to $T + \tau$) where the Libor rate L_t $(T < t < T + \tau)$ is above $K = 4\%$.

Decomposing it into a portfolio of asset-or-nothing call options, we would like to price

$$L_T 1_{L_t > K}.$$

Notice that we can write

$$E\lfloor L_T 1_{L_t > K} \rfloor = E\lfloor L_T 1_{L_T + (L_t - L_T) > K} \rfloor = E\left[X 1_{X + Y > K} \right],$$

where $X = L_T$ and $Y = L_t - L_T$ with X, Y uncorrelated (assuming that our processes are Markovian).

So, we can evaluate X, Y via a two-dimensional integral and avoid a full term structure model. This example shows how decorrelation comes about as we consider the same quantity but observe at different points in time.

Pricing Callable Accruals

As range accruals are path-dependent structures, Monte Carlo techniques are more suitable for handling them. If using PDEs, you might need to introduce auxiliary state variables (i.e. stacked PDEs) to store the amount of accrued coupons thus far.

If you have a callable range accrual, there are further complications. The callability condition is more naturally treated via PDEs. In this sense, stacked PDEs are ideal. If you are using Monte Carlo techniques, then some form of early exercise treatment is required. More on the treatment of callability will be seen in the appendix to Chapter 8 on early termination.

CHAPTER 8

There is quite a lot to be said on pricing early termination features., but this book contains enough space for only a few points.

Pricing Callables on PDEs

Callability is most naturally treated on PDEs. This is because, at each point in time, you need to decide if it is optimal to call, which involves comparing the value of exercise against that of holding (the latter being a conditional expectation of future values).

There has also been some interest in treating callables on trees. While trees illustrate certain aspects nicely (e.g. transition probabilities across branches), they are really just a type of PDE (namely explicit PDEs). So, I shall say little more on the subject.

For simplicity, let us illustrate with a local volatility model for a non-dividend paying stock. Specifically, let

$$dx_t = \left(r_t - \frac{1}{2}\sigma^2(x_t, t) \right) dt + \sigma(x_t, t) dW_t$$

$$S_t = \exp(x_t),$$

where

r_t is the risk-free rate of interest,
$\sigma(x_t, t)$ is the local volatility,
W_t is a Wiener process, and
S_t is the value of the stock at time t.

Then we have the PDE

$$\frac{\partial V}{\partial t} + \left(r_t - \frac{1}{2}\sigma^2(x, t) \right) \frac{\partial V}{\partial x} + \frac{1}{2}\sigma^2(x, t) \frac{\partial^2 V}{\partial x^2} = rV,$$

where V_t is the price of the derivative.

Let us discretise on the grid $\{x_i\}_{i=1}^n$, $\{t_j\}_{j=1}^m$. We solve the PDE by backward induction.

For a product callable at time t_j, we apply the following to each node (x_i, t_j):

$$V(x_i, t_j) = \max\left(V_{i,j}, E(x_i, t_j) \right),$$

where $E(x_i, t_j)$ is the exercise value at node (x_i, t_j), and $V_{i,j}$ is the value obtained at node (x_i, t_j) by backward induction on our PDE.

Pricing Callables on Monte Carlo

It may however be necessary to price callability using Monte Carlo methods. This can be because we are using models that are not Markovian in a small number of state variables (e.g. the BGM model). (After all, a PDE can handle up to three factors before becoming computationally prohibitive.) Alternatively, perhaps you have a path-dependent callable (e.g. a callable tarn) where the path-dependence is not too easily treated on a PDE.

The real issue of pricing callability on a Monte Carlo is that in order to decide on whether to call the deal, you need to know the expectation of the value of holding, conditional on your realised underlying value. But Monte Carlo methods produce random paths that are not related, so that conditional expectations are not easy to determine.

Two approaches are commonly resorted to. The Andersen method (see Andersen, 2000) requires that you come up with a functional form of your underlying and callability is then decided on the basis of whether this function breaches some level. For example, if the product pays out more as the interest rate curve steepens, you might choose to call if $10yRate - 2yRate > H$, where H is determined by optimisation runs prior to the actual pricing.

The algorithm of Longstaff–Schwartz (2001) requires that you come up with explanatory variables (that are a function of your simulated underlying). You do a pre-run of Monte Carlo scenarios to obtain values of your instrument corresponding to values of these explanatory variables. Then a regression is applied to determine the appropriate coefficients for use to predict realised instrument values from realised explanatory variables. In the pricing of Monte Carlo, you then apply this prediction to decide whether to call.

Both methods suffer from inherent suboptimality, in that you are deciding to call the option on the basis of less than a full evaluation of all probabilities conditional on a realisation of the underlying. As such, they will always underprice the call optionality, *vis-à-vis* PDEs. However, a good choice of functional form in the Andersen approach or regression variables in the Longstaff–Schwartz approach produces acceptably accurate prices for most derivatives of interest.

Some Tricks for Stability of Sensitivities

Monte Carlo methods involve random numbers. We typically compute sensitivities by a bump and revalue approach. For example, we get delta as

$$\Delta = \frac{f(S + \delta) - f(S - \delta)}{2\delta},$$

where $f(S)$ is the price of the derivative with initial spot S and $\delta \ll 1$ is a small shift. But if each of $f(S + \delta)$ and $f(S - \delta)$ is priced by Monte Carlo, then the random errors are not small and dividing by δ magnifies the errors significantly.

For callables, it is worse if we are using some optimisation to determine the optimal exercise boundary. The best approach for stable sensitivities is to "freeze the boundary", i.e. use the same exercise boundary in paths for the computation of sensitivities (even as we change initial variables). This can be justified as follows:

Consider a function

$$f(\eta, h(\eta)),$$

where the exercise boundary is $h(\eta)$, i.e. a function of η.

Taking the derivative with respect to η, we get

$$\frac{\partial f}{\partial \eta} + \frac{\partial f}{\partial h} \frac{\partial h}{\partial \eta}.$$

But if the exercise boundary is optimal, $\frac{\partial h}{\partial \eta} = 0$.

So, at least locally, our derivative with respect to η is just

$$\frac{\partial f}{\partial \eta}.$$

Another approach to having more stable sensitivities is to either differentiate the paths or apply maximum likelihood techniques. Basically, rather than bump and revalue, you do Monte Carlo simulations based on a different payoff. Benhamou (1999) describes the technique and shows how, if the payoff in a Black–Scholes world is $f(S_T)$, so that the Monte Carlo price is $\frac{1}{n} \sum_{i=1}^{n} f(S_i)$, then the delta is given as the average of the weighted payoff $f(S_T) \frac{W_T}{S_T \sigma T}$. Glasserman and Zhao (1999) show how this approach can be applied to the BGM model.

It must be said that it is not always possible to get an analytic form for the weighted payoff for more complex models. Furthermore, note that the $\frac{1}{T}$ in the weighted payoff for a delta can lead to significant instability for short-dated options, or more problematically, for a multi-period note just before the next coupon date. Overall, there is still ongoing research on such techniques to extend their usability.

Pricing Triggers

Triggers can be naturally handled by PDEs. In fact, suppose you have a product where the principal is repaid when the stock price is above a trigger level H. Then that automatically defines the upper boundary of your PDE and your boundary condition is the intrinsic value 1 (assuming your notional is 1). Naturally, a step-down trigger defines a PDE upper boundary that changes over time (see Figure A.2).

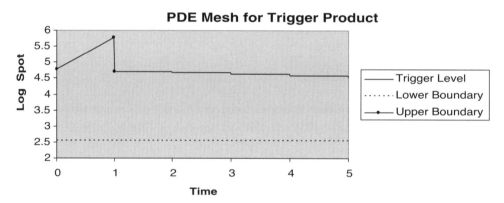

Figure A.2   PDE mesh for product with step-down trigger.

Monte Carlo methods are also well equipped to handle triggers. However, the discontinuity when the underlying crosses the trigger level leads to poor convergence in price, and even worse behaviour of Greeks. It is possible to smooth with the concept of partial trigger, i.e. define an ε-"sausage" around the trigger level, where the partial repayment of notional is possible (see Figure A.3). Piterbarg (2003b) describes this in detail in his document on Callable Libor Exotics.

Pricing Tarns

Monte Carlo is definitely a more convenient approach for pricing tarns as we need to keep track of the accumulated coupon, and that is clearly path dependent.

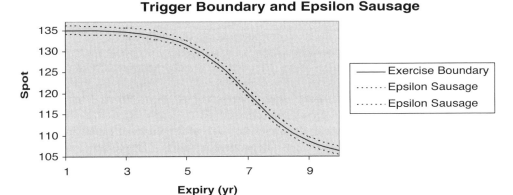

Figure A.3   Diagram showing epsilon sausage about trigger boundary.

However, it is possible to treat tarns on PDEs. One approach is to use auxiliary state variables. Basically, you have a bunch of PDEs each with a different auxiliary state variable (to represent the level of accumulated coupon) and these PDEs communicate with each other via joining conditions, as we backward induct to get the price today.

CHAPTER 9

It is worth addressing a few technical points on the modelling of pathological path-dependent products like the skyline and snowball. Our discussion will be centred in the interest rate world, even though there are snowballs in other assets (e.g. FX).

Pricing Pathologically Path-Dependent Products

Suppose you had to price a callable (fixed rate) bond. It is optimal to call only if interest rates fall below some level. Furthermore, the cost of hedging such an instrument tends to be fairly well represented by the quadratic variation, or loosely equivalent, the total variance. In that case, it is not so important which model you use to represent interest rates. Suppose you posit the Hull–White short rate model

$$dr_t = (\theta(t) - ar_t)\,dt + \sigma(t)dW_t.$$

You would calibrate it by choosing the volatility $\sigma(t)$ to match co-terminal swaptions of the appropriate expiry of your callable. (If you are worried about skew, you could choose a Cheyette model, or include stochastic volatility.) In any case, your total variance should capture the cost of hedging, so that your pricing of the callable bond would be acceptably accurate.

Even if you had to price a callable CMS spread, e.g. 10yRate – 2yRate, total variance is a good measure of your hedging cost. Admittedly, correlations are important here, mainly insofar as they affect the total variance of the spread (i.e. difference between the two rates). But capture the distribution of this spread correctly (via copula or a proper term structure model), and your hedging cost should be properly reflected.

The trouble, however, with pathologically path-dependent options (like skylines and snow-balls) is that whereas correlation matters, you cannot summarise the price dependence in a simple way. To be more precise, let us consider our skyline with barrier at 3%. Suppose your 2-year forward 3-month rate is 3%. Then the exact model you choose for it very much determines its probability of being above 3%. And for pricing purposes, it does not matter how much total variance there is, but much more on your model-implied distribution of this 2-year forward 3-month rate and, specifically, how much of it is above 3%. And this is heavily leveraged insofar as it affects all subsequent coupons.

It follows that your **exact model dynamics for each of the forward Libor rates is extremely important in pathologically path-dependent products**. This presents a very strong argument for using BGM models for skylines and snowballs, for example, where the exact correlation between forward rates is very important.

I remind you that the BGM specification for consecutive spanning Libor rates L_t^i is

$$dL_t^i = \mu\left(\left\{L_t^j\right\}_{j=1}^n, t\right)dt + \sigma\left(L_t^i, t\right)dW_t^i,$$

where $\sigma\left(L_t^i, t\right)$ are volatilities, $\mu\left(\left\{L_t^j\right\}_{j=1}^n, t\right)$ are drifts and W_t^i are Wiener processes.

In particular, **you are free to specify the correlations for all the Brownians**.

In practice, there are too many degrees of freedom, and you may resort to some long-correlation model, e.g. where correlations of longer expiries tend towards some long-term mean. Or you might go for some angular specification of correlation, e.g. $\cos\theta$ for some θ (as suggested by Rebonato (2004) since correlation has to be between -1 and 1.

But it cannot be overemphasised that the **prices of the above products are extremely model dependent**.

Monte Carlo and Callable Skylines/Snowballs

It is worth mentioning further that the strong path dependence of skylines and snowballs generally make Monte Carlo methods the algorithm of choice to treat them.

As such, if you have callability added, you are generally forced to resort to either the Andersen or Longstaff–Schwartz approach to estimate the optimal exercise boundary, and this will lead to more inaccuracies. I do not imagine very competitive pricing for such complex products in any case. Furthermore, such products are better suited to tarn features as they tend to be designed so that large coupons are paid initially, but the investor could be stuck with zero payoffs (or payoffs growing slowly from zero) after a few years. And it is hard to imagine an investor wanting to leave repayment decisions in such circumstances to the whim of the bank.

CHAPTER 10

The typical approach to long-dated FX modelling is to posit three processes for each of the spot FX rate, the domestic and foreign short rates. Traditionally, the rates were taken as Gaussian (for simplicity) and the FX is some (possibly parametric) form of local volatility.

The Basic Equations

Define the domestic and foreign short rates r_t and r_t^f respectively and the spot FX rate S_t. Then

$$dx_t = -ax_t dt + \sigma_x(t)dW_t^x$$

$$r_t = x_t + \varphi(t)$$

$$dy_t = \left(-by_t - \rho_{yz}(t)\sigma_y(t)\sigma_z(z_t, t)\right)dt + \sigma_y(t)dW_t^y$$

$$r_t^f = y_t + \varphi^f(t)$$

$$dz_t = \left(r_t - r_t^f - \frac{1}{2}\sigma_z^2(z_t, t)\right)dt + \sigma_z(z_t, t)dW_t^z$$

$$S_t = \exp(z_t),$$

where

a, b are respectively the domestic and foreign mean reversion speeds,
$\sigma_x(t)$, $\sigma_y(t)$ are respectively the domestic and foreign short rate volatilities,
$\sigma_z(z_t, t)$ is the local volatility for spot FX,
$\varphi(t)$, $\varphi^f(t)$ are drifts required to match the domestic and foreign curves, and
W_t^x, W_t^y, W_t^z are Wiener processes with correlations given by

$$dW_t^x dW_t^y = \rho_{xy}(t)dt, \, dW_t^x dW_t^z = \rho_{xz}(t)dt, \, dW_t^y dW_t^z = \rho_{yz}(t)dt.$$

Specifically, note that no-arbitrage requires for the price of a zero coupon bond

$$Z_{0,T} = E^Q\left[\frac{1}{B_T}\right],$$

which gives

$$\int_0^T \varphi_s ds = -\log(Z_{0,T}) + \frac{1}{2}\int_0^T \frac{\sigma_x^2(s)}{a^2}\left(1 - e^{a(s-T)}\right)^2 ds.$$

Similarly, no-arbitrage requires the price of a foreign zero coupon bond to satisfy

$$Z_{0,T}^f S_0 = E^Q\left[\frac{S_T}{B_T}\right],$$

which gives

$$\int_0^T \varphi_s^f ds = -\log\left(Z_{0,T}^f\right) + \frac{1}{2}\int_0^T \frac{\sigma_y^2(s)}{b^2}\left(1 - e^{b(s-T)}\right)^2 ds.$$

Notice that we need the **quanto-adjustment** of

$$-\rho_{yz}(t)\sigma_y(t)\sigma_z(z_t, t)$$

in our foreign drift to cancel the

$$
\int_0^T \rho_{yz}(u) \frac{\sigma_y(u)}{b} \left(1 - e^{b(u-T)}\right) \sigma_z(z_s, s) ds
$$

term that comes from the dW_t^y and dW_t^z cross.

Total Variance

Consider our FX process $S_t = \exp(z_t)$, with

$$
z_t = z_0 + \int_0^t \left(r_s - r_s^f - \frac{1}{2}\sigma_z^2(z_s, s)\right) ds + \int_0^t \sigma_z(z_s, s) dW_s^z
$$

$$
= z_0 + \cdots dt + \int_0^t \frac{\sigma_x(u)}{a} \left(1 - e^{a(u-T)}\right) dW_s^x - \int_0^t \frac{\sigma_y(u)}{b} \left(1 - e^{b(u-T)}\right) dW_s^y
$$

$$
+ \int_0^t \sigma_z(z_s, s) dW_s^z
$$

For the sake of easy exposition, let us assume that FX volatility is not spot dependent, i.e. $\sigma_z(z_t, t) = \sigma_z(t)$.

Then the total variance is

$$
\Sigma_t^2 = \int_0^t \left(\frac{\sigma_x^2(s)}{a^2} \left(1 - e^{a(s-t)}\right)^2 + \frac{\sigma_y^2(s)}{b^2} \left(1 - e^{b(s-t)}\right)^2 + \sigma_z^2(s)\right) ds
$$

$$
- 2 \int_0^t \rho_{xy}(s) \frac{\sigma_x(s)\sigma_y(s)}{ab} \left(1 - e^{a(s-t)}\right) \left(1 - e^{b(s-t)}\right) ds
$$

$$
+ 2 \int_0^t \rho_{xz}(s) \frac{\sigma_x(s)\sigma_z(s)}{a} \left(1 - e^{a(s-t)}\right) ds - 2 \int_0^t \rho_{yz}(s) \frac{\sigma_y(s)\sigma_z(s)}{b} \left(1 - e^{b(s-t)}\right) ds
$$

giving an implied volatility of Σ.

It is worth noting the interest rate contribution *vis-à-vis* the contribution of the volatility of the spot process $\int_0^t \sigma_z^2(s) ds$. In Figure A.4, we can see that, for long-dated FX options, a fair bit of the total variance may not be explained by spot volatility.

Other Processes

There has been some interest in parametric forms for the local volatility (e.g. CEV). This could make possible some approximations for calibrating the spot FX process (e.g. Piterbarg's Markovian projection and parametric averaging techniques (Piterbarg, 2005b). Bloch & Nakashima (2008) show, however, that a 3-factor model with Gaussian rates and local volatility FX (in its full generality) has a local volatility that can be seen as a bias added to the

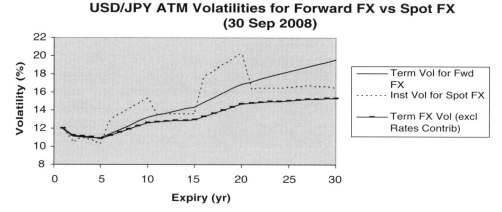

Figure A.4   USD/JPY at-the-money terminal vols for Forward FX versus instantaneous spot FX vols and terminal spot FX vols (with the interest rate contributions removed).

Dupire local volatility. This bias can be bootstrapped by solving a quadratic equation for each maturity.

Also, there is some interest in having rates skew, especially since there is already significant progress towards modelling FX skew, and most PRDCs at some time have to be hedged by out-of-the-money swaptions. However, it must be noted that there are not many skewed rates models that are Markovian in 1-factor, so we can easily end up with more than three factors and hence a problem not amenable to PDEs.

A few institutions have modelled the interest rate part via BGM, but this is not commonplace. The reason for this is that getting BGM to work properly (by proper control of forward volatility evolution and correlations between forward Libors) is already quite an effort in itself. Getting two BGM processes to work simultaneously and still have proper FX dynamics with skew (as well as sufficient stability of sensitivities) is no mean feat. Besides, PRDCs are much more sensitive to FX than the rates processes and the fact that they already have some form of stochastic rates accounts for much of the level dependence on rates.

Stochastic Volatility

Stochastic volatility has gained some popularity of late. This is partly because local volatility is known to have dynamics that are inconsistent with those observed in the market. The argument is as follows. If you have a smile volatility surface, then, as spot moves, you roughly expect the same smile to be centred about the new spot. This is what you indeed observe under stochastic volatility but in local volatility the smile moves the wrong way (Figure A.5). Hagan *et al.* (2002) have an excellent discussion of this "sticky strike" phenomenon in their paper on SABR.

The above leads to deltas that are even less accurate than the Black–Scholes delta without smile. Especially in pricing forward starting options (e.g. the cliquet of Chapter 12), the sticky strike phenomenon leads to too flat a surface in local volatility, so that stochastic volatility becomes quite important.

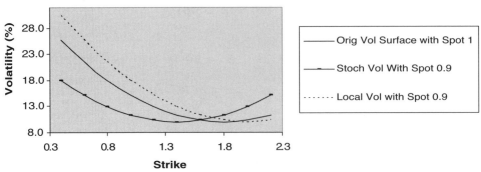

Figure A.5   Volatility skews under local volatility and stochastic volatility models when spot moves from 1 to 0.9.

Attempts have been made to introduce stochastic volatility (Heston style) and stochastic rates. This naturally leads to a 4-factor model (which cannot be priced on a PDE). The relevant equations follow:

$$dx_t = -ax_t dt + \sigma_x(t)dW_t^x$$

$$r_t = x_t + \varphi(t)$$

$$dy_t = \left(-by_t - \rho_{yz}(t)\sigma_y(t)\sigma_z(z_t, t)\right)dt + \sigma_y(t)dW_t^y$$

$$r_t^f = y_t + \varphi^f(t)$$

$$dV_t = \kappa\left(\theta(t) - V_t\right)dt + \eta(t)\sqrt{V_t}dW_t^V$$

$$dz_t = \left(r_t - r_t^f - \frac{1}{2}V_t\sigma_z^2(z_t, t)\right)dt + \sqrt{V_t}\sigma_z(z_t, t)dW_t^z$$

$$S_t = \exp(z_t),$$

where $\theta(t)$ is the long-run mean of variance, κ is the mean reversion speed of variance, $\eta(t)$ is the volatility of variance, and other quantities are as before.

Sometimes, simplifications are made (e.g. removing spot dependence of spot FX volatility, so that $\sigma_z(z_t, t) = \sigma_z(t)$).

It is worth mentioning that Andreasen (2006) has suggested a fairly efficient calibration procedure (to European calls and puts) based on Fourier transform solutions to the Heston model. This requires that processes correlated with rates are not also correlated with the stochastic variance.

Then each of the rate and variance parts can be treated separately by Fourier transforms.

PDE Methods

The local volatility and Gaussian rates 3-factor FX model can be represented by the following PDE in price P_t:

$$\frac{\partial P}{\partial t} = -ax\frac{\partial P}{\partial x} + \frac{1}{2}\sigma_x^2(t)\frac{\partial^2 P}{\partial x^2} - \left(by + \rho_{yz}(t)\sigma_y(t)\sigma_z(z, t)\right)\frac{\partial P}{\partial y} + \frac{1}{2}\sigma_y^2(t)\frac{\partial^2 P}{\partial y^2}$$

$$+\left(\varphi(t)+x-\varphi^f(t)-y-\frac{1}{2}\sigma_z^2(z_t,t)\right)\frac{\partial P}{\partial z}+\frac{1}{2}\sigma_z^2(z,t)\frac{\partial^2 P}{\partial z^2}+\rho_{xy}(t)\sigma_x(t)\sigma_y(t)\frac{\partial^2 P}{\partial x\partial y}$$

$$+\rho_{xz}(t)\sigma_x(t)\sigma_z(t)\frac{\partial^2 P}{\partial x\partial z}+\rho_{yz}(t)\sigma_y(t)\sigma_z(t)\frac{\partial^2 P}{\partial y\partial z}-rP$$

The existence of efficient methods for solving PDEs of up to three factors (e.g. by Craig & Sneyd, 1988) and the stable solutions and sensitivities have made it possible to turn callable and trigger PRDCs into flow products.

Rather curiously, since chooser PRDCs require at least five factors for pricing (i.e. the above three factors plus another foreign short rate and another spot FX process), product development has tended to focus on chooser tarns and triggers (which can be priced on MC) but not on callable choosers.

Choosers and the Correlation Triangle

The correlation between USD/JPY and AUD/JPY is not arbitrary. In fact, given the volatility for AUD/USD, the correlation is quite constrained.

Suppose we have the following lognormal processes, where for simplicity, we assume that the volatilities are not dependent on spot:

$$dS_t^{AUDJPY}/S_t^{AUDJPY}=\left(r_t^{JPY}-r_t^{AUD}\right)dt+\sigma_{AUDJPY}(t)dW_t^{AUDJPY}$$

$$dS_t^{USDJPY}/S_t^{USDJPY}=\left(r_t^{JPY}-r_t^{USD}\right)dt+\sigma_{USDJPY}(t)dW_t^{USDJPY}$$

Then

$$S_t^{AUDUSD}=\frac{S_t^{AUDJPY}}{S_t^{USDJPY}}.$$

Thus,

$$\frac{dS_t^{AUDUSD}}{S_t^{AUDUSD}}=\frac{dS_t^{AUDJPY}}{S_t^{AUDJPY}}-\frac{dS_t^{USDJPY}}{S_t^{USDJPY}}+\left(\frac{dS_t^{USDJPY}}{S_t^{USDJPY}}\right)^2-\frac{dS_t^{AUDJPY}dS_t^{USDJPY}}{S_t^{AUDJPY}S_t^{USDJPY}}$$

$$=\ldots dt+\sigma_{AUDJPY}(t)dW_t^{AUDJPY}-\sigma_{USDJPY}(t)dW_t^{USDJPY}$$

It follows that the total variance for AUD/USD up to maturity t is given by

$$\Sigma^2 t=\int_0^t\sigma_{AUDJPY}^2(s)ds+\int_0^t\sigma_{USDJPY}^2(s)ds-2\int_0^t\rho(s)\sigma_{AUDJPY}(s)\sigma_{USDJPY}(s)ds,$$

where $dW_t^{AUDJPY}dW_t^{USDJPY}=\rho(t)dt$.

But if

$$dS_t^{AUDUSD}/S_t^{AUDUSD}=\left(r_t^{USD}-r_t^{AUD}\right)dt+\sigma_{AUDUSD}(t)dW_t^{AUDUSD}$$

is the process for AUD/USD, then

$$\Sigma^2 t=\int_0^t\sigma_{AUDUSD}^2(s)ds.$$

Then the equation

$$2\int_0^t \rho(s)\sigma_{AUDJPY}(s)\sigma_{USDJPY}(s)ds = \int_0^t \sigma_{AUDJPY}^2(s)ds + \int_0^t \sigma_{USDJPY}^2(s)ds$$
$$-\int_0^t \sigma_{AUDUSD}^2(s)ds$$

completely determines $\rho(t)$.

Note that if we had local volatility processes for AUD/JPY, USD/JPY and AUD/USD, then our correlation would necessarily have been spot dependent, and the dimensionality of our integrals would increase. This also holds if we have rates skew or stochastic volatility. The point however remains that whatever correlation we assume between AUD/JPY and USD/JPY determines the volatilities of AUD/USD, and we should check that, at a minimum, any model for choosers produces reasonable prices for vanilla AUD/USD options.

CHAPTER 11

This technical appendix will discuss some aspects of pricing baskets and hybrid products.

Moments Matching for Baskets

A basket option comprises many underlyings with appropriate weights attached. Each of these underlyings can be described by a process and they can be jointly simulated (in a Monte Carlo) to price a payoff on the basket.

However, this is not ideal for the following reasons. First, this is too much of a black box approach and it gives little insight into the process and essential features (e.g. volatility) of the basket. Second, a basket involving 50 stocks (e.g. all stocks that comprise the STOXX 50 index) would be rather unwieldy to simulate (as it takes 50 times as long as for a single stock), and sensitivities (e.g. deltas, gammas, etc.) are likely to be rubbish. If instead, we treat it as one underlying, we can even stick it on a PDE.

The idea is basically that where possible we posit a process for the underlying and try to match moments of the process to what the moments would be of the basket. In a lognormal model, we can only match the first two moments (i.e. mean and variance). The drift of the process (i.e. which determines the mean) is dictated by no-arbitrage to be the risk-free rate.

For simplicity, let us posit lognormal processes where the volatility can depend on time but not spot. Then we have

$$dS_t^i = r_t S_t^i dt + \sigma_i(t) S_t^i dW_t^i,$$

as the process for underlying i, with volatility $\sigma_i(t)$, risk-free rate r_t, driven by Wiener processes W_t^i with $dW_t^i dW_t^j = \rho_{ij}(t)dt$.

If the basket is defined as

$$S_t^B = \sum_{i=1}^n w_i S_t^i$$

for weights w_i, then the process for the basket is

$$dS_t^B = r_t S_t^B dt + \sigma_B(t) S_t^B dW_t^B,$$

where

$$\int_0^T \sigma_B^2(u)\,du = \sum_{i=1}^n \int_0^T w_i^2 \sigma_i^2(u)du + 2\sum_{i=1}^n \sum_{j=1}^{i-1} \int_0^T w_i w_j \rho_{ij}(u)\sigma_i(u)\sigma_j(u)du.$$

This idea can be extended to more complex models, although the integrals may then involve spot (and hence be multiple integrals). Of course, for a skew model, it may be possible to match higher order moments (e.g. skewness and kurtosis), although whether such moments are stable is another issue.

Hybrid Models

Hybrid products often involve higher profit margins as opposed to simple products of one underlying. This is not surprising as there is more uncertainty (e.g. as to correlations across assets) and also because there is less competition. The higher profit margins mean that there is less need for accuracy in modelling each of the assets. Typically, if rates are involved, a short rate model (rather than BGM) is adequate, as it is usually only the total variance up to a coupon date that really affects the price (as opposed to the paths of individual forwards). Of course, this would be different if you had a hybrid snowball! But I think they are quite rare if they even exist.

It is, nevertheless, worth mentioning that once stochastic rates are introduced, skew modelling of the asset is more difficult. Consider, for example, the following CEV process for spot FX driven by Gaussian stochastic rates

$$dS_t = \left(r_t - r_t^f\right) S_t dt + \sigma_S(t) S_t^\beta dW_t^z,$$

where $\sigma_S(t)$ is the time dependent factor for FX volatility, β is the skew factor ($\beta = 1$ corresponds to lognormality, $\beta = 0$ corresponds to normality, and the lower the value of β the bigger the skew), and r_t and r_t^f are domestic and foreign short rates that follow Gaussian processes.

Note that the Gaussian rates contribute lognormally to the skew of the spot FX process. So, all things being equal, the greater the contribution of the Gaussian rates, the more lognormal the process (whatever of choice of β).

Calibrating our skew for the process then becomes a 3-factor integral (although Piterbarg (2005b), has some neat tricks on Markovian projection and skew averaging approximations in his PRDC paper). Of course, such neat tricks may not work if we have rates skew.

Similarly, if we had a local volatility process for FX, Bloch & Nakashima (2008) present an approach for calibration but that assumes Gaussian rates.

The other main consideration for hybrid modelling is correlation, which we touch on next.

Terminal Correlations

Consider a CMS-equity hybrid. We would like to price it using the following model

$$dx_t = -ax_t dt + \sigma_x(t) dW_t^x$$

$$r_t = x_t + \varphi(t)$$

$$dS_t = \left(r_t - r_t^f\right) S_t dt + \sigma_S(S_t, t) S_t dW_t^z$$

where a is the mean reversion speed, $\sigma_x(t)$ is the short rate volatility, $\sigma_S(S_t, t)$ is the local volatility for the spot process, $\varphi(t)$ is the drift required to match the domestic curve, and $dW_t^x dW_t^S = \rho_{xS}(t) dt$.

But what are actually being observed (even historically) are correlations on returns between the stock price and the swap rate, i.e. ρ that satisfies

$$\rho dt = dR_t dS_t,$$

where $R_t = \frac{Z_{t,t_0} - Z_{t,t_n}}{\sum_{i=1}^{n} \tau_i Z_{t,t_i}}$ defines a swap rate seen at time t, with $Z_{t,T}$ being a discount bond of maturity T as seen at time t (and being a function of the short rate r_t).

If we were implying ρ from a market-traded option, it would be for a specific expiry T, so that our correlation would be terminal, i.e. a number chosen so that the terminal processes for the swap rate and stock together give the price of the option.

So, we actually need to consider how to go from ρ as given to $\rho_{xS}(t)$ in our model. This need not be easy to achieve analytically. Nor is it necessarily the case that $\rho_{xS}(t)$ might be stable over time.

Correlations can be obtained from the market via quantoes (FX vs asset or rate) or baskets (between stocks or commodities), but that may not be very useful for hedging, since such instruments may not be too liquidly traded, especially for longer expiries. Alternatively, correlations can be estimated via historical data, although they may be unstable (see Figure A.6).

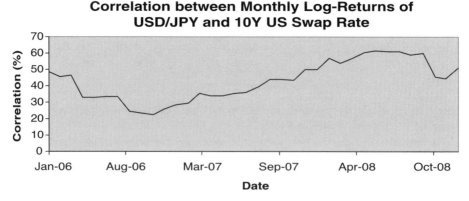

Figure A.6 Correlations between daily log-returns of USD/JPY and the 10-year dollar swap rate. *Source:* Bloomberg

Liquidity Considerations for very Long-Dated Options

Long-dated options are in general not liquid. The trader will make a market with a big margin and delta hedge while partially offsetting the gamma with shorter-dated options.

Needless to say, correlations across assets for long-dated options are even less likely to be available. However, if the product is not very sensitive to correlations, or the margin is big enough to absorb an adverse correlation impact, the deal may still be worth doing. It should be noted that there are products which are sensitive to correlations occurring under certain market conditions (e.g. for low stock value), and stress testing with a range of constant correlations may not fully reflect potential market losses. Care should be taken to identify potential situations of that sort.

CHAPTER 12

Various considerations arise in pricing and hedging the above exotic equity products. It is worth addressing some of them here, although this book cannot do justice in its coverage of relevant considerations. Quessette gives a very good discussion of mountain range products in his article of March 2002 in *Risk* (Quessette, 2002).

Cliquets and Forward Skew

In essence, the payoff of a cliquet is

$$\max\left(\frac{S_{t_i}}{S_{t_{i-1}}} - K, 0\right),$$

where S_t is the value of the underlying at time t, and K is strike.

So, we are interested in the distribution of $\frac{S_{t_i}}{S_{t_{i-1}}}$. Liquid options exist generally for each expiry, but this mainly gives the terminal distribution of S_T for each expiry T. What we need here are the transition probabilities of the underlying from time t_{i-1} to time t_i.

Calibrating different models to vanilla options only captures terminal skews, and forward volatilities need not be the same. Typically, equity skew flattens with expiry (see Figure A.7), since much more volatility is needed for short expiry out-of-the-money puts to compensate the bank for dangers of a stock market crash.

A local volatility model (i.e. $dS_t = r_t S_t dt + \sigma(S_t, t)S_t dW_t$) suggests that forward volatility flattens over time (and also becomes more like a smile); see Figure A.8. After all, the flattening skew just means that $\sigma(S_t, t)$ spans a tighter range as time increases. This makes it particularly unsuitable to model forward starting products (like cliquets). In contrast, a stochastic volatility model, for example, Heston, as specified by

$$dS_t = r_t S_t dt + \sigma(S_t, t)\sqrt{V_t} S_t dW_t,$$

$$dV_t = \kappa(\theta_t - V_t)dt + \eta\sqrt{V_t}dU_t,$$

$$dW_t dU_t = \rho dt$$

preserves somewhat better the shape of forward skew. Typically, a stochastic volatility model copes with the skew by having a very negative (e.g. -70%) correlation ρ between the spot and variance processes.

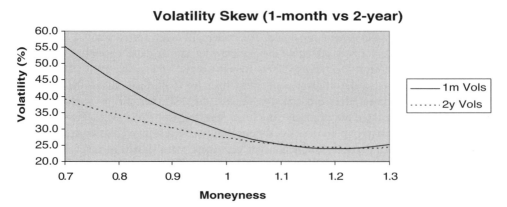

Figure A.7   Representative volatility skews for 1-month and 2-year options.

In FX, it is common to use a mixture of local and stochastic volatility to describe the process since the dynamics observed are somewhere between sticky delta and sticky strike.

Since forward volatility and skew is so important to pricing cliquets, it is desirable to have a model that can take forward skew as an input. Some research is ongoing on such a stochastic-implied volatility model. This is somewhat more intuitive than calibrating the Heston or local stochastic volatility model, much in the way that it is easier to see how the BGM model relates to caplet and swaption volatilities as opposed to a short rate model. Nonetheless, **the no-arbitrage condition fully constrains the forward of a stock to evolve based solely on spot and interest rate dynamics, so the extra flexibility to specify forward volatility must be fully supplied from a stochastic variance process**. That is why a model in equities that fits forward volatilities essentially requires stochastic volatility, whereas such a model in interest rates does not.

PDEs and Mountain Range Products

The simple observation is that PDEs are unsuitable for most mountain range products. Typically, PDEs require the payoff to be Markovian in a small number of factors. For path-dependent

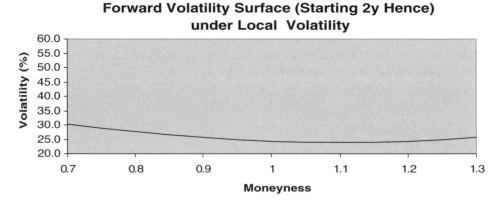

Figure A.8   Representative forward volatility surface starting in 2 years' time under local volatility.

products, PDEs are usable if you can have a small set of auxiliary states that describe the path dependence. But take a Himalaya on 10 stocks. At the end of each period, you record the best performer and exclude it. You have 10 states for the first fixing, 9 for the next, 8 for the next, ... and 1 for the last, i.e. $10 \times 9 \times 8 \times \ldots \times 1 = 3,628,800$. Better by far to stick to Monte Carlo!

Correlations and the Himalaya

The Himalaya is extremely sensitive to correlations, but the manner of the sensitivity is far from obvious and depends a lot on the returns of the stocks *vis-à-vis* each other. Overhaus (2002) has a nice article on the risks of this product in the March 2002 edition of *Risk*.

Consider the example of a Himalaya 1 day before the next fixing date, where stocks A and B have so far the highest returns of 12% and 12.5% say. Suppose stock A has a volatility of 40% and dividend yield of 0%, whereas stock B has a volatility of 20% and dividend yield of 2%. Then the product would be worth more if stock A were on the books (since it has higher volatility and higher forward). This is more likely if the correlation between stocks A and B was low (and especially negative). On the contrary, if stock A had a return of 13% thus far, it would be preferable for the correlation between the stocks to be high. This extreme sensitivity is definitely not welcome. This is especially so since correlation is not really hedgeable.

Stability of Sensitivities

The typical bump and revalue approach to sensitivities can work very poorly for mountain range products. (Again Overhaus (2002) covers this in his *Risk* article.) Take the delta, for example. You price a Himalaya by Monte Carlo. You then bump stock A by δ. If we had the case of stocks A and B producing very close returns (as above), then it may well lead to stock A being knocked out from the basket. This can lead to serious differences in the bumped price from the original price. So our delta is likely to be unstable.

An approach of course is to use Malliavin calculus to shift the differentiation to the density (as mentioned in Benhamou (1999) and also in Glasserman & Zhao (1999)). Since the payoffs are typically discontinous (involving choosing one stock in the basket), the pathwise differentiation approach is not likely to be of use.

More simply, perhaps we could ensure that if we bump the spot to get a finite difference, we should still record (and remove) the same stocks as in the "unbumped" version, so that we can eliminate noise from Monte Carlo. This is somewhat akin to using the same exercise boundary for callable products in Monte Carlo, when computing sensitivities (although with less theoretical justification).

Digital Risk for the Altiplano

The Altiplano involves a huge digital risk at the barrier. After all, the question is whether one stock among the basket breaches it. Suppose there is one stock close to the barrier and the risk-neutral value of the payoff in the event of a breach of the barrier drops significantly. This is a significant digital risk. In practice, a call spread executed with strikes around the barrier (should such be necessary) might help. Furthermore, the delta of an Altiplano with respect to this stock must be very negative in the vicinity of the barrier. Thus, hedging would require one to sell a huge quantity of the said stock in the vicinity of the barrier. If this were not a sufficiently large capitalised stock, hedging could depress the stock price significantly. Indeed, according to Quessette (2002), such hedging has led to transactions involving volumes of up to 10% of the market capitalisation of certain stocks at some point.

IR Risk for the Everest

The Everest is a long-dated (10 to 15 years) payoff based on a large basket of stocks. Being long-dated, it is worth pointing out that interest rates volatilities might be relevant. Perhaps with the complexities of properly dealing with cross correlations for a huge basket, interest rate volatilities would play second fiddle. But the longer the expiry, the less appropriate it is to ignore interest rate risk.

Cross Vega and Cross Stock Sensitivities

It is further worth mentioning that equity exotics often are sensitive to cross volatility sensitivities, specifically $\frac{\partial v}{\partial S}$ or even $\frac{\partial v_A}{\partial S_B}$ (where v is vega, S is spot, and A and B refer to two different stocks). In our Himalaya example above, both the volatility of stock A and the spot of stock B would significantly affect the final price.

CHAPTER 13

The technical appendix will touch on the static replication of variance swaps, as well as discuss issues on trading volatility swaps, and jump considerations when pricing options on variance swaps.

Variance Swap Replication

Consider a variance swap. The realised variance is

$$\frac{1}{N} \sum_{i=1}^{N} \left(\log \left(\frac{S_{t_i}}{S_{t_{i-1}}} \right) \right)^2 - \left(\frac{1}{N} \sum_{i=1}^{N} \log \left(\frac{S_{t_i}}{S_{t_{i-1}}} \right) \right)^2 = \frac{1}{N} \sum_{i=1}^{N} \left(\log \left(\frac{S_{t_i}}{S_{t_{i-1}}} \right) \right)^2 - \left(\frac{1}{N} \log \left(\frac{S_T}{S_0} \right) \right)^2$$

where, for convenience, take $t_0 = 0$, $t_i = \frac{iT}{N}$, $t_N = T$.

Consider the continuous process

$$dS_t/S_t = r_t dt + \sigma(S_t, t, \theta_t) dW_t,$$

where θ_t suggests that we do not preclude the dependence on another state variable, e.g. stochastic variance.

Then Itô's lemma gives

$$d \log S_t = \left(r_t - \frac{\sigma^2(S_t, t, \theta_t)}{2} \right) dt + \sigma(S_t, t, \theta_t) dW_t.$$

Now,

$$\sum_{i=1}^{N} \left(\log \left(\frac{S_{t_i}}{S_{t_{i-1}}} \right) \right)^2 = \sum_{i=1}^{N} \left(\log S_{t_i} - \log S_{t_{i-1}} \right)^2 \rightarrow \int_0^T (d \log S_t)^2 \text{ as } N \rightarrow \infty$$

(i.e. for continuous observations), giving

$$E\left[\sum_{i=1}^{N}\left(\log\left(\frac{S_{t_i}}{S_{t_{i-1}}}\right)\right)^2\right] \rightarrow E\left[\int_{0}^{T}(d\log S_t)^2\right] = E\left[\int_{0}^{T}\sigma^2(S_t,t,\theta_t)dt\right].$$

So we have to compute $E\left[\int_{0}^{T}\sigma^2(S_t,t,\theta_t)dt\right]$.

But Itô's lemma gives

$$d\log S_t = \frac{dS_t}{S_t} - \frac{(dS_t)^2}{2S_t^2} = \frac{dS_t}{S_t} - \frac{\sigma^2(S_t,t,\theta_t)dt}{2}$$

Thus,

$$\int_{0}^{T}\sigma^2(S_t,t,\theta_t)dt = -2\log\frac{S_T}{S_0} + 2\int_{o}^{T}\frac{dS_t}{S_t}.$$

So, we require to continuously maintain a position of $\frac{2}{S_t}$ in the spot, as well as a static hedge for the payoff $2\log S_T$ at maturity T.

To hedge the payoff $2\log S_T$ at maturity T, static replication can be used as per our discussion in Section 6.2.

Carr & Lee (2005) also discuss this in *Robust Replication of Volatility Derivatives*.

Jumps and the Options on Variance Swaps

These days, stochastic volatility models have already seen widespread use. This is because they have better volatility dynamics than local volatility models (see appendix to Chapter 12), and also because the forward volatilities they project do not flatten over time. This makes them suitable for pricing forward starting options (e.g. cliquets). Typically, such stochastic volatility models have high volatilities of variance and large mean reversion speeds to ensure that variance does not grow too fast over long expiries. (Even so, Andersen & Piterbarg (2007) show that stochastic volatility models can have infinite variance in finite time for some not uncommon parameter choices.)

For variance swaps, jumps have significant impact on realised variance. Whereas static replication is possible only in the absence of jumps, it may not be too inaccurate to use it for variance swaps themselves, especially if the size of the jumps is not likely to be too large (e.g. stock indices and FX as opposed to single-name stocks).

But options on variance swaps are far more sensitive to jumps than the variance swaps themselves, insofar as the volatility of variance affects their price. If our world were continuous, the volatility of variance for options on variance swaps would be akin to volatility for normal calls and puts. Higher jumps can be translated into higher volatilities of variance at the short end. But firstly prices of options on variance swaps are not liquid (indeed they are the result of the pricing and hence not observable). So, most likely if a stochastic volatility model were used, a choice of volatility of variance would be made, which would underprice by underestimating the effects of jumps.

CHAPTER 14

The technical appendix explains why a Constant Proportion Portfolio Insurance (CPPI) strategy should theoretically replicate a call option.

CPPI Strategy

The exposition below is based on ideas from Cont & Tankov (2007).

Let S_t be the price of a stock at time t, and $Z_{t,T} = \exp(-r(T-t))$ be the value of a zero-coupon bond of notional 1 with maturity T as seen at time t. (Here we have assumed that interest rates are constant at r.) Further let V_t be the value of the strategy at time t. Suppose we want to ensure that we get back a minimum percentage M of our principal of 1 at maturity T. This is worth $M Z_{t,T}$ at time t.

The strategy is as follows:

If $V_t > M Z_{t,T}$, then we hold an amount of stock equal to $\alpha(V_t - M Z_{t,T})$ for some constant multiplier α. Otherwise, the entire portfolio is invested in the zero-coupon bond.

Notice

$$dZ_{t,T} = r Z_{t,T} dt.$$

Further, suppose our stock process follows geometric Brownian motion. Then

$$dS_t = \mu S_t dt + \sigma S_t dW_t.$$

Let $H_t = V_t - M Z_{t,T}$ be the value of the portfolio in excess of the targeted minimum. Then

$$dV_t = \alpha H_t \frac{dS_t}{S_t} + (V_t - \alpha H_t) \frac{dZ_{t,T}}{Z_{t,T}} = \alpha H_t (\mu dt + \sigma dW_t) + (V_t - \alpha H_t) r dt$$

Thus

$$
\begin{aligned}
dH_t &= dV_t - M dZ_{t,T} \\
&= \alpha H_t (\mu dt + \sigma dW_t) + (V_t - \alpha H_t) r dt - r M Z_{t,T} dt \\
&= \alpha H_t (\mu dt + \sigma dW_t) + \left((V_t - M Z_{t,T}) - \alpha H_t\right) r dt \\
&= (\alpha \mu H_t + (1 - \alpha) r) H_t dt + \alpha \sigma H_t dW_t
\end{aligned}
$$

Note that under the risk-neutral measure $\mu = r$, so

$$H_t = H_0 \exp\left(rt - \frac{1}{2}\alpha^2\sigma^2 t + \alpha\sigma W_t\right).$$

Furthermore, $E[V_T] = \exp(rT)$ gives

$$\exp(rT) = M + H_0 \exp(rT).$$

Thus,

$$H_0 = 1 - M \exp(-rT) = 1 - M Z_{0,T}.$$

This gives the value of the portfolio at expiry of

$$V_T = M + \left(1 - M Z_{0,T}\right) \exp\left(rT - \frac{1}{2}\alpha^2\sigma^2 T + \alpha\sigma W_T\right).$$

Since exponentials are always positive, the second term on the right-hand side must be greater than 0 in theory, so that the portfolio value at expiry is at least M.

The above argument of course relies on perfect hedging for a diffusive process. In practice, the presence of stochastic volatility and especially jumps means that we are quite likely to fall below the minimum if markets fall.

Gap Risk

The issuer of a note with a CPPI strategy guarantees that the portfolio will be worth at least the floor at maturity. If the asset price follows a diffusive process, it is impossible in theory for the portfolio value to fall below this floor (as per the explanation above). To price the cost of such a guarantee to the issuer, it is therefore necessary to introduce a jump model for the process of the underlying.

Bibliography

This book is written to explain exotic products to the average investment professional. I have attempted to describe the products, the economic rationales for their existence and the risks attached to them. This is not a common theme among many financial books, many of which are instead targeted at an investment banking audience. I shall, however, attempt to list a few books that might be of interest to the typical reader (although some can require advanced mathematical knowledge). For a more quantitative reader there are many more useful books and papers regarding financial modelling and the pricing of derivatives, some of which are given below.

BOOKS ON PRODUCTS AND GENERAL READING

Benhamou, E. (ed.) (2007) *Global Derivatives: Products, Theory and Practice*. World Scientific, Singapore.
Chisholm, A. (2004) *Derivatives Demystified: A Step-by-Step Guide to Forwards, Futures, Swaps and Options*. John Wiley & Sons Ltd, Chichester.
De Weert, F. (2008) *Exotic Options Trading*. John Wiley & Sons Ltd, Chichester.
Hull, J.C. (2008) *Options, Futures and Other Derivatives* (seventh edition). Prentice Hall, Englewood Clifts, NJ.
Smithson, C.W. (1998) *Managing Financial Risk: A Guide to Derivative Products, Financial Engineering, and Value Maximization*. McGraw-Hill Professional, New York.

BOOKS ON FINANCIAL MODELLING AND DERIVATIVES PRICING

Baxter, M. and Rennie, A. (1996) *Financial Calculus: An Introduction to Derivative Pricing*, Cambridge University Press, Cambridge.
Brigo, D. and Mercurio, F. (2006) *Interest Rate Models: Theory and Practice*. Springer Finance, Berlin and Heidelberg.
Brzezniak, Z. and Zastawniak, T. (1998) *Basic Stochastic Processes*. Springer-Verlag, London.
Duffy, D.J. (2006) *Finite Difference Methods in Financial Engineering: A Partial Differential Equation Approach*. John Wiley & Sons Ltd, Chichester.
Gatheral, J. (2006) *The Volatility Surface: A Practitioner's Guide*. John Wiley & Sons Ltd, Hoboken, NJ.
Glasserman, P. (2004) *Monte Carlo Methods in Financial Engineering*. Springer-Verlag, New York.
Haug, E.G. (2007) *The Complete Guide to Option Pricing Formulas*. McGraw-Hill, New York.
Hunt, P.J. and Kennedy, J.E. (2004) *Financial Derivatives in Theory and Practice*. John Wiley & Sons Ltd, Chichester.

Joshi, M. (2003) *The Concepts and Practice of Mathematical Finance*. Cambridge University Press, Cambridge.

Karatzas, I. and Shreve, S.E. (2001) *Methods of Mathematical Finance*. Springer-Verlag, New York.

Karatzas, I. and Shreve, S.E. (2004) *Brownian Motion and Stochastic Calculus*. Springer-Verlag, Berlin, Heidelberg and New York.

Lewis, A.L. (2000) *Option Valuation under Stochastic Volatility: With Mathematica Code*. Finance Press, Newport Beach, CA.

Morton, K. and Mayers, D. (1994) *Numerical Solutions of Partial Differential Equations*. Cambridge University Press, Cambridge.

Musiela, M. and Rutkowski, M. (2007) *Martingale Methods in Financial Modelling (Stochastic Modelling and Applied Probability)*. Springer-Verlag, Berlin, Heidelberg and New York.

Neftci, S.N. (1996) *An Introduction to the Mathematics of Financial Derivatives* (second edition). Academic Press, San Diego, CA.

Oksendal, B. (1998) *Stochastic Differential Equations* (fifth edition). Springer-Verlag, Berlin.

Pelsser, A. (2000) *Efficient Methods for Valuing Interest Rate Derivatives*. Springer Finance, London.

Rebonato, R. (2002) *Modern Pricing of Interest Rates Derivatives: The LIBOR Market Model and Beyond*. Princeton University Press, Princeton, NJ.

Rebonato, R. (2004) *Volatility and Correlation: The Perfect Hedger and the Fox*. John Wiley & Sons Ltd, Chichester.

Rebonato, R., McKay, K. and White, R. (2009) *The SABR/LIBOR Market Model: Pricing, Calibration and Hedging for Complex Interest Rate Derivatives*. John Wiley & Sons Ltd, Chichester.

Shreve, S.E. (2005) *Stochastic Calculus for Finance: Binomial Asset Pricing Model*, Volume 1. Springer Finance, New York.

Shreve, S.E. (2005) *Stochastic Calculus for Finance: Continuous-Time Models*, Volume 2. Springer Finance, New York.

Wilmott, P., Howison, S. and Dewynne, J. (1995) *The Mathematics of Financial Derivatives: A Student Introduction*. Cambridge University Press, Cambridge.

Wystup, U. (2006) *FX Options and Structured Products*. John Wiley & Sons Ltd, Chichester.

PAPERS ON FINANCIAL MODELLING AND DERIVATIVES PRICING

Andersen, L. (2000) A simple approach to the pricing of Bermudan swaptions in the multi-factor Libor market model. *Journal of Computational Finance*, **2** (3), 5–32.

Andersen, L. (2007) *Efficient simulation of the Heston stochastic volatility model*. Working paper, Bank of America.

Andersen, L. and Andreasen, J. (2000) Volatility skews and extensions of the LIBOR market model. *Applied Mathematical Finance*, **7**, 1–32.

Andersen, L. and Andreasen, J. (2001) Factor dependence of Bermudan swaption prices: Fact or fiction? *Journal of Financial Economics*, **62**, 3–37.

Andersen, L. and Brotherton-Ratcliffe, R. (2005) Extended LIBOR market models with stochastic volatility. *Journal of Computational Finance*, **9** (1), 1–40.

Andersen, L. and Piterbarg, V. (2007) Moment explosions in stochastic volatility models. *Finance and Stochastics*, **11** (1), 29–50.

Andreasen, J. (2000) *Turbo charging the Cheyette model*. Working paper, Gen Re Securities.

Andreasen, J. (2006) *Long-dated FX hybrids with stochastic volatility*. Working paper, Bank of America.

Assefa, S. (2007) *Calibration and pricing in a multi-factor quadratic Gaussian model*. Research paper 197, University of Technology Sydney, Quantitative Finance Research Centre.

Baxter, M.W. (1997) General interest-rate models and the universality of HJM. In *Mathematics of Derivative Securities*. Cambridge University Press, Cambridge.

Benhamou, E. (1999) *Faster Greeks for discontinuous payoff options (A Malliavin calculus approach in Black world)*. Working paper, London School of Economics.

Benhamou, E., Gruz, A. and Rivoira, A. (2008) *Stochastic interest rates for local volatility hybrids models*. Working paper.

Black, F. (1976) The pricing of commodity contracts. *Journal of Financial Economics*, **3** (March), 167–179.

Black, F., Derman, E. and Toy, W. (1990) A one-factor model of interest rates and its application to Treasury bond options. *Financial Analysts Journal* (January–February), 33–39.

Black, F. and Karasinski, P. (1991) Bond and option pricing when short rates are lognormal. *Financial Analysts Journal* (July–August), 52–59.

Black, F. and Scholes, M. (1973) The pricing of options and corporate liabilities. *Journal of Political Economy*, **81**, 637–654.

Bloch, D. and Nakashima, Y. (2008) *Multi-currency local volatility model*. Working paper, Mizuho Securities.

Brace, A., Gatarek, D. and Musiela, M. (1997) The market model of interest rate dynamics. *Mathematical Finance*, **7**, 127.

Carr, P. and Lee, R. (2005) *Robust Replication of Volatility Derivatives*. Courant Institute and Bloomberg.

Carr, P. and Madan, D. (1999) Option valuation using the Fast Fourier Transform. *Journal of Computational Finance*, **2** (4), 61–73.

Castagna, A. and Mercurio, F. (2005) *Consistent pricing of FX options*. Working paper, Banca IMI.

Craig, I. and Sneyd, A. (1988) An alternating implicit scheme for parabolic equations with mixed derivatives. *Computers and Mathematics with Applications*, **16** (4), 341–350.

Cheyette, O. (1992) *Markov representation of the Heath–Jarrow–Morton model*. Working paper, BARRA.

Cox, J., Ingersoll, J. and Ross, S.A. (1985) A theory of the term structure of interest rates. *Econometrica*, **53** (2), 385–407.

Cont, R. and Tankov, P. (2007) *Constant proportion portfolio insurance in presence of jumps in asset prices*. Report No. 2007-10, Columbia University Center for Financial Engineering.

Derman, E. and Kani, I. (1994) Riding on a smile. *Risk* (February), 32–39.

Derman, E. and Kani, I. (1998) Stochastic implied trees: Arbitrage pricing with stochastic term and strike structure of volatility. *International Journal of Theoretical and Applied Finance*, **1**, 61–110.

Dupire, B. (1994) Pricing with a smile. *Risk* (January), 18–20.

Dupire, B. (1997) *A unified theory of volatility*. Working paper, Banque Paribas.

El Karoui, N., Viswanathan, R. and Myneni, R. (1991) *Arbitrage pricing and hedging of interest rate claims with state variables*. Working paper, Université de Paris IV and Stanford University.

Geman, H., El Karoui, N. and Rochet, J.C. (1995) Changes of numeraire, changes of probability measures and option pricing. *Journal of Applied Probability*, **32**, 443–458.

Giles, M. and Glasserman, P. (2006) Smoking adjoints: Fast Monte Carlo Greeks. *Risk* (January), 88–92.

Glasserman, P. and Yu, B. (2004) Number of paths versus number of basis functions in American option pricing. *Annals of Applied Probability*, **14** (4), 2090–2119.

Glasserman, P. and Zhao, X. (1999) Fast Greeks by simulation in forward Libor models. *Journal of Computational Finance*, **3**, 5–39.

Hagan, P.S., Kumar, D., Lesniewski, A.S. and Woodward, D.E. (2002) Managing smile risk. *Wilmott magazine* (July), 84–108.

Harrison, J.M. and Pliska, S.R. (1981) Martingales and stochastic integrals in the theory of continuous trading. *Stochastic Processes and their Applications*, **11**, 215–260.

Heath, D., Jarrow, R. and Morton, A. (1992) Bond pricing and the term structure of interest rates: A new methodology for contingent claims valuation. *Econometrica*, **60**, 77–106.

Heston, S.L. (1993) A closed-form solution for options with stochastic volatility with applications to bond and currency options. *Review of Financial Studies*, **2** (6), 327–343.

Ho, T.S.Y. and Lee, S.B. (1986) Term structure movements and pricing interest rate contingent claims. *Journal of Finance*, **41** (5), 1011–1029.

Hull, J.C. and White, A. (1987) The pricing of options on assets with stochastic volatilities. *Journal of Finance*, **XLII** (2), 281–300.

Hull, J.C. and White, A. (1990) Pricing interest rate derivatives securities. *Review of Financial Studies*, **3**, 573–592.

Hull, J.C. and White, A. (1994) Numerical procedures for implementing term structure models I: Single-factor models. *Journal of Derivatives* (Fall), 7–16.

Hunt, P., Kennedy, J. and Pelsser, A. (2004) Markov-functional interest rate models. *Finance and Stochastics*, **4** (4), 391–408.

Jamshidian, F. (1989) An exact bond option pricing formula. *Journal of Finance*, **44**, 205–209.

Jamshidian, F. (1991) Bond and option evaluation in the Gaussian interest rate model. *Research in Finance*, **9**, 131–710.

Jamshidian, F. (1997) Libor and swap market models and measures. *Finance and Stochastics*, **1** (4), 293–330.

Longstaff, F.A. and Schwartz, E.S. (2001) Valuing American options by simulation: A simple least-squares approach. *Review of Financial Studies*, **14** (1), 113–147.

Longstaff, F., Schwartz, E. and Santa-Clara, E. (1999) *Throwing away a billion dollars: The cost of suboptimal exercise in the swaption market*. Working paper, The Andersen School, UCLA.

Lucic, V. (1998). *Boundary conditions for computing densities in hybrid models via PDE methods*. Working paper, Barclays Capital.

Margrabe, W. (1978) The value of an option to exchange one asset for another. *Journal of Finance*, **33**, 177–186.

Milterson, K., Sandmann, K. and Sondermann, D. (1997) Closed form solutions for term structure of derivatives with log-normal interest rates. *Journal of Finance*, **52** (1), 409–430.

Overhaus, M. (2002) Himalaya options. *Risk* (March), 101–104.

Pedersen, M.B. (1998) *Calibrating Libor market models*. Working paper, SSRN.

Pedersen, M.B. (1999) *Bermudan swaptions in the LIBOR market model*. Working paper, SimCorp Financial Research.

Pelsser, A. and Pietersz, R. (2005) *A comparison of single-factor Markov-functional and multi-factor market models*. Working paper, SSRN.

Pelsser, A., Pietersz, R. and van Regenmortel, M. (2004) Fast drift-approximated pricing in the BGM model. *Journal of Computational Finance*, **8** (1), 93–124.

Piterbarg, V. (2003a) *Computing deltas of callable LIBOR exotics in a forward LIBOR model*. Working paper, SSRN.

Piterbarg, V. (2003b) *A practitioner's guide to pricing and hedging callable Libor exotics in forward Libor models*. Working paper, SSRN.

Piterbarg, V. (2005a) Stochastic volatility model with time-dependent skew. *Applied Mathematical Finance*, **12** (2), 147–185.

Piterbarg, V. (2005b) *A multi-currency model with FX volatility skew*. Working paper, Bank of America.

Piterbarg, V. (2009) Rates squared. *Risk* (January), 100–105.

Quessette, R. (2002) New products, new risks. *Risk* (March), 97–100.

Ritchken, P. and Sankarasubramanian, L. (1995) Volatility structure of forward rates and the dynamics of the term structure. *Mathematical Finance*, **5**, 55–72.

Savine, A. (2000) *A theory of volatility*. Working paper, Reech.

Tezier, C. (2005) *Short rate models. Linear and quadratic Gaussian models*. Working paper, Barclays Capital.

Vasicek, O. (1977) An equilibrium characterization of the term structure. *Journal of Financial Economics*, **5**, 177–188.

Wilmott, P. (2002) Cliquet options and volatility models. *Wilmott magazine* (December), 78–83.

Index

Index compiled by Terry Halliday